Ancestral Grace

Broken

Ancestral Grace

Meeting God in Our Human Story

Diarmuid O'Murchu, MSC

ORBIS BOOKS

Maryknoll, New York 10545

Second Printing, March 2009

Founded in 1970, Orbis Books endeavors to publish works that enlighten the mind, nourish the spirit, and challenge the conscience. The publishing arm of the Maryknoll Fathers and Brothers, Orbis seeks to explore the global dimensions of the Christian faith and mission, to invite dialogue with diverse cultures and religious traditions, and to serve the cause of reconciliation and peace. The books published reflect the views of their authors and do not represent the official position of the Maryknoll Society. To learn more about Maryknoll and Orbis Books, please visit our website at www.maryknollsociety.org.

Published in 2008 by Orbis Books,
P.O. Box 308, Maryknoll, NY 10545-0308.

Copyright © 2008 by Diarmuid O'Murchu.

Manufactured in the United States of America.

Library of Congress Cataloging-in-Publication Data
Ó Murchú, Diarmuid.
   Ancestral grace : meeting God in our human story / Diarmuid O'Murchu.
      p. cm.
   Includes bibliographical references and index.
   ISBN-13: 978-1-57075-794-5
   1. Theological anthropology – Christianity. 2. Africa – Religion. 3. Christianity – Africa. I. Title.
BT701.3.O24 2008
233 – dc22   2008012652

Contents

Foreword   xi

Preface   xvii

Part One
THE HUMAN AS HUMAN

1. By the Grace of God...   3

    Dualistic Overtones / 3
    Grace and the Fundamental Flaw / 5
    Grace Revisited / 6
    Our Graced Story / 8
    Our Graced Orientation / 9

2. Creatures of Imagination   11

    The Cult(ure) of Rationality / 11
    The Suppressed Imagination / 13
    Invoking the Imagination / 14
    Imagination as We Trace Our Origins / 15
    Imagination and Paradox / 17
    The Wisdom to See Differently / 19

3. Gazing into Deep Time   20

    Chimp or Human? / 21
    Chimp or Bonobo? / 22
    The Counter-Culture of Deep Time / 24
    The Joy of Sex / 25
    Factoring in Another Time Scale / 26

4. Interdependence and the Will to Life   29

    The Urge to Explore / 29
    The Living Planet / 30
    The Tradition of Gifting / 31
    What about Sexual Interdependence? / 32
    Relating Nonviolently / 34

5. Our Home in Africa   36

   The African Connection / 36
   Walking on Two Feet / 38
   Africa: Our Collective Home / 40
   The Upright Stride / 42

6. Creative Innovation and the Awakening Artist   44

   Oldowan Technology / 45
   The Awakening Artist / 46
   The Cave Walls / 47
   Strange Statuettes / 48
   Art and Spirituality / 48
   Religious Endorsement of Our Creativity? / 50
   An Original Synthesis / 51

7. Working Our Way with Paradox   52

   Our Delight in Work / 53
   Man the Hunter / 54
   Befriending Ambiguity / 56
   Learning from Ergaster / 58

8. The Wise Species   59

   Intelligence Revisited / 59
   Humans Appropriate the Enveloping Intelligence / 62
   Enter Synaesthesia / 63
   The Communal Challenge / 64

9. The Peril of European Promise   66

   Developed Skills / 66
   Colonial Arrogance / 67
   Is There a European Archetype? / 68
   Can the Neanderthals Inspire Us Today? / 70

10. The Discovery of Language   72

   Proto-language / 73
   Theories of Language / 75
   Language and Social Bonding / 76

11. Pagan Spirituality   78

    Paganism Reinstated / 78
    Ritualizing the Spiritual / 79
    Enter the Great Mother / 81
    Earth Spirituality Today / 83
    Wisdom from Deep Within / 84

12. Agriculture and Its Discontents   85

    Agriculture as an Axial Moment / 85
    The Rise of Anthropocentrism / 87
    Religious Validation / 88
    Agriculture and Ancestral Grace / 89

Part Two
THE HUMAN AS CHRISTIAN

13. Jesus, Disciple of Ancestral Grace   93

    Creatures of Ancestral Grace / 94
    Rescuing Jesus from Patriarchy / 95
    Jesus as Archetypal Human / 97

14. The God Who Incarnates   99

    The Divine as Spirit Power / 99
    The Divine as Creator / 101
    The Feminine Face of God / 102
    Jesus as a Model of Inspired Birthing / 104
    Wisdom Has Set Her Table / 105

15. Jesus as an Archetypal Human   107

    Reclaiming the Human Face of God / 109
    Soulful Living / 110
    Reclaiming the Dream / 111

16. Jesus in Evolutionary Context   113

    The Two-Thousand-Year Benchmark / 113
    Jesus in the Big Picture / 115
    Savoring the Enlarged Context / 117

17. Humans at Home in God's Creation   119

    Exile and Alienation / 120
    A New Metaphor / 121
    Coming Home to Our Human Story / 122
    The Kingdom Reenvisioned / 123
    Healing and Empowerment / 125
    Creation and the Kingdom / 126

18. Jesus beyond Patriarchy   128

    Dislocating Stories / 128
    Disrupting Regimes of Normalcy / 130
    Is Jesus Still a Dangerous Memory? / 131

19. Being Human — Being Person   133

    The Person in Aristotle / 134
    An Alternative Paradigm / 135
    What Kind of Person Was Jesus? / 136

20. Incarnation Embracing Paradox   138

    Naming Our Reality Afresh / 139
    Jesus Embracing Paradox / 141
    Humans Embracing the Paradox / 142

21. Christian Incarnation and Other Religions   144

    Parallels in Other Faiths / 144
    Commonalities Rather Than Differences / 146
    Jesus among the Religions / 148
    Through Religion and Beyond / 149

22. Jesus as Ritual Maker   150

    A Culture of Ritual / 150
    Ritualization in Word / 154
    Ritual in Our Time / 155

23. Wholesome Holiness — Incarnational Spirituality   157

    Jesus: Religious or Spiritual? / 157
    Christian Spirituality and Ancestral Grace / 159
    From Orthodoxy to Orthopraxy / 161

Part Three
THE HUMAN LURED
TOWARD THE FUTURE

24. The Grace of Evolutionary Becoming   165

   Beyond the Limits of Old / 166
   Enter Evolution / 167
   Human Emergence / 168
   Co-creating the Future / 170
   Adapting to a New Way of Being / 172

25. Technology and the Protean Self   175

   Mechanizing the Human / 176
   Artificial Intelligence (AI) / 177
   Altering Human Behavior / 178
   Posthuman, Protean, or Transhuman? / 178
   Transpersonal Wisdom / 180
   The Shadow Side / 181
   Conclusion / 182

26. Toward Bioregional Networking   184

   The Dwindling Nation State / 184
   Beyond the Nation State / 186
   Global Governance / 188
   When the Time Is Ripe... / 191

27. Embracing the Adult   193

   The Adult in Creation / 194
   The Adult and the Inner Child / 195
   Beyond the Preoccupation with the Child / 196
   Being Adult for the Future / 197
   Learning and Transformation / 198

28. Learning to Relate Laterally   200

   Commonalities and Differences / 200
   The Identity Question / 201
   Relational Dislocation / 203
   Relating Laterally / 205

29. Apocalyptic Cataclysm or Eschatological Breakthrough?   207
        A Lurid Fascination / 208
        The Apocalyptic Mind-Set / 210
        The Eschatological Outlook / 211
        Christian Hope / 213

30. The Spirit Will Lead You Forth   216
        The Inspiring Life Force / 217
        Our Spirit-Filled Age / 218
        The Spirit That Lures Us Forth / 219
        Fulfilling the Promise / 220
        Dreaming an Alternative Future / 222

31. Preoccupied with Death and the Afterlife   224
        The Demonization of Death / 224
        Befriending Death / 226
        Death in the Cosmic Matrix / 227
        Death and Our Graced Future / 229

32. Will We Actually Make It?   231
        Possible Scenarios / 231
        Beyond Our Denial / 233
        Hanging On to Hope! / 235

Notes   237

Bibliography   247

Index   259

Foreword

MY FAMILY AND I live in a place of thatched cottages in the bushveld of Mpumulanga, looking over the Crocodile River to the Kruger National Park of South Africa. There are no fences! Game wander freely: zebras and warthogs crop the lawn, mongooses peep at us sitting on our step with a group of friends eating and drinking, reading or singing, or working away at theology, politics, and economics, with kudus and giraffes looking on.

Often, as earth drops the light and heat of the sun below the western horizon, talk ceases. Cicadas take over; the genets jump silently from the roof. The cough and roar of a lion, the squeal of hyenas, make night audible. It is awesome.

Nothing comes between us and the light from a million stars millions of light years away. What has happened since that light left them? We are poised in time, reaching back through evolving earth. The work and plans, the tragedies and joys, have been handled for now. Wonder and hope grip us as earth turns eastward, moving toward the dawning promise coming back from tomorrow. Grace speaks to us from our ancestral past and from the promise of the future. There are no fences!

We have built many barriers around our human and spiritual stories. Diarmuid O'Murchu's *Ancestral Grace* reminds us of a time when we lived out of a different kind of wisdom, long before we erected the fences that marginalize and divide. This is the deep truth we long have known, and often neglected: our human story, our Christian story, and in a very special way our African story!

Reclaiming Ancestral Values

The scramble for Africa, seeking plunder and slaves, minerals and markets, and eventually colonies, was mounted by waves of explorers and traders, and by religions, couched in the dictates of imperialism. They found no sign of religious institutions: no churches, mosques, or temples; no scriptures, colleges, or priests, and concluded that Africa was a heathen, dark domain. The guns and greed of colonial military and technical power, blessed by colonial religions, subjugated the continent.

Few missionaries ever sensed that Africa, the birthplace of the human race itself, retained some of the earliest motivations of the human spirit. We may have missed centuries of northern religious civilizations, but thousands of African communities were still rooted in the early experience of human understanding. That quest for fulfillment fired the struggle for liberation, and by the close of the twentieth century Africa had shed the fetters of colonial political and social oppression.

Today this vast continent, where community was conceived in the genesis of the human story, desperately needs to free its spirit from the oppressive cultures of colonial religions and rediscover the thrust of spiritual power in *Homo sapiens sapiens*. Much of Africa still stands on those foundations of human community, the vital force, the secular spirituality, the revolutionary morality, the faith-energy, the stuff of life, aptly described by Diarmuid O'Murchu as "ancestral grace."

Ancestral grace is no fancy formulation of the noble African savage: blacks can be as brutal as whites and neocolonial Africans as dictatorial and oppressive. But African traditional insight indicates three crucial characteristics of ancestral grace. It is focused on earth, not heaven; on community, not individuals; and it is holistic, not dualistic.

1. Earth-Focused

In the introduction to *An African Prayer Book* (1995), Archbishop Desmond Tutu writes: "The African worldview rejects the common dichotomies between the sacred and the secular, the material and the spiritual. All life is religious, all life is sacred, all life is of a piece."

Traditionally, humans in Africa look to earth, not to heaven. They hear God in nature, a saddle in the hills, a stone in the circle, a thundering waterfall. They seek the good news of a vision and values for this life, not speculation on the next. They seek liberation now, not paradise hereafter. "There was no hell in our religion," wrote Steve Biko in 1978. "The great powers of the world may have done wonders in giving the world an industrial and military look, but the great gift still has to come from Africa — giving the world a more human face."

2. Communal

According to the Ghanian theologian Mercy Amba Oduyoye, Africans recognize life as life-in-community. We can truly know ourselves only if we remain true to our community, past and present. The concept of individual success or failure is secondary. The ethnic group, the village, the locality are crucial in one's estimation of oneself. Our nature as beings-in-relation is a two-way relation: with God and with our fellow human beings.

The African concept of *ubuntu* is about the discovery and enjoyment of one's person through other persons. Canon Luke Pato claims that the African person has a sense of the wholeness of life. In traditional African religion there is no separate community of religious people, because everyone who participates in the life of the community also participates in its religion.

This communality is the experience of all peoples still in touch with their human roots, from Inuit to Maori. It is the custom of the so-called "Indians" of North America to hold their meetings in a circle, not fenced off by rows of pews. Both individuals and large congregations have their place in the economy of humanity, but the power is in small community groups. One could argue that Jesus did well on his own: he coped with huge crowds but the heart of his message was developed with his small group of disciples.

3. Holistic

One of our African theologians, Dr. J. S. Mbiti, claims that traditional religions permeate all the departments of life. There is no formal distinction between the sacred and the secular, between the religious and the nonreligious, between the spiritual and the material areas of life. Wherever Africans are, there is their religion.

That wealth and poverty are two sides of the same coin of an oppressive economic system demanding religious change was recognized from Amos to Jesus to Marx. The South African National Congress sees the quest for vision and values as vital to what it calls the National Democratic Revolution. Spirit and votes and money cannot be kept in separate compartments. Holiness, housing, hustings, and jobs go together. Sectionizing humanity leads to oppression and superstition. Human community is one.

The True Ancestral Spirit

The Western world, which kept grace and politics in separate compartments, closed the horrors of the Nazi era with the Nuremberg Trials, which saw justice in terms of punishment. South Africa, inheriting a secular spirituality from its ancestors, ended the horrors of apartheid with the Truth and Reconciliation Commission, which saw justice in terms of reconciliation.

Religious truth is evolutionary. It is not given once and for all in particular traditions. Rather, these traditions undergo decisive changes as modern people cannot view them in the same way as people from past times. These unfolding insights, related to the exigencies of their times, have to be assessed in the light of ancestral grace, whether we are liberating humanity from Christian, Muslim, or Hindu fanaticism, African dictators, or the oppressive Western empire.

Traditional Africa resisted being trapped in religious institutions. Grace is personal: it flows through persons in community, not through systems designed to enhance the power of institutions. We must liberate ourselves from those religious traditions that subvert the good news of Jesus in the quest to bolster their own kingdoms on earth. We often evidence this in the current manipulation of Pentecostal-type institutions and in the fanatical developments of other religions. The machinations of right-wing fundamentalists, whether promoted by Tel Aviv, Al Qaeda, or Washington, have nothing to do with the prophets of Israel, Jesus or Mohammad, and are barriers to the liberating power of ancestral grace.

The evolutionary nature of religious truth is clearly seen in the New Testament itself, where the early Christians sometimes got it wrong, and for two thousand years the church has struggled through one reformation after another to recover the original insights of Jesus. Another prophet must come to reclaim that gift of grace again. Hopefully, the expanded vision of ancestral grace offered in this book will contribute to that evolving process.

A Landscape without Fences

Diarmuid O'Murchu traces the pathway of ancestral grace in the struggles and achievements of humans over a timespan of 7 million years. And all this happened primarily in Africa! Long before religious institutions came to be, or Holy Scriptures were created, what Paul describes as the harvest of the Spirit (Gal. 5:19) flourished in Africa. The earthy, communal, and holistic routines of daily life knew the communal gifts of the Spirit.

We reap the fruits of ancestral grace through an interplay of communal endeavor, not merely as a solo performance seeking individual salvation. Love needs someone else. Joy is something shared. Peace is mediated. Patience is interactive. Generosity is toward! These communal activities have no reality except with another. Ancestral grace is not a solitary rosy glow but an experience of deep communal solidarity.

I welcome the expansive horizons depicted by Diarmuid O'Murchu. I appreciate particularly the African contribution to that unfolding, liberating process. As we begin to reclaim a landscape without fences, may we know once more a grace-filled humanity, learning to cherish more deeply the blessings of our ancient and unfolding story.

Cedric Mayson
Religious Affairs Commission,
African National Congress

Preface

*Let's forget the assumptions that betray our hugeness. Let's have
a great story in our pocket for every time we meet.*

— JAN PHILLIPS

THIS BOOK AIMS AT an unusual synthesis of three rather divergent
fields of exploration. First, I record the remarkable achievements
of a group of researchers many people never hear of, namely, *paleoanthropologists,* scholars who devote their study and time trying to
uncover our origins as a human species. This is a field of research
that has intrigued me for several years. Although it is often described
in terms of fossils and bone deposits, I am far more enamored by the
underlying curiosity and mystic-type analysis that the scholars adopt.

That brings me to the second strand. Findings and facts are merely
the external expression of a deeper story. Rational analysis often hides
and even undermines archetypal insight. What is conscious is often
the mere tip of an unconscious iceberg. Drawing on imagination and
intuition, I want to unlock the deeper wisdom behind and within the
scientific research. In that way, I believe we come to see humanity in
an exciting new light, one that can offer greater hope and meaning
for our time.

Third, I revisit our Christian story in the light of the great human
story. If the coming of God in the flesh (incarnation) reveals to
us some deep truths about our human condition, presumably this
includes every stage of human emergence throughout the entire evolutionary story of 7 million years. That being the case, we need to
re-vision the Christian narrative so that it honors the more ancient
wisdom we are uncovering today.

The title of the book, *Ancestral Grace,* clearly confirms my bias,
but also, I hope, my deep convictions. I believe God has been fully

with humanity on the whole evolutionary journey of 7 million years, and not merely during the recent five thousand years of formal religion. Every moment of that story is a graced experience. In other words it is imbued with a foundational goodness and a power for creativity. It is not perfect, and never will be, but nonetheless, it demonstrates an elegance, wonder, and empowerment that we have neglected to our personal and earthly detriment.

And just to set the record straight: I do not see myself as a nostalgic, deluded new ager, forever yearning for a lost idyllic past. I believe our past is an integral dimension of our lives — personally and collectively. If we fail to honor it, and its ancestral wisdom, it is likely to haunt us. If we integrate it in a creative and imaginative way, it can become an empowering resource for the new and challenging future we are all asked to embrace.

In a word, I have tried to write a book full of gratitude for the past and full of promise for the future.

Part One

The Human as Human

We are not saying we know where the cradle of humanity is, but the cradle is much larger than we thought.

— MICHEL BRUNET

Once upon a time — but this is neither a fairy tale nor a bedtime story — we knew less about the natural world than we do today. Much less. But we understood that world better, for we lived ever so much closer to its rhythms.

— DANIEL SWARTZ

Chapter 1

By the Grace of God...

I know nothing except what everyone knows —
if there when Grace dances, I should dance.
— W. H. AUDEN

Grace is the secret essence of all eligible reality.
— KARL RAHNER

I N THE CHILDHOOD formation of my Christian faith, "grace" was an important word. It described the state of one's soul, defining whether or not one was in a right relationship with God. One went to communion only if one's soul was in a state of grace. When lost, it could be regained by going to confession. By God's grace one avoided committing sin, and when one did, we prayed for the grace to be forgiven.

Affiliation to the church was crucial to all this. Yes, grace was a gift from God, but effectively it could be dispensed only through the church, especially by participation in the sacraments. And the dispenser was the priest, really the only one who could mediate grace on behalf of sinful humans. Ordinary people could grow more fully in grace by doing good works; the ability to do so was itself a benefit of God's grace.

Dualistic Overtones

Dualistic overtones rumble in the background. The great perfect God and the flawed human are juxtaposed. How much of this belongs to God and how much is a human projection? There is no one word corresponding to grace in the Hebrew Scriptures. Two words tend to be

3

used: *chesed,* meaning loving-kindness, and *hanam,* best translated as the spontaneous gift of affection. The Greek word used in the New Testament is *charis,* which literally means gift. In all cases, grace is understood as an expression of divine graciousness (see Duffy 1993, 18ff.).

Eastern Christianity seems to be more faithful to the biblical foundations. Grace is associated with the divine energy, sustaining and empowering everything in being. It does not deny sin and fragility but it reconsiders them within a larger picture in which the relationship between God and creation (including humans) is fundamentally benign.

Western Christianity often fell foul of the dualistic divide between the divine and the human, grace and nature, salvation and sin, grace and good works.[1] The all-good God and the fundamentally flawed human were often portrayed in a struggle to regain a lost harmony. A language of "earned" and "unearned" grace begins to develop (grace and merit). Categories of "actual" and "sanctifying" grace were invoked, the former, a temporary enlightened state of mind or strength of will to remain sinless; the latter, the supernatural nature of grace infused by God into the soul enabling humans to serve God faithfully. The debate between Pelagius and St. Augustine is just one of several weighty diatribes that ensued (see Duffy 1993; Haight 1979).

As we sift our way through the theological complexities, a few basic elements can be identified:

1. Above all else grace denotes *giftedness,* a primary expression of divine *graciousness,* described many years ago by the late Karl Rahner (1966) as the nearness of the abiding mystery.

2. God's gracious giftedness is expressed through everything in creation, especially the abundance with which God endows creation (see Dreyer 1990, 190–211).

3. Grace also denotes the sustaining energy with which God infuses the whole of creation. Some people identify this with the Holy Spirit (e.g., Wallace 2002; 2005).

4. Grace could be defined as God's unconditional love for everything in creation — "...the grace of God plunges us into the world" (Johnson 2003, 110).

5. Grace also denotes a central element in the strategy whereby God rescues sinful humanity. Christianity states this explicitly; it is less explicit in the great Oriental religions.

6. "Rather than something that can be easily lost by sin and regained by repentance, grace remains as God's permanent offer of love and thereby of salvation to the creature, an offer that cannot be extinguished by the grossest sin" (Johnson 2003, 109).

Grace and the Fundamental Flaw

Grace becomes problematic when we enter the human realm. In the great story of creation things seem fine with God until humanity comes along. Then things seem to fall into disarray, particularly in a catastrophe called "the Fall."

The Christian version goes like this: There was a rebellion in the heavenly realm (above and beyond the earth) between two groups of warring angels, vying for power and domination, it seems. The losers were deemed to be evil and were expelled by God from paradise. They landed on planet earth and began to propagate through sexual reproduction. Thus the evil force that led to the rebellion in heaven is endemic to this species called humanity, and the evil is passed on primarily through sex. Moreover, everything affected by these sinful creatures, including the whole of creation, becomes contaminated. Consequently, everything in creation is now fundamentally flawed.

Humans are the culprits. They are the first to be fundamentally flawed, the first to fall foul of Original Sin. Everything else in creation suffers the negative fallout. In this scenario, we need to note that humans are considered superior to everything else in creation. And God is postulated as being concerned primarily with humans.

The breakthrough for humans is activated and facilitated through the salvation wrought by Jesus. This is the great rescue — not just for Christians but allegedly for all humans. Whether or not it is a rescue for the rest of creation has not preoccupied scholars down through the ages.

As people of faith, we are expected to believe this preposterous myth, because Christianity declares it to be revealed truth. It is the very truth of God himself, and in Christian theology, only the Christian church has full access to that truth. When we realize that historically the Christian church defined revelation exclusively within a male context — half of God's creatures, namely, women, had no say whatever — then we begin to glimpse the shaky foundations on which the whole theory rests.

Beyond the specific domain of Christian theology, people argue that we need some theory to make sense of human waywardness. Ormerod (2007, 68–89) opts for the theory of an inherited "universal victimhood," drawing on the social-psychological groundwork of theorists such as René Girard, Alice Miller, and Karen Horney. Obviously, we are not perfect, and history painfully reminds us of the consequences of our recklessness, violence, and immorality. Others go on to suggest that not only are we prone to evil, but in and of ourselves we seem unable to do anything much about it. Therefore, the theology of redemption makes enormous sense. Without belief in a rescuing God, we are all condemned to absolute meaninglessness and ultimate despair.[2]

Grace Revisited

It is against this perverse background that grace came to be understood as a supernatural power of rescue, and Jesus came to be understood as the great rescuer. We began to lose sight of the blessed, empowering love of God, which had flourished in creation for billions of years. Religious reductionism ossified an otherwise empowering and liberating endowment. But, as I shall attempt to illustrate in the present work, that is only a development of the past few thousand years. Grace has been triumphant throughout the billions of years of creation's evolution and throughout the 7 million years of our great human story.

In the contemporary world, concepts like sin and grace have lost a great deal of meaning. And despite the horrendous suffering and injustices of our time, people are not convinced that this is a hopelessly flawed creation. In fact, more than ever before, people strive to make the world a better place because innately and intuitively we know it can be better and should be better. What still haunts us in trying to achieve this noble goal is the same anthropocentrism that propagated the notion of a fundamental flaw in the first place.

In the closing decades of the twentieth century, as we began to realize the precarious state of life on planet earth, numerous movements arose seeking to reclaim the sacredness of creation in relation to both the cosmic and earthly realms. A disturbing insight came to the fore: humans themselves have construed ways of dealing with creation that are no longer politically, economically, or culturally sustainable, and often the root causes of so much meaningless suffering seem to be fueled by *forms of religion that are inherently destructive* (see Harris 2005). In other words, it may be religion itself — or the inherited concept of civilization (see Crossan 2007) — rather than humanity or creation that is fundamentally flawed.

In reclaiming the great story of the cosmos and of planet earth, we have come to realize that our conventional human story has become grossly distorted by separating ourselves from the bigger story and, in recent millennia, setting ourselves over it. We construe our human narrative largely in terms of two thousand years and trace many central notions of what it means to be human to the Greek culture of twenty-five hundred years ago. We abort humanity from the womb to which it integrally belongs. Little wonder that we behave in such dysfunctional and destructive ways.

By resituating humanity within the larger cosmic and planetary context where we — like all other creatures — integrally and intimately belong we stand a much better chance of re-visioning the human enterprise with meaning and renewed hope. Then we can reclaim grace for what it foundationally means in both the Hebrew and Christian scriptures: the great gifting power of God nourishing and sustaining everything in being, described by Miroslav Volf (1998) as the double movement of embrace and covenant. Redemptive rescuing makes sense no longer. Grace abounds, grace sustains, and grace enables us to live gracefully with the paradoxes that characterize creation's great story.

Our Graced Story

The present work does not begin with an angelic rebellion in the heavenly realm, a far-fetched myth that makes little sense to intelligent people of our time — even to children! My story strives to honor God's starting-point. Where does God begin with humanity's story, as we know the story today from history and science? And what might our story begin to look like when we honor more authentic origins?

If we assume that God is fully at work in creation at every stage — and I certainly do — then God was fully with us, in the power of unconditional grace, when we first evolved as a human species a few million years ago. There has never been a time in which our God was not fully present to us, nor has there ever been a time when God's grace was not abundantly and generously bestowed upon us.

Endowed abundantly with such grace, which is also the grace-filled energy sustaining everything in creation, for most of our time on earth we responded well to God's Grace. As intimated by W. H. Auden in the opening quotation: we did participate in the dance, even to the extent of dancing our religion long before we composed creeds or developed legally enforced religious dogmas.

Contrary to so many theories that problematize the human endeavor, the evidence of the larger story suggests that *we got it right for most of our time as an earth-based species*. We got it right because we lived in a close, convivial relationship with the earth in which our graced God has grounded us. Only when we began to distance ourselves from the earth, over the past few thousand years, have things got badly out of kilter.

The oft-quoted remark of the late Stephen J. Gould (2000, 51), "...any replay of the tape (of life) would lead evolution down a pathway radically different from the road actually taken," has rightly been challenged by several other scholars, notably the Cambridge (UK) paleobiologist Simon Conway Morris (2004). Morris claims that convergence more than anything else characterizes organic and human evolution, suggesting that in all probability we would continue to evolve constructively and creatively on what we have already achieved throughout our long story. In other words, there is an ancient and foundational "rightness" to who we are and to what we have been about in our evolutionary story. I wish to suggest that it is the theological concept of *grace,* more than anything else that enables us to grasp the deeper significance of this meaning-laden emergence.

The critical issue at stake here is the interpretative frame of reference we use. We tend to regard the academic sphere as the ultimate custodian of truth and meaning. And for most disciplines this means adopting the insights of classical Greek times as the basis for rational discourse and foundational truth. Anything predating twenty-five hundred years ago is considered suspect, unreliable, and not to be taken seriously.

The interpretative context is further trivialized by several unquestioned assumptions belonging to the cult(ure) of *patriarchy.* I use this term to denote the shadow side of the agricultural revolution, dating back some ten thousand years from the present time. Faced with a new social complexity arising from the development of agriculture, a predominantly male subgroup fragmented the land and sought to control both the land and its users with a firm hand, one that became progressively more domineering and violent. Validated by a self-created sky-God, the patriarchal system set out to conquer and control all before it. It prevails to the present time, although now facing decline and the ensuing disarray we notice in so many major institutions today.

The patriarchal value system has been the subject of much criticism in recent decades, and the more criticism is launched the more robust the defense even to the point of demonizing the critics. While I believe that the patriarchal system is running its course and is now a wearied force, I want to cherish its achievements while also acknowledging its serious limitations. Nor is it likely to have been the first time in human evolutionary history in which humanity opted for a cultural response with such a destructive vein to it.

Our Graced Orientation

In evolutionary terms we have never got it totally right; had we achieved that we would have been gods unto ourselves. Blessed as we are with freedom and creativity, *we get it right most of the time* — in terms of the big story — and occasionally we get it badly wrong. Yet the evolutionary story, infused by the guiding grace of divine wisdom, tends to bring things back to a more wholesome way of living and behaving.

Our great mistake today is to judge our entire story by the standards of the past eight thousand years. Intellectually and spiritually we have been conditioned into thinking small. The figure of two thousand years has taken on an archetypal significance never intended by God. Its importance belongs to the patriarchal cult of minimalism; it is easier to exert control when we keep things small, and the control is powerfully enhanced when we can religiously validate the context.

But when we learn to embrace a bigger picture, we then find ourselves in the amazing and liberating quandary Philip Yancey must have been pondering when he wrote: "Grace makes its appearance in so many forms that I have trouble defining it" (1997, 70). Grace is our abundance, our blessedness, our most enduring survival skill. Gratitude is our default mode! "In grace we see ourselves as peers," writes Elizabeth Dreyer (1990, 239), "not only with all peoples, but with the earth itself." Deep inside we know this, and hopefully the reflections of this book will empower us to reclaim and honor that which we know at the heart of our being.

We begin these reflections with the challenge of honoring and adopting God's time scale — which in human terms is 7 million years and not two thousand years. When we adopt the big picture, we stand a better chance of outgrowing the minimalism that is choking us to death. We stand a better chance of honoring God's big story revealed in the whole of creation and in our own embodied existence. We begin to realize that beyond all our flaws, sins, and limitations we are first and foremost the beneficiaries of God's unconditional love, a love that needs to be reclaimed in its rightful context, namely, the realm of *ancestral grace*.

Chapter 2

Creatures of Imagination

Most species do their evolving, making it up as they go along, which is the way nature intended. This is all very natural and organic and in tune with the mysterious cycles of the cosmos, which believes there is nothing like millions of years of evolving to give a species moral fibre and, in some cases, backbone.

— TERRY PRATCHETT

WHILE WE CLING TO THE THEORY of a fundamental flaw and the need for special grace to rescue us from it, inevitably we view humanity as depraved and corrupt. This begets a type of helplessness and a culture of despair that plunges us further into anomie and alienation. The rescuing God begins to look more and more like a punitive father, keeping the wayward children well under his thumb, while all the time eroding the confidence and trust of growing adults. We begin to suspect that projections abound; the controlling culture of patriarchy dominates and perverts the scene. Alienation poisons the landscape.

Alienation begets more alienation. People get worse, not better. Creatures begotten and called forth by a creative God are consistently robbed of their capacity for mystery, growth, and wholeness. We resolve the dilemma by creating preposterous theories like that of the fundamental flaw, but it does not illuminate our plight; it darkens it. The solution does not rest outside us, but within us. That is the relocation attempted in this book.

The Cult(ure) of Rationality

For a few thousand years now, humans have been indoctrinated in an excessively rationalistic way of comprehending reality. As long as we

11

use our reason and act upon it, we are deemed to be on safe ground. And the dark and sinister side of life is best rationalized in a dark and sinister way. Ironically, rationality generates its own fundamental flaw, which David Korten (2006) vividly describes as he invites us to outgrow the culture of empire in favor of the earth community!

The emphasis on rationality is based on a number of cultural assumptions that are widely approved and, therefore, rarely critiqued in an enlightened or comprehensive way (see Lerner 1986; Plumwood 2002). These assumptions include:

1. Man is the measure of all things (anthropocentrism).

2. Humans are the most highly evolved creatures in the whole of creation.

3. Humans alone possess developed intelligence.

4. Humans alone can make rational, moral decisions.

5. To make those decisions intelligently, we use only information we can verify objectively and quantitatively.

6. Objective knowledge requires us to take seriously things that have happened closer to our time rather than those of the distant past. Mythology is mere myth and of little use to rational human beings.

7. Imagination, intuition, feelings, and emotions are suspect, difficult to control, and not to be taken seriously. Cherish hard science and dogmatic religion rather than artistic expression.

8. The earth, and all of creation, is an object for human use and benefit.

9. To master creation and manage human affairs in a rational way we need hierarchical structures of governance.

10. Religion, based on a sky-God, hierarchically ruling over all human hierarchies, is our ultimate referent point.

11. Creation is fundamentally flawed, but concerted human effort can mold it into something reasonably good.

12. Those who work hard will be rewarded either in this life or in the next.

These are among the leading assumptions of our dominant patriarchal culture, one that has thrived since the agricultural revolution of about ten thousand years ago. It is an evolutionary cycle that has largely run its course and, as I have indicated elsewhere, is now entering its wave of decline and disintegration. It has had its moments of glory, but for the greater part it has been something of a dark age for humanity, and darker still for the surrounding creation because of dysfunctional human interference.

The rational mind is reluctant to look at big pictures because they cannot be subjected to rational evaluation. Ten thousand years is too far-fetched to be taken seriously. All that matters are the past few thousand because those we can manage and control — with the rational mind. There is little room here for ancestral grace. And despite the catechetical rhetoric that God created the world and sustains everything in it, only the reduced God of the past few thousand years is taken seriously. The divine grandeur in the cosmic-planetary story, or in the human story of 7 million years, is fine for mystics, but not for us advanced rational people.

The Suppressed Imagination

The most damaging impact of this patriarchal cycle is its tendency to undermine and underestimate the role of the human imagination. Rationality triumphed, and correspondingly imagination and intuition were either suppressed or repressed. Not surprisingly, therefore, we have witnessed cultural breakthroughs of compensatory significance, as in the great geniuses of music, art, and literature. Rarely, however, did these people play leading roles in the overall culture, and many individual artists struggled to survive financially and materially. No matter how significant the creative outburst might have been, it was always contained, and often subdued, within the dominant rationalistic culture.

In our time, imagination and intuition are back with a vengeance. We see it in the popular culture, often in chaotic and outrageous ways, but we also detect it in the scholarly world as larger horizons of research and exploration tease our curiosity. In the present book,

I look specifically at the work of paleoanthropologists, particularly those who have borne the heat and dust of East Africa in search of our origins. This can be tedious, unrewarding work, and were it not for a subconscious driving force, deeply mystical in my opinion, it would not be pursued with such fervor and resilience.

Furthermore, I want to suggest that the allurement points not merely to a spiritual hunger in the scholars themselves, but a realignment of deep desire evoked by the story of evolution itself — a thesis I develop at length elsewhere (O'Murchu 2007). This is a story carved out of mystery and potential of which we are only vaguely aware at this moment in our human history. And our addiction to rationality may well be the single greatest obstacle inhibiting us from making the deeper connections.

Invoking the Imagination

We make the connections when we set free the creative imagination and learn to trust insight and intuition with fresh transparency. This is what scholars like Carl Jung, Henri Corbin, and Edward Casey have been calling us to do. Carl Jung believed that *soul* and *image* are one and same and that they exist as a mediating factor between body and mind.

The French scholar Henri Corbin (1972; 1998) developed the concept of the *mundus imaginalis* (the imaginal realm), which he describes as a vast intermediate sphere of image and representation that is just as ontologically real as the worlds of sense and intellect. In the domain of the imagination things are *real,* not in the sense that they are being "imagined" by someone but are images that have a quality of integrity and existence in their own right. The imagination is a phenomenon we need to cherish and affirm for its inherent worth (see also Casey 2000, 32).

Corbin describes images as the thoughts of the heart, understanding heart to be the seat of the imagination. In this sense, images are not something that a person sees — they are not necessarily visual — but rather a perspective, a way of seeing, comprehending, and understanding reality. All of this makes sense only when we adopt a different understanding of the imagination and its role in human living.

Most importantly, we need to distinguish imagination from mind (see Casey 2000). The psychologist James Hillman consistently claims that the mind is in the imagination rather than the imagination in the mind. Imagination belongs not just to the head but to the entire body, and in human terms it is grounded in the human body as it functions interactively with the creative energy of the universe.[3] Obviously, for humans our own evolutionary story provides a more immediate link with the larger story of the home planet and the entire cosmos.

While we continue to define imagination as a mere processor of perceptions or, worse, as a sphere for daydreaming and wild fantasy, we subvert its more central role as the domain in which we appropriate, channel, and process images in our desire to connect creatively with the rest of creation. In the words of Carol Frenier (2005, 13): "We inhabit the image in order to grow from it."

All the scholars cited thus far acknowledge the transcendent and archetypal dimension of imagination and readily connect psychic processes with spiritual aspirations. Imagination of its very nature is transparent to spirit-power. Hillman suggests that the value found in images is in regard to how they present the "gods" to us, not so much as concrete appearances but rather in what the deities represent for us as metaphors constructed by the human imagination. Imagination at all times is in pursuit of meaning, of viable connection and life-giving relationship. What the divine desires is ultimately what the imagination is seeking. And for much of our evolutionary time, I suggest, we were a species deeply attuned to the lure of the divine!

Imagination as We Trace Our Origins

Like most other scientists, paleoanthropologists approach their research with great caution. That which closely resembles humanity as we know it today we assume to be the basis of all human evolution. The further back we go in tracing human origins the more reluctant scholars are to attribute authentic human identity.

One discovery, however, is beginning to serve as a revolutionary bridge between the prevailing rationalism and the more imaginative construct I am proposing, namely, the micro-organism known as *mitochondria*. First reported in 1974 in horse-donkey hybrids by the geneticist and jazz pianist Clyde Hutchinson, and poetically described as tiny powerhouses within human cells, mitochondria are considered by Nick Lane (2005, 1) to be the clandestine rulers of the world.[4] Whereas the DNA in the chromosomes of the cell nucleus is inherited from both parents, everyone gets their mitochondria from one parent only, namely, the *mother*. The cytoplasm of the human egg cell is stuffed with a quarter million mitochondria! Fathers pass on nuclear DNA, but mothers pass on the crucial information that connects us with deep time.

"Mitochondrial Eve" has entered the imperial world of sophisticated science, and by implication puts women, rather than men, at the heart of our evolutionary story — so different from the male prerogative highlighted by Aristotle about twenty-five hundred years ago. This new slant on our great story forms the basis of Bryan Sykes's popular work *The Seven Daughters of Eve* (Sykes 2004), which indicates that we can now trace our genetic origins back through the female line to some 170,000 years ago. That is as far as the rational scientist is prepared to go. The more imaginative researcher wishes to probe further into deep time.

Currently, we distinguish between the *Ardipithecines,* the *Australopithecines,* and the genus *Homo.* Both *Ardipithecus* and *Australopithecus* are considered to be more ape-like than human, while *Homo* is considered to be so humanly advanced as to have outgrown its ape-like characteristics. Scholars have never established a clear demarcation line between these two developments, indicating that commonalities are far more significant than differences, a prospect that feels very threatening for patriarchal humans, seeking to establish an absolute uniqueness for humans.[5]

For the purposes of the present work, I want to embrace continuity rather than discontinuity and explore commonalities rather than differences. I like to think of our primate ancestors as *anthropoids,* from the Latin "human-like." I believe our humanity will actually be enriched if we work toward a greater integration of our primate (and even our animal) ancestry. For this reason, I want to view our *Australopithecus* ancestors as human rather than nonhuman (proto-human, if you wish). Their underdeveloped humanness was an evolutionary stage in the process of further emergence, something fluid and evolving rather than rigidly determined biologically or genetically. Our authentic humanity can be retrieved and reclaimed only when we choose to work with our entire story, and not merely with its evolution in more recent millennia.

These insights are potentially enriching and empowering for people of religious disposition but also for those of no religious persuasion. For religious folks, I want to suggest that the divine creativity (what I am calling "ancestral grace") has been at work *at every stage* of our evolutionary becoming, and therefore all the stages deserve our discerning attention, despite the paucity of hard fact. For the nonreligious believer, I want to suggest that every stage of human evolution carries distinctive meaning for who we are today as a human species. Meaning is embroidered in the grand narrative, and we need the big picture to access and appreciate its elegance and creativity.

We can view our history as a piecemeal accumulation of rather disconnected episodes, illustrating various developments — fire, tools, language, art, etc. — as illustrations of Darwinian-based evolutionary necessity. This is a partial explanation in a narrative that has deeper meaning and hidden elegance. Aided with imagination and intuition, with which we are abundantly blessed, we can, and must, aim deeper and higher.

Imagination and Paradox

Evolution thrives on wild creativity. It is full of surprises. In the grand story of cosmic unfolding, things often reach frightening levels of disintegration, as in the great extinctions. Annihilation seems to be the only resolution, but total annihilation is *never* registered, because this wild creative Spirit swings the pendulum as novel breakthroughs herald a new wave of vitality and future possibility. It makes no rational or logical sense, and I suspect it never will. This is paradox writ large;

it makes sense to the creative imagination, and without imagination it spells ruination, despair, and nihilism.

As a human species we too have known this paradoxical mix throughout every stage of our existence. It is important therefore that we do not glamorize the past or excessively idealize it. At every stage of creation and throughout the various epochs of human unfolding, nature has consistently been red in tooth and claw (Tennyson). How we humans coped with this is something upon which we can only make reasonable guesses, which is quite different from mere specu-lation. We are richly endowed with wisdom, resilience, and survival skills, and these provide clues to how we would have coped. But of much more central importance is our convivial relationship with nature itself. That, more than anything else, is the clue to human meaning, past and present.

Even today, anthropologists and psychologists tend to view the past rather negatively, alleging that because humans were so im-mersed in nature and its processes, they were largely unable to attain human distinctiveness and allow human uniqueness to evolve. For most of our time on this earth, we viewed ourselves as dimensions of the natural world and learned to live convivially with it. The rule of patriarchy insists that we had to separate ourselves from nature, learn to stand over against it and be different from it. That is the source and ongoing sustenance of the deep alienation that bewilders the human species today. That is the strategy through which we lost our ances-tral wisdom, leaving us with a cultural and spiritual emptiness that haunts us in various spheres of contemporary life.

It is not the cruel paradoxes of nature that undermine our integrity and meaning. Rather it is the culturally imposed dislocation that sets us at variance with creation and strips us of the integral wisdom through which we can comprehend the paradoxes and befriend them in a more meaningful way. The media recorded the story of the Mor-gan fisherfolk of Thailand, who on December 26, 2004, used their imagination and intuition to discern the imminent tsunami. Their inner wisdom told them that massive waves would hit their shoreline in a matter of hours. Gathering most of their meager possessions, they eloped to the hills. None of their members was killed.

Our civilized world describes such people as ignorant, primitive, even barbaric, words that anthropologists no longer use in describing indigenous cultures. The Morgan fisherfolk cannot function in our technologically developed world, but they are imbued with ancestral grace, with a quality of wisdom and insight that is probably crucial if *Homo sapiens* stands any chance of surviving amid the precarious conditions we have created on the earth today.

The Wisdom to See Differently

This is a book about reconnection, not regression. It is about re-claiming the deep wisdom of our ancient past in order to be better equipped to embrace the future that beckons us forth. Past-present-future form an unbroken web. The present is the seminal moment in which we weave past and present, in which we rework the integration that makes progress possible. As in every other age, what we need more than anything else for that onerous task is an abundance of imagination.

Beyond the artifacts, the fossils, skeletons, and bone collections, is a way of seeing reality, imbued by what I call ancestral grace, facilitated primarily through what Guy Claxton calls the "intelligent unconscious" (see also pp. 59ff.). This is a wisdom of engagement, with cooperation and interdependence deeply interwoven. In all probability our ancestors were not into the tasks of conquering and controlling that have become endemic to our patriarchal culture. They certainly were not passive, nor were they the helpless victims of ignorance and savagery. While not educated like us moderns, they were blessed with a wisdom that we have largely lost. Let's investigate more deeply what that wisdom looks like.

Chapter 3

Gazing into Deep Time

We are the local embodiment of a cosmos grown to self-awareness. We have begun to contemplate our origins —
star-stuff pondering the stars! — CARL SAGAN

PALEONANTHROPOLOGISTS ARE SCHOLARS with a fascination about human origins. With Buddhist-like concentration and mystical intuition they meticulously examine bone and limb remnants that most of us would not even notice. They gaze long and hard until meaning begins to divulge clues an average researcher would never even suspect. Painstakingly and religiously, they unravel the great revelations of ancestral grace. And their day's work is never finished — particularly in an infinite universe like ours.

The oldest graced ancestor on our family tree today is *Toumai;* in the indigenous Goran language of his birthplace, the name means "hope for life." Even before the skull was subjected to thorough analysis, it was already confirmed as being a male. One day we may be able to access the DNA of fossils as old as that of Toumai, and if we can identify the strands of mitochondria what will be all important is not the male Toumai but the female progenitor that birthed him.

Wild and speculative though this may sound to readers of a more scientific ilk, I want to intuit and anticipate those further breakthroughs. I do this in the desire to honor the wildly liberating power of ancestral grace. Throughout this chapter, therefore, I write about *Lady Toumai,* the as-yet-undiscovered ancestor with the creative wisdom of our graced origins. Like Lady Wisdom in the Hebrew Scriptures, I suspect she was there when he created the world (of human becoming). She has important things to say to all of us.

20

Toumai, the offspring of Lady Toumai, was discovered in July 2001 in the Goran region of Chad, North Africa. The discovery consisted of a relatively small cranium, two pieces of jaw, and some teeth, excavated by the French paleoanthropologist Michel Brunet and his colleagues. The skull was actually located by Chadean undergraduate Ahounta Djimdoumalbaye. On August 31, 2001, Michel Brunet and his colleague Alain Beauvilain carried the skull to the Chadean president, Idriss Deby, who proposed the name Toumai, explaining that it was a favored name for babies born in the harsh conditions of the hot dry season in the desert. It is the oldest artifact for human ancestry thus far known in the search for human origins. Lady Toumai existed more than 7 million years ago.[6]

Chimp or Human?

In terms of classification, Lady Toumai is neither *Australopithecus* nor *Homo;* the discovery tends to be classified as *hominin* (see Gibbons 2007, 250), and may be an ancestor common to both chimpanzees and humans, yet with some unique human characteristics, categorized initially by Tim White and colleagues as *Ardipithecus* (Gibbons 2007, 152). While the braincase has distinctive chimpanzee features, and measures merely 350cc, the teeth are closer to those of humans, and the face includes brow ridges, a human feature not found in any living great ape. Examination of the neck muscles indicate that this species may have walked upright (see Brunet et al. 2005; Gibbons 2005).

Lady Toumai belongs to that ancient time of evolutionary transition when the primate was yielding pride of place to the human, representing the recurring cycle of everything in creation: birth-death-rebirth. In Toumai we see the twilight of our primate ancestors and the birthing forth of the new — always radically new, yet inescapably linked to the great chain through which everything in creation holds common allegiance.

It is not by accident that the Toumai family was discovered at a time of intense research on our primate ancestors.[7] Sadly, many people are not even aware of this research. We have long outgrown the popular notion of being descended from apes — some people think from monkeys. We don't know who we are descended from; in fact seeking a direct line of descent is a pursuit based on a dangerous and misguided literalism.

At every level of creation evolution does not follow a linear line of succession, but something more akin to quantum leaps. Neils Eldredge (1999) describes it as a process of punctuated equilibrium: long periods of relative stability punctuated with sudden outbursts that defy rational explanation. Our human species is one such outburst, which chronologically may have taken a few million years, but cannot be pinpointed to a precise moment in time.

We are *not* descended from the apes. They share with us a common unidentified ancestor. The chimpanzees, bonobos, orangutans, and gorillas are better described as *our first cousins,* with whom we share over 98 percent of the same DNA. While scholarship generally likes to focus on differences, in conjunction with a growing body of contemporary research I want to focus on commonalities. We bring with us — even to this day — numerous features of our ancestral cousins, and those endowments are central features of our graced uniqueness. The apes are also God's creatures and the connections we share with them are channels through which God's grace works in us — for much longer than we care to acknowledge.

Chimp or Bonobo?

Most of the research on our primate origins focuses on the chimpanzees. Endowed with intelligence and resilience they intrigue and baffle those who study them intimately. But there is a disturbing feature to this fascination, a dangerous type of self-fulfilling prophesy rarely challenged or subjected to a more informed critique. Chimpanzees, by nature, are quite violent, highly competitive, and streamlined very much along patriarchal lines and norms. They powerfully endorse the values of our dominant, patriarchal culture. We give them a high priority because they validate so much of what reinforces our desire for power and control.

And what do we miss in the process? The wisdom to realize that there are other prototypes we could use and adopt, some of which are far more congruent with our deeper story as a human species. Of particular interest are the bonobos, first discovered in 1929 by a German anatomist, Ernst Schwarz. These are highly cooperative creatures whose prevailing behavior exhibits distinctive egalitarian features, with females, and not males, dictating the guiding values. For an alternative view see Raffaele (2006).

Frans de Waal (1996; 2001; 2005) is the world renowned authority on bonobo life and culture. To date, these apes have been discovered only in the Wamba Forest of the Democratic Republic of the Congo, and much of the research has been done with those domesticated in the San Diego Zoo in the United States. "Had the bonobo been known to science first and the chimpanzee second," writes de Waal (2001, 41), "we might today have different ideas about the inevitably of violence in human society, about male dominance and male bonding in hunting and warfare, about the role of technology, and about the social significance of sex."

Bonobo communities are peace-loving and generally egalitarian; they share extensively. The strongest social bonds are those among females, although females also bond with males. The status of a male depends on the position of his mother, to whom he remains closely connected for her entire life. Three major issues differentiate the bonobo from other well known primates, particularly chimpanzees. First, the strong matriarchal leadership; second, the distinctive lack of aggression and violence; third, a prolific sex-life, serving bonding and peace-making rather than reproductive success. Given such rare and distinctive characteristics, one wonders why bonobos have received so little scholarly attention. Sadly, we have to concur with de Waal (2005, 30) when he notes:

Believe me, if studies had found that they massacre one another, everyone would know about bonobos. Their peacefulness is the real problem.... Bonobos act as if they had never heard of the idea [of violence]. Among bonobos, there's no deadly warfare, little hunting, no male dominance, and enormous amounts of sex.

The Counter-Culture of Deep Time

Harold S. Burr (1889–1973), who worked at Yale University, is credited with an intriguing piece of research on the nature and function of energy fields (Burr 1991; *www.wrf.org/news/news0003.htm*). When he examined the energy field of a tiny seedling, he discovered that the surrounding field was not that of a tiny sprout but rather that of a fully mature adult plant. The field represented the entire future destiny of the plant, a kind of template for what the fully mature plant could become. Our ultimate destiny seems to be written into the fabric of our embryonic origins.

Lady Toumai carries a strong memory of the primate world upon whose shoulders we stand, but also the field-potential of our final maturation. The critical question facing humanity is how we best access and discern those primate origins. How much of our attention to the chimps is actually a self-fulfilling prophesy useful to endorse an aggressive, competitive, patriarchal dominance? Perhaps our deep story carries a very different orientation, for which the bonobo serves as a much more authentic model. I wish to suggest that the bonobo belongs strongly to the counter-culture of ancestral grace; the chimpanzee represents what we might consider the shadow side of that endowment.

Obviously, we carry both features, the light and the dark, throughout our entire evolutionary story. But have we honored both? In prioritizing the violent, aggressive chimpanzee, not merely are we left with a rather lop-sided view of our human potential, but much more seriously, we may well have neglected that which constitutes our more authentic development, our bonobo inheritance.

I don't wish to depict an idyllic picture simply to offset our negative characteristics as a human species. At the very least, I wish to reclaim a creative balance and call to greater transparency our human preoccupation with violence and patriarchal power. Even those who prioritize the chimpanzees as models for human behavior concede

that they also exhibit remarkable levels of care, kindness, and cooperation, a dimension largely ignored until Jane Goodall (2001) began
to counter the leading violence-based hypothesis.

The Joy of Sex

The psycho-sexual foundations are much more formidable and require a quality of discernment unprecedented in recent millennia.
Ever since the classical Greek period, we have lived with sexual
self-understandings now under severe strain. For Aristotle, sex is a
biological function for the procreation of the species, with the man
endowed with the life-giving seed and the woman a mere biological
receptacle for the fertilization of the male seed. For the bonobos, sex
is a bonding and reconciling mode of behavior, largely beyond gender distinctions (bonobos are basically bisexual). Although most of
their sexual intimacy is not aimed at reproduction, their reproductive
success is on par with that of chimpanzees.

Primordially, serious questions arise here on what is the purpose
of sexuality in both the primate and human domains. How do we
re-vision sexuality within the context of ancestral grace? And within
that context, how did humans express and articulate their sexual desires throughout our long evolutionary gestation? We can no longer
assume that sex was a function primarily for reproduction. As with
the bonobos it may have had a counter-cultural significance of enormous life-enhancing quality, something largely lost to our biologically
driven culture, leaving us with the repressed burden of the sexual pain
and confusion we experience in the modern world.

The bonobos are models of sharing commonalities rather than
competing over differences. This, too, may well be a graced endowment of deep time in our evolving human story. While the rational
scholarship of our time likes to prioritize the human, often validating
our dominance over every other life form, our evolutionary emergence consistently informs us that we are an integral dimension of
an ancestral line that informs everything we are and everything we
desire to achieve. Ours is fundamentally a narrative of belonging and

interdependence. What we share with others — in deep time — is far more significant that what defines our differences.

Factoring in Another Time Scale

Symbolically, Lady Toumai represents our human identity as creatures of *deep time*. We have been around much longer than most of us suspect, and during all that time, not merely have we survived, we have actually thrived! Yet today we persist in judging ourselves and everything around us in terms of the two thousand years of Christendom or the mere five thousand years of so-called civilization. The academic world attributes unquestioned allegiance to the latter; rarely is research based on anything before five thousand years ago. And for most of us of the Western and Christian heritage, the benchmark of two thousand years signals a time restriction in urgent need of reevaluation.

These time constraints severely damage not merely the potential of humans themselves but also our way of dealing with the enveloping creation. Our delusion that we are somehow the masters of time, and therefore we tend to deal only with what we can chronologically control, is the source of an enormous amount of alienation and meaningless suffering. We become far more humble, grounded, and real when we acknowledge our appropriate time scale. We begin to glimpse the cosmic and planetary mystery to which we belong, the great narrative that has molded us as much as we mold it, the interactive evolutionary process within which we are called to be co-creators.

Currently, scholars tend to use the notion of *deep time* in reference to our cosmic and planetary origins (e.g., Dowd 2007). We are creatures who carry within us ancient stardust and the wisdom to appropriate the nourishing potential of sunlight, with the cosmic giftedness it confers upon every living organism. We are programmed to live and thrive as cosmic-planetary creatures (see Edwards 2006, 7–26). Without the integration of this larger life-giving context, we stand little chance of realizing our God-given, graced potential. While fully endorsing the need to embrace this larger context, for the purposes of the present work I reserve the term "deep time" to the human evolutionary story of the past 7 million years.

When we are dealing with deep time, we need to remain open to the fact that evolution is primarily about new horizons, not established boundaries. Even the Darwinian notion of the survival of the fittest works with the assumption that change is of the essence, and with each new change enlarged horizons of engagement open up. Culturally, spiritually, and educationally, we have not been well prepared to deal creatively with deep time.

When reflecting on deep time we need to allow for the fact that co-evolution was probably the norm that guided much of our ancient behavior, that we co-evolved collaboratively with other organisms in a mutually enhancing way — to a degree that is difficult to entertain in our highly competitive world. A useful example, belonging to a more recent phase in our evolutionary story, comes from our original stone-based technology known as the Acheulean age. Describing some intriguing parallels, Ervin Laszlo (2004, 93) writes:

> The Acheulean axe, a widespread tool of the Stone Age, had a typical almond or tear-shaped design chipped into symmetry on both sides. In Europe this axe was made of flint, in the Middle East of chert, and in Africa of quartzite, shale, or diabase. Its basic form was functional, yet the agreement in the details of its execution in virtually all traditional cultures cannot be explained by the simultaneous discovery of utilitarian solutions to a shared need: trial and error is not likely to have produced such similarity of detail in so many far-flung populations.

Current scholarship assumes that the nearer events and experiences are to our time the more they can be subjected to rigorous analysis, and, therefore, the more they stand the test of credibility. But in our allegiance to such rigorous testing might we not be at risk of abetting a dangerously misleading reductionism? As Laszlo suggests, the manufacture of stone tools in this earlier epoch seems to exhibit some intriguing commonalities, especially if we bear in mind that travel over long distances did not exist and none of the modern means of communication were available. Did ancestral grace link up people (and minds) in ways that defy all our scholarly theories? Is this morphic resonance several millennia ahead of its time?

The biologist Rupert Sheldrake (1988; 1999) has championed the case for *morphic resonance,* the tendency for successful past forms to build up a resonance, bringing an organism, species, or movement to a critical threshold, activating a quantum leap in either new awareness or new behavior. This is popularly known as the hundredth monkey syndrome, from a famous experiment in Japan in the 1950s.

What we humans observed only in the 1950s may well be a feature of our life form, and others, over several millennia. From the growing body of research on emergence, scholars are beginning to reconnect with the underlying consciousness that may well be the glue holding together not merely organic life but also the entire web of cosmic and planetary life (Morowitz 2002; Clayton 2004; Clayton and Davies 2006; Laszlo 2004). Now we realize that the deep time that envelops the human is one and the same with what prevails throughout the entire spectrum of creation.

All of this leaves us with an inescapable conclusion: because we are creatures of deep time, ancestral grace works best in us when we are deeply grounded in this world, and not when we seek to escape to the nirvana or fulfillment of life in another realm. Of all the possible realms favored by ancestral grace, this seems to be the one where humanity — in life and death — is likely to realize its deepest potentials. When we learn to live convivially within the framework of deep time, then indeed we can begin to experience heaven on earth.

Chapter 4

Interdependence and the Will to Life

*The move from seeing ourselves as separate beings placed on
Earth ("the world is made for us") to seeing ourselves as self-
reflective expressions of Earth ("we were made for the world")
is an immense transformation in human identity.*

— MICHAEL DOWD

I N THE 1990s scholars exploring human origins began to stretch
the time scale deeper into the dim and distant past. Foremost
among these visionaries were Tim White and his colleagues from the
University of California, Berkeley. In 1992 they discovered the skull
fragments of *Ardipithecus ramidus* (*ramid* is the Afar word for root)
at a site near Aramis in the Middle Awash region of Ethiopia and
proceeded to date the discovery to 4.4 million years ago. That was
almost one million years older than previous discoveries. However,
more recent excavations, made between 1997 and 2001, indicate an
original date for *Ardipithecus ramidus* (or *Ardipithecus kadabba*),
possibly as far back as 5.8 million years ago.

Meanwhile, in 2000, another very ancient fossil, known as *Orrorin
tugenensis,* was unearthed near the village of Tugen in western Kenya.
It was discovered by Martin Pickford of the Kenya Palaeontology
Expedition and Brigitte Senut of the Museum of Natural History in
Paris and has been dated between 6.1 and 5.8 million years ago.

The Urge to Explore

Orrorin (literally, the original human) is of particular interest for its
bone structure and teeth. The thigh bones (especially the femur) evidence a species that walked upright. This poses a substantial challenge

to the widely held view that we first learned to walk when we moved away from tree-land and began to occupy the open spaces of the savannahs. The fossil evidence shows that *Orrorin* dwelt in woodland, presumably still climbing trees, but nonetheless walking upright (for further detail, see Gibbons 2007, 197ff.). With upright mobility, the human urge to explore took a kind of quantum leap. Ancestral grace expanded into the discovery and exploration of new horizons, particularly the ecological and environmental surroundings.

And the teeth structure suggests a diet quite similar to modern humans. It would have consisted largely of fruit and vegetables, possibly meat on rare occasions. It looks like *Orrorin* explored its environment with a degree of intelligence that has rarely been attributed to these early human ancestors. And as with the animals and primates of previous times, nature consistently nourishes and supports her own, particularly those who act congenially within the supporting web of life.

With bipedalism (moving on two feet) gracefully evolving so early in our great story, humans adopt a sense of mobility that deeply nourishes our innate creativity. To this exploration we bring not just our brains and senses, but our whole embodied existence. And we do that, thanks particularly to our newly acquired skill to walk and run, travel and engage with the wider creation.

The Living Planet

From earliest times, the emerging human species relates interdependently with the surrounding creation. It would be millions of years yet before humans began to treat creation as an object to be conquered and controlled. Deep in our collective psyche we, humans, know the earthly creation as a creature we love and cherish, an organism to work with, a resource to befriend, the primal home to which we all belong. The objectification of the natural world severely damages our inner beings and our outer capacity to connect and relate interdependently.

In our essential nature, we are primed for interdependence, not for independent domination. The groundbreaking research of microbiologist Lynn Margulis (1998) indicates that our primary orientation is toward cooperation, not toward competition. Scholars such as John Stewart (2000), Michael Dowd (2007), and Bruce Lipton (2005) persuasively illustrate that we are programmed for cooperation — of a type in which legitimate self-interest can be accommodated and fostered. The patriarchal culture that requires us to be separate and different so that we can lord it over everything else in creation is increasingly seen to be deleterious to creation's future. Somehow, many theorists fail to see that it is even more destructive to the human race itself.

Our survival as earthlings will not be determined merely by a radical change toward living more sustainably and using earth's resources with greater discretion. The conversion so urgently needed at this time is not just about external reform; much more urgent is the internal renewal to which we are called. We need to forego our anthropocentric imperialism, standing outside and above all other inhabitants with whom we share this planet. We belong integrally as do all others. It is in our sense of belonging, and not in our isolation, that we come home to who we really are. Our interdependence, and not our self-centered independence, is the doorway to survival and fresh meaning.

The Tradition of Gifting

Ever since its publication in 1950, Marcel Mauss's *Essai sur le don* (see Mauss 1990) has been considered an anthropological classic. Tracing the custom of gift exchange across various contemporary indigenous cultures, Mauss seeks to reclaim a practice that characterizes the human species into the dim, ancient past. Anne Primavesi (2003, 112ff.) locates the significance of gifting in the gratuitousness of creation itself. Contrary to the contemporary trend of bestowing gifts for special occasions, gifting in our distant past was a cultural norm with distinctive social, moral, and economic implications (see *www.en.wikipedia.org/wiki/Gift_economy*).

Mauss (1990, 39) summarizes three dominant features: *to give, to receive, to reciprocate*. For much of human history, gifting was a type of social contract. There was no such thing as a free gift. Everything

"freely" given carried the widely recognized obligation of reciproca-
tion. The sense of obligation arose from community expectation, not
something to be arranged among individuals (see Hyde 1983, 74ff.).
Gifting was seen as a central dynamic in the whole fabric of social
and economic life, possibly arising from a deeply unconscious conviction that everything in creation exists primarily as gift. In the words
of Mary Douglas in her introduction to Mauss (1990, xv), "every
single relationship had its substantiation in a gift."

Bernard Lietaer (2001, 181ff.) in his pioneering analysis of alternative economic systems, suggests that a readiness to gift is the
foundation stone of every thriving community and also essential to
every viable economic system. He highlights that the use of money in
former times had a symbolic spiritual significance, as demonstrated
by the imagery on coins (Lietaer 2001, 34ff.); Hyde (1983, 143ff.)
claims that commerce initially was spiritually motivated as well. Gifting is the unwritten rule that binds people together in solidarity and
fellowship, motivated for the greater part by subliminal forces of
great age and depth. Lietaer surmises that such a widespread exchange of goods belongs foundationally to our African origins rather
than to our Neanderthal ancestors.

As indicated in our opening chapter, the word "grace" itself means
"gift," the generous outpouring whether understood to be from a divine source or from the prodigious creativity of creation itself. The
notion of ancestral grace seeks to highlight the deep and ancient
values and behaviors that have sustained our species for millions
of years. Increasingly from diverse sources — economic, ecological,
social, religious — we are hearing echoes of this ancient wisdom,
inviting us to reclaim once more that which we have neglected or
forsaken from our deep past.

What about Sexual Interdependence?

Gender complementarity is a primary aspiration of our time. It is
likely to dominate our evolutionary emergence for quite some time
to come. While we cannot draw on viable models from the past —
because they have been suppressed — we can make intelligent guesses

on how people would have related interdependently. And we have uncovered some significant corroborative evidence from our primate ancestors.

As indicated in chapter 2 above, our adoption of chimpanzees as role models for our evolutionary development is seriously deficient on several fronts. Instead, the bonobos provide a far more congruent blueprint, beneficial to person and planet alike. In a world immersed in so much mindless violence, the example of the bonobos, as peace-loving and highly cooperative creatures, leaves us in little doubt that there is another way forward, that allegiance to ancestral grace can liberate us from our destructability and inspire us to opt for more creative and constructive alternatives.

In this alternative model, females and matriarchal modeling are of central importance. And we have good reason to assume that such female prerogative was a frequent occurrence in our great evolutionary story; tragically, most of the evidence has been subverted and in many cases totally destroyed.

This alternative interdependent way of engaging our world, with women often serving as primary instigators, is the model we now need to adopt, despite the paucity of hard evidence. Intuition and insight point us toward resources we know have been there; when we add corroborative evidence of glorious epochs like the Paleolithic era (see chapter 6 below), we know we have other choices and other models that promise a different and better strategy for engaging creation in a way that honors ancestral grace. Frans de Waal (2001, 109) echoes a similar sentiment when he writes:

> We now view most primate societies as female centered rather than male controlled, based on the strength of the female bonds present. Females are also the "ecological" sex. Their own reproductive gains are more intimately tied to the physical environment than those of males.

The stereotype of the robust male hunter and the domesticated subdued female is a caricature for which there is little substantial evidence, other than the historical fact that male fossils tend to be significantly larger than female ones. When dealing with the wisdom of ancestral grace, we do not rely solely on external measurements, particularly those supporting dominance and control. We need to read the evidence so that we can also embrace insights of the creative imagination, and especially the alternative wisdom that tends to be subverted in our inherited patriarchal interpretations.

In conjunction with much of rational science, male discoveries tend to dominate the archaeological record, Lucy being one notable exception (see p. 37 below). Imaginatively and intuitively we need to fill the gaping chasm, because without doing so, we cannot appreciate nor contemplate the full scale of ancestral grace. In this enterprise there are several starting points, including the commitment to nonviolence that has featured strongly in our ancient past and evokes a fresh sense of urgency in the violence-ridden culture of the present age.

Relating Nonviolently

We can never hope to retrieve the past in a rationally objective way, but a growing body of alternative insights entitles us to weave a narrative that seeks to honor a deeper meaning and a more ancient truth. Central to this alternative story is a convivial way of being in the world, a foundational interdependence, begetting a much more gentle and cooperative mode of existence on earth. I wish to submit that our evolutionary story for most of our historical existence exhibits this relational orientation long ahead of the recent millennia when we became a much more violent and adversarial species.

Geoffrey Carr (2005, 11) indicates that violent behavior among humans in itself cannot be invoked as evidence for a violent species. In social and cultural systems over several thousand years humans have punished their own members for deviant and unjust behavior. Humans are hardwired to detect injustice and consistently strive to set it right. Altruistic behavior, including even the sacrifice of one's own life, occurs in every ancient culture. In fact, Carr (2001, 10) claims that we can locate evidence for it in animal populations. Contrary to all the wanton and violent behavior exhibited by humans today, there is another dimension to our story, revealing a peace-loving, reconciliatory species. And these interdependent characteristics are not merely features of rare occurrence in our ancient story. They comprise the bulk of our graced story over several thousand years.

This alternative mode can be studied under numerous contemporary expressions, the *way of nonviolence* being to the fore (see Dear 2004; Wink 1998; Zinn 2002). Associated mainly with the pacifist views of Gandhi and Martin Luther King, nonviolence signifies a great deal more than just the absence of conflict or violence, or the socio-political option for pacifism. Nonviolence denotes a set of values prizing the central role of dynamic, flourishing relationships (see *www.nonviolence.org*). Among other things it includes the awareness:

- that life will flourish only when all the constituent elements interact creatively and dynamically;

- that cooperative endeavor is the most empowering strategy for life at every level;

- that our skills for dialogue and negotiation need frequent and transparent review;

- that conflict in itself is not bad or destructive, but to resolve it constructively we humans need to acquire the wisdom and skills for conflict resolution;

- that forgiveness is not just a religious disposition, but a crucial ingredient in all evolutionary unfolding (where it often is manifest as altruistic behavior);

- that warfare is a patriarchal invention that rarely achieves a just or beneficial outcome and serves power for the sake of power;

- that wanton violence tends to beget further violence, making it increasingly difficult to halt or break the cycle of violence.

In a word, nonviolence is a whole way of life characterized by respect and deep attention to the unfolding patterns of evolution. It seems remarkably close to how our ancient ancestors lived under the inspiring guidance of ancestral grace. Perhaps it carries a strong contemporary resonance precisely because we know it intuitively in the deep recesses of our inner being.

Chapter 5

Our Home in Africa

Be nice to whites, they need you to discover their humanity.
— ARCHBISHOP DESMOND TUTU

Never, never and never again shall it be that this beautiful land will again experience the oppression of one by another.
— NELSON MANDELA

MOST OF THE GREAT DISCOVERIES related to early humans come out of Africa, particularly the countries along the eastern seaboard. Africa is our birthplace as a human species. It is our primordial home, the place where we struck deep roots and laid the foundations for the evolutionary trajectory that has brought us to where we are today. Outside of Africa, the oldest known hominids are dated merely at 1.8 million years (Gibbons 2007, 232).

We climbed the trees of East Africa and in due course roamed the wild savannahs. We encountered — in both play and conflict — the kindred species with whom we share the planet. It was in Africa that we first created fire, fashioned primitive tools, danced our religion, and created the first art and sculpture. The soil of Africa knows intimately the human soul, and as the African people themselves intuit, the African air breathes the living spirit of the ancestors.

The African Connection

Two different discoveries, dated almost a million years apart, acknowledge the African connection. First, there is *Australopithecus afarensis,* existing possibly as far back as 3.5 million years ago, a creature with an apelike face, a skull similar to that of a chimpanzee,

36

human-like teeth, and a pelvis and leg bones quite similar to those of modern humans.

The first skeleton was discovered in the Hadar region of Ethiopia in November 1973 by Donald Johanson of Arizona State University (Johanson 2006; see *www.becominghuman.org*). As the skeleton was being pieced together it turned out to be that of a young woman, which Johanson nicknamed Lucy after the Beatles song "Lucy in the Sky with Diamonds." Lucy was only three feet eight inches tall, with a small skull similar to that of a chimpanzee. But her pelvic structure proved that she had walked upright, and her teeth were distinctively human.

Overnight, Lucy became a household name among those searching for human origins, causing great excitement and no small measure of controversy. Today, a plaster replica of the skeleton is preserved in the national museum in Addis Ababa, Ethiopia. Her reputation was further enhanced in December 2000, when the Ethiopian paleo-anthropologist Zeresenay Alemsgeded unearthed a virtually intact skull of a three-month old infant at a site called Dikika in the Afar region of northern Ethiopia. Formally named Salem, it is much more widely known as Lucy's Baby, providing one of the most intact skulls representing *A. afarensis* (see Gibbons 2007, 94ff.; Wong 2006a).

Next there comes *Australopithecus africanus*, of slender build like *A. afarensis* but significantly more evolved with a more human-like cranium, a slightly larger brain, and more humanoid facial features. This discovery belongs largely to South Africa and is dated between 2 and 3 million years ago. The initial evidence is that of a child's skull, discovered by quarryman M. de Bruyn and categorized by Raymond Dart at Kimberley, South Africa, in 1924. It came to be known as the Taung Child. The second substantial piece of evidence, believed to be the skeleton of a middle-aged woman — the celebrated Mrs. Ples — was discovered at Sterkfontein, South Africa, by Robert Broom and John T. Robinson in April 1947.

Scholarly opposition arose because most scientists and anthropologists in the early twentieth century favored Asia as the best location for the origin of the human species. New evidence was mounting for

Africa, and in our time no serious scholar doubts or disputes our African origins. This raises serious cultural questions for humanity today, most of which are not even clearly articulated, never mind confronted. Sadly, millions of people in Africa itself are totally ignorant of this deep and profound ancestral tradition.

Sterkfontein is one of South Africa's best known fossil sites. Less well known are sites like Swartkrand, Dreimulen, and Kromdraai, excavated by Robert Broom in 1938 and producing a set of bones that have been named *Australopithecus robustus.* This creature has been dated to about 2 million years ago, similar to *A. africanus* but significantly more robust in terms of skull and teeth. Closely resembling *A. robustus* is *A. boisei* (popularly known as Zinj), discovered in 1959 by Mary Leakey in the Olduvai (Oldupai) Gorge in Tanzania. The Leakey family, particularly Louis and Mary along with Richard and Meave, are internationally recognized as the trail blazers in the search for human origins (see Morell 1996).

Walking on Two Feet

For many years now, bipedalism has been extensively researched in anthropological studies (see McHenry 2004). First, various attempts have been made to date the emergence of walking upright, in order to distinguish between our occupation of woodlands and our transition into the plains of East Africa. As long as we remained in the woodlands, it is assumed that our developmental status was closer to that of the great apes, still climbing trees, and behaving in a way similar to primates. The movement to the savannah lands strongly suggests that the transition to being human had happened.

The oldest verified date for bipedalism is based on a set of footprints excavated in 1978–79 in Laetoli, northern Tanzania. The expedition was led by the great Mary Leakey, although the discovery was made by team member and geochemist Paul Abell (see Agnew and Demas 1998). The find proved to be another benchmark in the story of ancestral grace. After detailed analysis, the footprints were dated at 3.7 million years, assigning a new chronological threshold for *Homo erectus,* the person who walks uprightly.[8]

Throughout the 1980s and into the 1990s, scholars adopted this new date for the origins of upright walking. Then things began to change as new fossils were discovered and new techniques for analyzing the fossils came to the fore. Evidence for bipedalism surfaced in ever more ancient finds right back to Toumai, tentatively dated to 7 million years ago. Walking characterizes not merely the *Homo* genus, but the *Australopithecines* as well (see also Gibbons 2007, 202ff; 232ff.). In March 2008, two American researchers, Brian Richmond of George Washington University in Washington, D.C., and William Jungers of Stony Brook University in New York published their analysis of a thigh bone of *A. Orrorin* (discovered in Kenya in 2000), indicating many features of an upright walking creature (6 million years ago) (Richmond and Jungers 2008).

How did *Homo erectus* engage with the local environment? What was survival like for these ancient peoples? Toolmaking thus far has been dated to the successors of *Erectus*, namely, *Homo ergaster* and *Homo habilis* (treated in the following chapters). *Erectus* probably remained closely aligned to the earth, drawing nourishment from natural foods and grasses. Natural resources were also used for shelter. The relationship with other animals would have been mutual for the greater part, with humans themselves being hunted (rather than hunting) at times. Bruce Bower believes that *Erectus* may have built rafts and traveled on sea, a controversial claim still under review (*www.sciencenews.org/articles/20031018/bob8.asp*).

Since 1960 evidence for *Erectus* has been found extensively throughout eastern Africa, suggesting a migrant species that may have traveled widely. Why did they travel? In pursuit of meat is the standard response. It seems to me that hunting is a much later development (see chapter 8 below); at this early stage, and indeed for long after, food was procured by gathering, not by killing. *Homo erectus* traveled — possibly on sea as well as on land — because the human spirit is programmed to roam and explore. We are restless creatures and have been from earliest times. And that restlessness belongs to that dimension of our human-divine becoming that I name as ancestral grace.

We begin to glimpse a species feeling confident and at home in creation. *Homo erectus* is the human holding head high, a planetary stance of paradoxical import. This is the species that knows it is endowed with power, an ancestral capacity capable of extensive empowerment. In all probability, the power was used benignly, with the safeguards provided by a convivial way of living largely in harmony with the surrounding environment. Present-day humans, immersed in a world so afflicted by violence and greed, have much to learn from those ancestors who illustrate another way to live meaningfully and gracefully upon the earth.

Africa: Our Collective Home

The study of genetics has brought a new sophistication to the work of paleontology. If the interpretation of the fossil record is corroborated by DNA evidence, obviously a more objective and accurate assessment can be made. Scientists opt for the more rigorous data. While this is important in terms of pursuing scientific credibility, it runs the risk of losing something of the myth and mystique that also belong to the pursuit of human origins. The creative story can suffer at the hands of excessive rationalism.

We evidence this hunger for accuracy and precision in the heated debate between the *multi-regionalists* and those backing the *"Out of Africa"* hypothesis. The former acknowledges the dispersal of *Homo erectus* from Africa to other parts of the planet, emerging as the Zhoukoudians (Peking man) in China, the Ngandong (Java man) in Indonesia, and the Neanderthals in Europe. Modern Chinese therefore are assumed to have sprung form this ancient line and modern Europeans are assumed to be the offspring of the Neanderthals.

The alternative theory, favored by a majority of paleoanthropologists, is called the "Out of Africa hypothesis" (see Stringer and McKie 1998; *www.actionbioscience.org/evolution/johanson.html*). According to this view, *Homo erectus* became extinct in the different parts of the planet in which he had evolved. A new shoot from Africa evolved between 150,000 and 100,000 years ago. Known as *Homo sapiens,* it spread across the planet branching into Europe, Asia, and elsewhere. The genetic corroboration for this view is substantially in excess of the multi-regional position.

In both cases, Africa plays a crucial role, the main point I wish to highlight. Even if there are no physical links between modern humans and the more ancient strands postulated by the multi-regionalists, I wish to propose that there is a psychic and spiritual connection of immense significance. Cultural progress cannot be reduced to merely external observable fact. Spirit-power works according to different principles, rarely entertained by rational science but nonetheless essential to the poetics that bring zest and meaning to life.

African spirituality vibrates with ancestral enthusiasm.[9] Stories abound on the immediacy and intimacy of the ancestors. Rituals record the achievements of the ancestors and invoke their healing and liberating power. Every mountain and valley, lake and river, plant and animal carries the embodied power of the ancestors. In the power of ancestral grace, everything is interconnected; interdependence thrives.

Christian missionaries have often dishonored the deep soul of African spirituality. Imperial arrogance and dogmatic religiosity prevented them from seeing the deeper and larger story. Africa is home to the human race. Human ancestry imbues every dimension of African life and culture. The incarnation of God in human life first happened in Africa. The whole spiritual story of our species belongs more to Africa than to any other part of planet earth.

Yet today Africa is the most tortured part of the Gaia Planet[10] — torn apart by internal strife and horrendous suffering and exploited from without by ruthless transnational corporations. The pain and anguish of Africa reverberates throughout the entire human species. When our home is suffering, we all suffer. We carry within us our African roots, and when that foundation is so "up-rooted" then inevitably we all feel the pain and the ensuing alienation.

It is in our collective interest that we try to resolve the plight of African nations today. The call to such engagement is not about charity — for refugees, AIDS sufferers, war victims, starving children — but rather about *justice*. And not just for Africa, but for the entire human race, so that mutually we can begin to reclaim our collective home and treat it with the love and dignity that it deserves.

The Upright Stride

Africa is the earthly space in which we first learned to walk uprightly. Initially this may have been demanding of energy and skill, but with time it became the graceful and elegant stride we use today. Except in Africa, of course, where so many of our fellow humans find walking difficult, weighed down by so many burdens. What a cruel contradiction: the place that empowered us to hold our heads up with dignity, joy, and pride is now the very part of the planet where such dignity and pride are not easily maintained.

Developing the capacity to walk uprightly awakens the desire to explore in a radically new way. A new pride enters the human endeavor. A legitimate pride indeed, but one that all too easily translates into a dangerous arrogance. Positively, it is the energy and vision that leads to new discoveries: new landscapes, biodiversity, alternative food sources, new encounters with danger, and fresh skills to cope with those challenges. Ancestral grace learns to deal with newness, as humans gradually learn that the new is what we are called to embrace each day. While we build on the old, we grow and change by embracing the new.

The emergence of bipedalism would also have evoked a whole new range of social and interpersonal skills, which at this distance we can only reconstruct imaginatively. New challenges and encounters would have evoked a stronger sense of group cohesion, as collective wisdom was sought to resolve challenges and difficulties. New modes of communication would have evolved, although verbal speech would not emerge yet for several thousand years. And we must not assume that males took all the prerogatives and females looked after the home bases; such role differentiation may not even have existed in these early times.

We stand erect and hold our heads high! And we have done so for most of our time on earth. Not to lord it over others, however, but rather to rejoice and celebrate the fulfilling achievements that ensue when we make our contribution to the mutually empowering force of evolution itself. That enduring gift of ancestral grace is still at our disposal. Are we humble and wise enough to surrender to its guidance as we did for most of our time on earth? And can we muster it afresh for the crushed people of Africa today? That is the formidable spiritual and cultural challenge facing our species now.

Chapter 6

Creative Innovation
and the Awakening Artist

*Beauty and grace are performed whether or not we will or sense
them. The least we can do is try to be there.*

— ANNIE DILLARD

A LITTLE-KNOWN SPECIES was discovered by Y Haile-Salassie in
the Bouri formation of Ethiopia in 1997; it was named *Australo
Garhi* in April 1999. Dated to some 2.6 million years ago, Garhi
(meaning "surprise" in the local Afar language) is the first species
thus far discovered to have used tools. This is a new benchmark in the
fascinating story of human evolution, an embryonic artistic upsurge
that will pursue the human species throughout the entire evolutionary
story. Ancestral grace takes another quantum leap.

Most of this chapter is devoted to Ice Age art, a development that
in evolutionary terms belongs to relatively recent times, the Upper
Paleolithic era (35,000–10,000 BCE). I want to highlight the two
features of surprise and continuity. Ever since our ancestors first excavated beauty out of a piece of stone (ca. 2.5 million years ago) we
have continued to surprise ourselves by what we are capable of in-
venting. I suspect there has never been a time in which the artist in us
was not alive and active. Ice Age art serves as a high point of something unfolding over millions of years. Let's pick up the fascinating
story!

According to current scholarship, *Habilis* was the first hominid
to use stone tool technology. *Habilis,* denoting skill of hand (hence
handy man), was the name adopted in 1964 by Louis Leakey, South

African paleoanthropologist Philip Tobias, and British primate researcher John Napier. Initially unearthed in 1961 by Louis Leakey and his colleagues in the Olduvai (Oldupai) Gorge in Tanzania and enhanced by later fossils discovered by other researchers, particularly Richard and Meave Leakey excavating the Koobi Fora in Kenya, this ancestor is believed to have existed as far back as 2.4 million years ago. Proportionately short in body, *Habilis* was gifted with long arms, ably employed to use the first stone flakes to manipulate the local environment and begin to shape it more congenially to human need.

Oldowan Technology

The oldest tool-manufacturing culture known to humans dates back to about 2.6 million years BP.* They were first excavated in the Gona and Omo basins in Ethiopia. Two categories of tool have been identified: chopped stones with sharpened edges and flakes used primarily as cutters, possibly to dismember game carcasses and to strip tough plants. The flakes were struck from crystalline stones such as basalt, quartz, or chert, indicating that early humans were aware of rock types and their potential uses.[11]

Most of the evidence for such tools comes from East Africa, particularly from the Olduvai Gorge in Tanzania. Mithen (2005, 314 n. 5) records the findings made in the Riwat Plateau in Pakistan in 1987, cobbles of stone almost identical to Oldowan chopper tools. Stone tools, possibly 1.9 million years old, have also been unearthed in the Longuppo Cave in China. Whether these artifacts were fashioned by humans or formed by natural forces is a conundrum that still remains unresolved.

We can only hazard a guess at the various uses of such tools. About five hundred thousand years later we witness a much more sophisticated use of tools in what came to be known as Acheulean industry (to be reviewed in chapter 7). My interest is more in creative skill than in precise usufruct. It is the earliest evidence we have of the human capacity to create and innovate, to engage with the environment, to

---

*BP: an archeological term used in radiocarbon dating to indicate a specified amount of time or at a specified point in time before 1950 CE.

articulate the human need to work and co-create. Ancestral grace was molding a creature that would be useful, and in its usefulness would draw forth the creative potential not just of its own species but of numerous other life forms as well.

The Awakening Artist

Our artistic potential tends to be reserved to the achievements of the Great Ice Age of Paleolithic times, but there were various earlier precedents. Rock painting is generally considered to predate cave paintings by several thousand years. To date, the largest concentration of rock paintings in the world is that located in the Tsodilo Hills, in a sparsely inhabited area, Ngamiland, in northwestern Botswana. This is also the location for the now famous source of ancient ritual discovered by Prof. Sheila Coulson in the summer of 2006 (see the web pages *www.stonepages.com/news/archives/002172.html* and *www.thinkingseriously.com/gpage4.html*).

While in our time painting is viewed as a recreational activity, for our ancestors it seems to have carried strong spiritual significance. As intimated by Rappaport (1999, 384), "Art and religion seem ancient or even primordial companions, and it seems abundantly clear that representations appearing in ritual may evoke emotion and may affect cognition through their aesthetic qualities."

Art in the more formal sense did not begin in the Paleolithic era; it was already flourishing in Africa, and we are continuing to make some remarkable discoveries like, for example, (a) scraped, heat-treated red ochre, possibly used in ritual burial acts, from the Qafzeh in Israel, estimated to be ninety-two thousand years old; (b) a bone harpoon from Katanda in the Democratic Republic of the Congo, estimated to be eighty thousand years old; (c) shell beads from Blombos Cave in South Africa, about seventy-seven thousand years old (clothing seems to have appeared about the same time); (d) an ostrich eggshell bead from Loiyangalani in Tanzania, estimated to be seventy thousand years old (see Wong 2006b). Nor must we fail to include Australia, where rock art flourished sixty thousand years ago.

The Cave Walls

The Upper Paleolithic era, dating from around 35,000 down to 10,000 BCE, was one of incredible artistic achievement. Art, sculpture, engravings, and music seem to have flourished throughout this period, and it seems to have been happening throughout the populated world of the day.[12]

The first of the famous cave paintings was discovered in 1879 in a cave at Altamira in the Cantabrian mountains of northern Spain, and has since been dated to 14,330 years BP. The discovery was made by Don Marcelino de Sautuola, a Spanish aristocrat and amateur archaeologist. Sadly, he died without being able to convince his contemporaries of the distinctiveness of what he had found.

Next we encounter the set of caves known as Lascaux located near the village of Montignac, in the Dordogne region of southwestern France. Initially discovered in September 1940 by four teenagers and a dog, the wall paintings date somewhere between 17,000 BP and 25,000 BP. It is believed that the initial paintings were done with natural pigments such as ochre, charcoal, and iron oxides.

Altamira and Lascaux are household names in the world of Ice Age art. More recent discoveries, matched with more specialized dating techniques, have brought other locations into the limelight. Foremost is the Chauvet Cave in the Ardeche in France, discovered only in 1994, and dated to 32,410 BP. At the time of writing, this is the oldest known site for Ice Age art.

While the production of such art seems to have been most prolific in Europe, it flourished all over the populated world after 30,000 BP. In southern Africa the painted slabs from Apollo Cave are at least 27,000 years old while wall(rock) engravings in Australia have been dated to 40,000 BP (*www.aboriginalartonline.com/art/rockage.php*). Similar artifacts have also been unearthed in China, India, and elsewhere in the Far East. It is truly amazing that this prehistoric artistic spirit flourished wherever humans existed. Here we obtain unique access to the marvels of ancestral grace.

Strange Statuettes

While much of the cave art depicts animals — horses, ibexes, bison, deer, and sea animals — and stenciled hands, the more controversial discoveries are those strange female statuettes known as Venus figurines. One of the earliest discoveries was made in 1931, in the Vogelherd caves, at Ulm, Germany. However, the most famous of these figurines is the Venus of Willendorf, a limestone statuette, excavated in Willendorf, Wachau, Lower Austria, and dated around 25,000 BP. These statuettes have become the subject of intense debate as we continue to unravel the artistic marvels of the Great Ice Age.

Various attempts have been made to unravel the meaning and significance of these statuettes, nor can we establish with any certainty whether they were created by men or by women. The exaggerated breasts, sexual organs, hips, and buttocks tend to be interpreted as symbols of fertility. The more controversial claim links the images with the cult of the Great Goddess (a topic I explore in chapter 10 below).

The central role of the woman in these ancient images, while impossible to establish accurately, is an issue we must not bypass due to lack of objective data. Interpretation of art is essentially a task of discernment, and to varying degrees with matters of archetypal intent that cannot be explained in a rational way. These images celebrate womanhood, either as an invocation to bring the female more into the cultural scene, or to affirm a crucial role she already plays. My hunch is that we are dealing with the latter — women carried substantial archetypal significance in Upper Paleolithic times, an icon of ancestral grace, which in this rational age we find difficult to accept or appreciate.

Art and Spirituality

One notes a progression in the earliest European artifacts: rather simple drawings, including vulvas from 35,000 to 30,000; then simple outline drawings between 26,000 and 21,000; finally, more painted three-dimensional figures after 18,000 years BP. In all cases, important cultural aspirations are being articulated.

First, there is the relationship between the human and the animal. This interdependence cannot be reduced to the exigencies of the hunt, in which the animal is depicted as the object that needs to be subdued and killed to provide food in the face of precarious conditions. Throughout this period, northern Europe was covered in ice (ca. 60,000–20,000 BP); living conditions were harsh and demanding. Throughout the rest of the inhabited planet, weather conditions seem to have been quite favorable, and potential food supplies were more than ample. The animal drawings depict something much more sophisticated than merely a human struggle with adversarial weather conditions. Instead we are evidencing a celebration of the spirit world in which human and animal "co-create" an interdependent relationship, evoking further connection with the nurturing Spirit, animating and sustaining all life.

To suggest, therefore, that these images are another form of totemism, or that they belong to some rite of passage related to sympathetic magic — both theories initially propounded in James Frazer's *The Golden Bough* (1890) may be quite accurate. Also relevant is the suggestion that this ancient art world belonged to, and was influenced by, the practices of shamanism. But the modern mind, conditioned by rationality on the one hand and religiosity on the other, finds it hard to discern the deeper meaning of these insights. Our judgmental tendency to dismiss as "pagan" anything that does not fit our preconceived theories makes ours a rather hostile environment for the wisdom I am describing as ancestral grace. Not surprising, the modern artist also struggles to survive in such an environment.

Writing in the British newspaper *The Telegraph* (February 23, 2005), archaeologist Peter Bahn states: "I believe that recent efforts have uncovered compelling evidence that motivation for some Ice Age art — though by no means all — was religious." This, too, is the view of the French prehistorian Abbé Henri Breuil, one of the first people to examine the finds at Lascaux. Without invoking a religious motif, we can never hope to decipher the deeper and richer meaning of these ancient artifacts.

However, our discernment needs to be broadly based and deeply rooted. The religious significance of Ice Age art — drawings and statuettes — cannot be determined by what constitutes formal religion. We are in a time zone several thousand years before formal religions evolved. Spirit-power was flourishing long before the evolution of formal religion. Ancestral grace is abundant but is not being mediated through churches or religions. Spirituality, and not religion, is what will guide us in our exploration.

Religious Endorsement of Our Creativity?

Unfortunately, religion has played a leading role in the suppression of human creativity. All the religions, to one degree or another, perpetuate the myth of a flawed species, the victims of Original Sin. The theory suggests that humans have been sinful and destructive from the beginnings. According to this view, our nasty side is much more basic than our positive endowments, and our creative and artistic abilities tend to be given scant attention.

René Girard (1977; 1986) is a leading proponent of this negative view. He claims that humans have been violent from time immemorial, backing up his conviction with source material none of which is more than five thousand years old. This is the great delusion of the academic world, a telling example of what Brueggemann (2005, 40) calls "the tyranny of the academy," a widespread assumption that in getting it wrong in recent millennia we have been in error and sin for all or most of our earthly existence. Ironically, theorists like Girard present a slanted picture because they focus excessively on the personal and interpersonal spheres, giving scant attention to the impact of the social and systemic forces so persuasively documented by scholars like Zimbardo (2007).

Only the big picture — the graced picture of our creative God — can rescue us from this minimalist delusion. When faced with preposterous allegations of this nature, our evolutionary story serves as a timely and urgent corrective. Viewed in the large scale — whether it is 1 million or 7 million years — there is little to verify a flawed destructive species. Instead, what we encounter, time and again, is a species of enormous creativity with an unceasing propensity for innovation. Throughout the long aeons we witness creatures who are the beneficiaries of an original blessing and not the victims of an original sin.

We are not perfect; we never have been and never will be. If we were perfect we would not be free and could not act creatively thus contributing to the unfolding nature of creation itself. One of the consequences of this freedom is that we will get it wrong from time to time, and I suspect that is not a big problem for the divine Creator. Indeed, there may have been timespans of ten thousand years or longer when we got it basically wrong and did not fare well as a co-creative species. In human terms that is less than 1 percent of our 7-million-year story. I suspect that the God of ancestral grace will not hold that against us. So why are we so punitive toward ourselves? Does it not make more sense to build on our strengths and forgive ourselves for our occasional folly?

An Original Synthesis

As a cherished ancestor, *Homo habilis* launched us on the road of artistic discovery. We trace that creative trail through *Homo ergaster, sapiens,* and the Neanderthals, reaching an exquisite threshold in the achievements of Paleolithic times, a process of integration that had been maturing for several thousand years. Prehistoric historian Steven Mithen (2005) attributes the breakthrough to a new stage of "cognitive fluidity." The Cro-Magnon human was quite a genius, mentally intelligent, artistically creative, and spiritually enlightened. Ancestral grace was transforming humanity into another aperture of the divine grandeur.

In an age when paradox confronts us on every front, we need the resilience of the artistic soul. We need to invoke the imagination, not merely to survive, but to thrive amid the bewildering contradictions of life. But such contradictions are not new; creation has known them from time immemorial, and our ancient ancestors mobilized resources to engage the great paradoxes. That is the topic of our next chapter.

Chapter 7

Working Our Way with Paradox

From the view of modern physics, the entire world may be seen as the manifestation of a broken symmetry. If the symmetries of nature were actually perfect, we would not exist.

— HEINZ R. PAGELS

I F THE SYMMETRIES OF NATURE were perfect, there would in fact be no intimations of that wonder and awe that evoke notions like that of beauty and perfection. Nor would there be anybody around to marvel at the unfolding mystery within which everything is held. What baffles humans of our time are the massive contradictions all around us. And they seem to be multiplying by the day!

At this juncture the wisdom of ancestral grace is so crucial for our future evolution that one can scarcely exaggerate its significance. We, like everything else in creation, are begotten out of paradox, and paradox is the source of our enduring transformation. In the words of Michael Dowd, "When I look at cosmic history through sacred eyes, I see that the chaotic, destructive side of the Cosmos is consistently held within the larger arc of creative evolution. *Crises call forth creativity. Breakdowns catalyse breakthrough. Emergencies evoke emergence*" (2007, 270).

In the mass extinctions of the past 500 million years (see O'Murchu 2002, 209 n. 9), it looked at times as if we were heading for total annihilation. But it never happened, and I suspect it never will. Ancestral grace embodies an inexplicable affirmation of the will-to-life. Despite the paradoxes, the extinctions and the ensuing chaos, life always wins out in the end. And amazingly, long before the education and enlightenment of the present time our ancient ancestors recognized this thrust toward meaning. We detect it at work in our ancestor *Homo ergaster.*

Our Delight in Work

Turkana Boy (or Nariokotome Boy) is the legendary figure launching this new quantum leap. Named by Richard Leakey, Kimoya Kimeu, and Tim White in 1984, he is considered to have provided us with the most complete skeleton of *Homo ergaster,* who flourished in eastern and southern Africa between 1.9 and 1.4 million years ago. *Ergaster* is also deemed to be the first of our ancestors to migrate in large numbers to other continents, initially, it is believed, to Dmanisi in ex-Soviet Georgia and possibly as far as the Indonesian island of Java.

Ergaster literally means "the person who works." Humans have always worked, not just to manufacture something or to earn a living, but for the sheer joy of doing so. Sigmund Freud uncovered a subliminal streak in human life and meaning when he asserted that humans evidence two very deep needs: the need to *love* and the need to *work*. Work is the dimension through which we express our God-given creativity. Work is the medium through which we co-create with the divine life force, as together we shape and mold God's creation.

As distinct from *Habilis, Ergaster* used more sophisticated tools associated with Acheulean industry, such as hand axes and cleavers. The name is derived from the region of St. Acheul in France, where Boucher de Perthes discovered the first flint hand axes in the 1830s. Two key innovations come to light: (a) the shaping of an entire stone to a stereotyped tool form, and (b) chipping the stone from both sides to produce a symmetrical cutting edge. The most common tool materials were quartzite, glassy lava, chert, and flint. Acheulean tools show a regularity of design and manufacture that is maintained for over a million years (1.5 million years BP down to five hundred thousand years ago).

A new wave of artistry unfolds, but also a deepening engagement with the raw materials of creation. While lacking concrete evidence, we can readily surmise that *Ergaster* cultivated soil and produced food, although predominantly the food supply would have been

acquired directly from the natural environment. Work satisfaction
came naturally to *Ergaster,* not in any way conditioned to modern
expectations of working for a wage, often in fabricated and superficial environments into which people cannot take their best selves.
Ergaster serves as a perpetual reminder that work should not be
drudgery, even in hard times, but the creative outlet for the energy of
the living spirit at work in every aspect of creation.

Man the Hunter

The charred animal bones found in the Acheulean fossil sites provide
a reliable indication of hunting and meat-eating. Various studies highlight our killer instinct and consider it a very ancient acquisition in
our evolutionary development. A plethora of unexamined assumptions arise at this point, to the fore being the conviction that just
as our primary ancestors, the chimpanzees, are highly aggressive and
violent, so are we. Our blood-thirstiness is the basis of numerous well-
known monographs, for example, *Man the Hunter* (Lee and DeVore
1968), *Demonic Males* (Peterson and Wrangham 1997), *The Imperial Animal* (Tiger and Fox 1971), *The Dark Side of Man* (Ghiglieri
1999).[13]

"Man the Hunter" has become a kind of slogan for the perceived
aggression and violence that characterizes our species. By instinct we
kill, not just for food and not merely for domination, but because
we are endowed with a killer instinct forever seeking expression.
It sounds so true to reality, and yet is far from the whole truth.
As various studies of recent decades reveal, hunting among our ancient ancestors is a complex phenomenon that cannot be explained
on the basis of any one single cause. Social reinforcement, bonding, and ritualization all play a major role. The more we investigate
this controversial issue the more the evidence is pointing us *away
from,* rather than toward, the myth of the violent killer (see Hart and
Sussman 2005).

Scholars have also challenged the male prerogative in the traditional analysis of hunting. The female is never considered. Adrienne
Zihlman (1996) was among the first to challenge this gross oversight,

claiming that women not only participated in food provision but in all probability were the primary food gatherers, as is still the case among hunter-gatherers in various parts of today's world. In many cases, Zihlman claims, hunting plays quite a small role. It is plant life rather than meat that provides the bulk of daily diet.

Reinforcing Zihlman's insights, Frans de Waal goes on to suggest that the killing and procuring of meat was more a social activity than a source of diet. Humans were not so much scavengers as social manipulators. As has been noted among the chimpanzees, hunting provides status and enhances social ranking: "Males use meat to secure and maintain political alliances, to publicly snub rivals, and at times to attract oestrous females" (de Waal 2001, 110).

The ability to cook meat would have made it more palatable for humans and probably increased its dietary significance. It is quite difficult to date precisely when this might have happened. Karen B. Strier claims that the fossil record for meat-eating is unambiguous, and she dates it to 2.5 million years ago (de Waal 2001, 257, n. 1). On the other hand, Richard Wrangham claims that the cooking of food is unlikely before 1.9 million years ago, when humans first learned to master the use of fire (de Waal 2001, 138).

Ergaster is likely to have been the first human to have hunted on a regular basis, but the nature and purpose of such activity needs a much more nuanced interpretation, congruent with the influence of ancestral grace. Our ancestors were essentially peace-loving people and not violent scavengers. Diet seems to have been predominantly vegetarian throughout our long evolutionary history. Hunting and capturing animals seems to have been much more a social activity, guaranteeing greater recognition within social and interpersonal ranking.

When an animal was captured for food, Joseph Campbell (1959) claims, it was typically killed in a ritualistic way, recognized as a convivial life form deserving of dignity and respect. Campbell suggests that the holy person, the Shaman, oversaw the entire process. The animal was lured to the edge of a cliff and pushed over while the Shaman engaged in frenzied ritualistic behavior. After the animal died, the hunter removed the meat under the supervision of the

Shaman, who then took the bones and formally buried the carcass. *Ergaster* seems to exhibit special regard for life and death even when dealing with animals.

Ergaster probably used fire for a variety of purposes, including social gathering and possibly ritualistic ceremonies for which we have no precise evidence at the present time. We glimpse our human ancestors beginning to understand the environment much more intimately, passing on traditions and skills over a long period of time. We can surmise that they would also have had their first insights into creation's paradoxes, particularly the universal paradox of creation and destruction.

Befriending Ambiguity

Paleontologists attribute an enormous significance to brain size, and with it comparative guesses at intelligent behavior. Few would attribute such behavior to any of our ancestors who lived beyond ten thousand years ago. Although social scientists have long abandoned the derogatory use of the word "primitive," disparaging projections onto our past are still surprisingly common.

Endowed with ancestral grace from the very beginning, humans have recognized and coped with *ambiguity* from earliest times. We may never comprehend the "intelligence" with which they did it, because conventional understandings of intelligence may have little to offer in this discernment. We are dealing with perception based on intuition and imagination, features that predate and outstrip intelligence as a neurological concept (see Haught 2006). Immersed in the natural environment, *Homo ergaster* would have had intimate awareness of the cycle of *birth-death-rebirth*. And the intimate connection between birth and death may have been much more transparent in this preintelligence age than for people of our time. All around them, our ancestors saw natural cycles in which things come forth, blossom, mature, and die. Baffling and bewildering it may have been at times, but intuitively our ancestors recognized a fundamental paradox characterizing not merely human life but creation at every level.

In all probability, death would not have been the problematic issue it is for modern peoples. The notions of the curse of death coming into the world through a specific human being, and being resolved through a human-like creature (1 Cor. 15:21ff.) or the belief of death being a punishment for sin (Rom. 6:23) are rather primitive views compared to the more integrated understandings of our ancient ancestors. Contemporary fears linking death with judgment, or postulating death as the final and enduring end, are views that would not have been shared by *Homo ergaster.* Death was an integral part of a process, and in all probability it was discerned as a stage on an ongoing journey. This becomes more explicitly conscious several thousand years later when we see the Neanderthals burying their dead with elaborate rituals.

What many today experience as ambiguity, indeed as a great curse, would have been viewed in a much more benign way by *Homo ergaster.* The ambiguity would have been viewed more as a *paradox* than a *contradiction. Ergaster* did not need a rational explanation for everything as we do today. In the human cycle of birth-death-rebirth, our ancestors would have seen a mirror-image of what happens throughout the whole of creation. Nature's paradoxical cycles are reflected in the human life cycle.

The attitude to suffering would have been very different. To people of our time it seems like fate or fatalism. But not necessarily for *Homo ergaster.* Suffering would have been embraced as an integral aspect of the great life cycle. Humans at that time would not have been happy about the paradox, and like ourselves may have performed rituals (magic) to resolve it, but they would not have been caught up in the compulsive urge to control as evidenced in the anthropocentric world of our time.

Nor would our ancient ancestors have looked to the gods to resolve the dilemma for them. Long ahead of process theologians, *Homo ergaster* would have considered the divine to be part of the great cosmic and planetary life cycles, suffering in solidarity with all who are struggling and fructifying the efforts of every new birth. Thankfully, there were no evangelists around to accuse the ancients of pantheism.

Learning from Ergaster

These are not merely empty speculations. In terms of ancestral grace we must give the benefit of the doubt to our ancestors and not simply judge them by the standards of our time. As a theological concept, grace requires openness and transparency in the human spirit. This is much more likely to be present in those who live close to nature and behave convivially with creation's organicity. How that grace might have worked as they faced life's ups and downs is what I am briefly reviewing in this chapter.

In our modern world we do not deal well with paradox and ambiguity, nor with the suffering and disintegration that often ensue. Compared with our ancestors, we seem poorly equipped to deal with paradox. All the destruction we witness in the surrounding creation is put down to human ineffectiveness: one day we will be able to control these bizarre events (like earthquakes) and conquer their destructibility. Precisely by adopting this arrogant stance we exacerbate the meaningless suffering all around us, while consistently inflicting damage on the planet we inhabit.

In our arrogantly "enlightened" state, we create horrendous suffering for ourselves, other species, and the planet on which we are supposed to feel at home. In this regard we have much to learn from ancient peoples. I am not suggesting we revert to former times; evolution never regresses, but it can progress only by bringing with it the cumulative learnings of the past. By appropriating the wisdom of *Ergaster,* the graced awareness to live with ambiguity, transcending the compulsive urge to change everything to our liking, we would be a more fulfilled species and in turn would help to fulfill creation's own desire to grow and flourish.

Chapter 8

The Wise Species

To a remarkable extent, we are accidental tourists as we cruise through Nature in our bizarre ways. But, of course, we are nonetheless remarkable for that. — IAN TATTERSALL

THE EARLIEST VERSION of *Homo sapiens* (archaic) is dated to 500,000 years ago, while modern *Sapiens* first evolved about 200,000 years ago. Primary evidence for the modern form came initially in 1967 when Richard Leakey and his colleagues located a skull and partial skeleton near the town of Kibish in southern Ethiopia; the fossils were dated as being 130,000 years old. Thanks to the painstaking analysis of Tim White of the University of California in Berkeley and his colleague Berhane Asfaw, the dating was pushed back to 160,000 years, based on findings in 1997 near the village of Herto in Ethiopia (see *Nature*, June 12, 1997). Finally, geologist Frank Brown and colleagues revisited the 1967 sites between 2001 and 2003 and discovered additional fossils that now enable scholars to push the dating back even further — to 195,000 years ago (see *Nature*, February 17, 2005).

Intelligence Revisited

The appellation *sapiens*(whether archaic or modern), while measured by external features such as skull size, or by external achievements such as handmade artifacts, is in effect a subliminal characteristic that probably cannot be adequately described in human language. Contemporary attempts at investigating and defining consciousness provide significant clues (see Wallace 2007). Perhaps most important of all is the Jungian notion of the "collective unconscious."

59

For Jung, the collective unconscious can simply be described as an envelope of wisdom embracing everything in creation, humans included. For Jung, it is essentially of God and may well be considered as the wise and enduring power of divine Spirit infused throughout the whole of creation (see esp. Edwards 2004; Wallace 2002). Long dismissed as an esoteric illusive fantasy, the collective unconscious begins to look very similar to the notion of the creative vacuum, or pure space, in modern physics (see Conforti 1999; Laszlo 2004; Swimme 1996, 90ff.).

Among the most accessible writers on this subject is the systems theorist Ervin Laszlo (1993; 1998; 2004). Many of his seminal ideas, articulated with the average reader in mind, come together in his description of the "Akashic field,"[14] the interactive realm of quantum fluctuations, culminating in a supercoherent state empowering all structures in creation, whether atoms, organisms, or galaxies. Laszlo goes on to raise a crucial question, central to the deliberations of this book: "Could it be that our consciousness is linked with other consciousnesses through an inter-connecting Akashic field, much as galaxies are linked in the cosmos, quanta in the microworld, and organisms in the world of the living?" (2004, 44). The link with contemporary brain-studies is informatively reviewed by Wallace (2007).

Of related interest is Guy Claxton's notion of the "intelligent unconscious" (Claxton 2005). A cognitive scientist from Bristol University in the UK, Claxton claims that the human mind exhibits potentialities far beyond the basic functions of rational reasoning that we extol in modern Western societies. These capabilities have been at work in human life from earliest times and connect us with the deeper forces of planet and cosmos in ways we scarcely understand as yet. We appropriate the larger wisdom unknowingly; I guess Laszlo would wager that we do so through our inescapable immersion in the Akashic field. The abundance of such wisdom will always outstrip our rational minds and at times will baffle and confuse us because, among other reasons, this cosmic intelligence is also infused by the paradox we reviewed in the last chapter.

The amorphous nature of this intelligence and its potential for connectedness across various spheres of life challenge us to discern not merely its usefulness for ourselves, but the wisdom about all creation with which we are endowed. In our preoccupation with self-aggrandizement, we often miss the empowering richness of being connected to other dimensions of this great life force.

For several centuries we have regarded human intelligence as superior to every other form of wisdom in creation. Moreover, scholars of all disciplines tend to postulate that creation at large is intelligible only to the human mind. This often translates into the human right to exploit everything in creation for our own benefit. The inflated ego seems unable to entertain any understanding of creation other than that which feeds its own deadly delusion. No room here for grace, understood in ancient or modern terms!

Several scientific discoveries throughout the twentieth century hint at an innate intelligence within creation at large (Bennett et al. 2003; Regan and Kelly 2002; Primack and Abrams 2006; McTaggart 2007). And many of the oft-quoted insights of the astronauts, spiritually jolted by their observations of the earth from outer space, support this notion of a wise creation. From a vast range of statements, I quote three:

> Having seen the sun, the stars, and our planet, you become full of life, softer. You begin to look at all living things with trepidation and to be more kind and patient with the people around you. (Boris Volynov, USSR)

> On the return trip home, gazing through 240,000 miles of space toward the stars and the planet from which I had come, I suddenly experienced the universe as intelligent, loving, and harmonious. My view of the planet was a glimpse of divinity. (Edgar Mitchell, USA)

> The first day we all pointed to our own countries. The third or fourth day we were pointing to our continents. By the fifth day, we were aware of only one earth. (Prince Sultan Bin Salman al-Saud, Saudi Arabia)

In short, we are describing a wisdom that imbues the whole of creation. This is a basic endowment of ancestral grace. God was at work in creation for billions of years before our evolution. We inherit human intelligence from this primordial resource, and we are likely to use our intelligence wisely and responsibly when we consistently align it with the foundational source from which we obtained it in the first place.

Humans Appropriate the Enveloping Intelligence

In terms of the human imagination, we access and appropriate the wisdom of the collective unconscious through archetypes, dream analysis, symbols, and rituals. Undoubtedly, it is also mediated through a range of brain processes. These have been extensively studied over the past hundred years. While they offer important insights, our capacity to function intelligently cannot be reduced to such neurological or biochemical structures (see Haught 2003).

We are naming an internal capacity rather than a power that determines external achievements. We are naming and celebrating a wisdom we share with all other organisms that inhabit creation including the earth itself. In the human, we see embodied wise capacities that powerfully remind us of the mysterious yet intelligent universe to which we all belong. These include issues already reviewed, like our convivial relationship to nature and to the land, the development of tool technologies, our exploration of art. In subsequent chapters we will highlight our capacity for spirituality, language, and music that existed many thousand years before formal education ever came to be. Characterized by insight, intelligence, intuition, and imagination, we are dealing with what may be the core elements of ancestral grace. In contemporary spirituality this inner foundational wisdom is described as "soul," or "soulfulness" (see chapter 15 below).

Homo sapiens is an icon of the holy wisdom that graces all creation and becomes manifest intimately for us humans through our graced ancestors. We all reflect this ancient source, but it is revealed more explicitly in seminal figureheads of all the great ages known to humankind. Sadly, we remember only a few of these outstanding personalities: Krishna, the Buddha, Jesus, Mohammed. These are all male examples, which in itself should alert us to the incompleteness of the list and the anthropocentric bias that has prevented us from honoring great females.

Much more controversial and fretful for our contemporaries is the suggestion that we should transcend the individual models in favor of communal ones. Outstanding and inspiring though they may have been, Krishna, the Buddha, Jesus, etc. represent a phase in human evolution when only patriarchally approved models stood any chance of flourishing. Ancient wisdom was suppressed. Cosmic intelligence was suffocated, but not eliminated. Not surprisingly, ancient truth in the power of ancestral grace is revisiting our world with a timely vengeance.

Enter Synaesthesia

We appropriate knowledge and wisdom through our senses. Through sight, smell, taste, hearing, and touch we comprehend what is happening in the environment. We process our experience through the senses and integrate into our lives and actions the wisdom we appropriate from the surrounding environment. This is quite a complex process and one we take very much for granted.

Today we consider the human senses in isolation. Seeing, hearing, smelling, tasting, and touching are widely assumed to be different bits of behavior governed by their respective brain centers. This is quite a recent perception and not congruent with the experience of many indigenous peoples around the planet. Among modern researchers, the philosopher Maurice Merleau-Ponty boldly counters this widely accepted view. Our senses are not totally separate, but can overlap in significant ways.

"Synaesthesia" refers to the ability to experience reality through the interpenetration of sense experience. We hear colors, smell shapes, and see sounds. Metaphorically, people speak of "loud" colors, "soft" music, the "odor" of sanctity. These are subliminal echoes of earlier times when, apparently, we were all endowed with synaesthetic giftedness. What today is considered a rare gift and frequently dismissed as pathological has in fact been our dominant experience for thousands of years, enhancing our ability to engage life wisely and creatively. David Abram (1996, 60), quotes Merleau-Ponty:

> Synaesthetic perception is the rule, and we are unaware of it only because scientific knowledge shifts the center of gravity of experience, so that we have unlearned how to see, hear, and generally speaking, feel, in order to deduce, from our bodily organization and the world as the physicist conceives it, what we are to see, hear, and feel.

The Communal Challenge

What is particularly disconcerting for us moderns is the apparent threat to the status of the individual in this reframing of human and cosmic culture. The emphasis is no longer on the distinctive uniqueness of the individual — person, system, tribe, religion, nation, planet. The iconic wisdom of *Homo sapiens* prioritizes the relational web out of which every individual substance is born and without which it cannot flourish or even survive. We inherit identity and uniqueness not from isolation but from relationality, a recurring topic throughout the pages of this book.

We learn best when we learn together. And we learn on a larger, more liberating scale when that togetherness includes everything inhabiting creation including planet earth itself. In this communal endeavor, the distinctions between teacher and pupil become quite secondary. The primary concern is about appropriating and celebrating the vastness of the wisdom that unites us, simply by being creatures sharing the one God-given creation.

The wisdom of our wise ancestors is not just about clever manipulators standing a better chance of surviving than their more primitive predecessors. Rather, *Homo sapiens* represents the cumulative wisdom of all that had gone before, bringing such wisdom to a new critical threshold named in our time as "the capacity for self-reflexive consciousness." Yes, when it comes to intelligence we humans are uniquely endowed (as is every other organism in the diversity of creation), but that giftedness is not given for imperial management; rather it is to enhance the mutual giftedness that nourishes the dynamic diversity without which creation would come to nought. We humans act intelligently when we share from our uniqueness, not when we hoard it to subdue and control others.

"Realignment" is the word that springs to mind. We are out of tune with our true purpose, because we have disconnected ourselves from the universal web of cosmic and planetary life. Robust individualism is our great sin; cultural isolation is our curse. We are programmed for intelligent cooperation, not for individualistic competition. We have betrayed the inheritance of our wise ancestors.

But ancestral grace never gives up. The awakening of our world today, battered and bruised by so much unwise self-aggrandizement, pushes us to reclaim that which we have ignorantly subverted. Not an easy challenge for such an arrogant species, but one we cannot escape from if we stand any reasonable chance of living intelligently once more on the home planet.

Chapter 9

The Peril of European Promise

If we knew the unwritten story of our past, especially the pre-historic past, its fascination would cut the history of kings and queens, wars and parliaments, down to proper size.

— JOHN MCLEISH

I N 1977, José Bermúdez de Castro, of the National Museum of Natural Sciences in Madrid, began excavating fossils at the Spanish cave of Atapuerca and dated them to 780,000 years ago. The juvenile skeleton came to be known as *Homo antecessor.* The same site yielded an amazing discovery in June 2007, a partial jawbone and some teeth, suggesting that indigenous Europeans are at least 1 million years old. The fuller story can be read in *Nature* 452 (2008): 465–69 or online at *www.sciencecentric.com/news/08032618.htm.*

Europe, however, is associated primarily with the Neanderthals, creatures with a large brain and a robust figure capable of withstanding the colder climates of the time and inhabiting the European mainland as far back as 230,000 years ago. The oldest known skull for this group was discovered in Forbes quarry in Gibraltar in 1848, eight years prior to the more significant find in a limestone quarry in the Neander Valley (near Dusseldorf, Germany) in 1856. Over four hundred specimens have been found since then. The name "Neanderthal" was originally coined in 1863 by the Irish anatomist William King.

Developed Skills

Neanderthals performed a sophisticated set of tasks normally associated with humans alone. For example, they constructed complex shelters, controlled fire, and skinned animals. They used a range of stone weapons, including hand axes and spears. Faced with often harsh weather conditions, the Neanderthals coped and survived with remarkable ingenuity. Quite likely, they adopted something of the role-modeling we know today, with the men doing the hunting and more physical kinds of work, and the women caring for the young.

The Neanderthals are the first humans known to us to bury the dead and seem to have adopted elaborate rituals in doing so, dating back as far as a hundred thousand years ago. They may also have celebrated seasonal changes and created other rituals for special occasions. And they certainly used proto-language, but strangely did not go on to develop the complex speaking abilities of our time, as did the contemporary *Homo sapiens* in other parts of the planet.

According to Steven Mithen (2005), the Neanderthals loved their song and music. They may well have been the inventors of *hmmmmm,* a melodic precursor to articulate speech, developed in its more sophisticated form by *Homo sapiens,* but without the celebratory repertoire that Mithen claims was unique to the Neanderthals:

> I believe that all modern humans are relatively limited in their musical abilities when compared with the Neanderthals. . . . We place ballerinas on a stage and very few of us watch them more than once a year; the Neanderthals watched their ice-age dancing equivalents on a daily basis by firelight within their caves. (Mithen 2005, 245)

Colonial Arrogance

For much of the twentieth century scholars debated the links between Neanderthals and *Homo sapiens.* Were they a subspecies of *Sapiens* or an independent development following the multi-regional hypothesis (see p. 40 above)? The debate continues, with a growing consensus that the Neanderthals are an offspring of *Homo sapiens,* which initially emerged in Africa.

The Neanderthals carry archetypal significance for Europeans, ancient and modern. They are our primal ancestors, who molded something of the Europe we know today. That legacy has been subjected to some questionable assessments, particularly throughout the nineteenth and twentieth centuries. They were perceived to be more advanced, intelligent, and cultured than any of their African counterparts, particularly the earlier strands. This perceived superiority in subtle ways became the basis of European colonialism. The Neanderthals of white skin were deemed to be more sophisticated and advanced than the black primitive peoples. The seeds of modern racism and ethnicity were sown; the disturbing consequences endure to our own time.

For contemporary Europeans, the Neanderthals embody a heritage characterized by hard work, innovation, and survival strategy, as well as cultural advances in communication, musicality, and ritual-making. It is a heritage we can rightly and proudly cherish. We grossly dishonor it when we use it to lord it over others and possibly condemn others to the fate that the Neanderthals themselves eventually encountered.

It appears that they may have become extinct due to cultural isolation. By keeping to themselves and not traveling extensively as *Erectus, Ergaster,* and *Habilis* may have done, they cultivated a closed culture that began to implode. There is no evidence to show that they gave birth to *Homo sapiens.* That happened through a fresh influx from the African subcontinent.

For the Neanderthals it sounds like a sad ending. A powerfully creative group, endowed with an enormous capacity to transcend hardship and shape culture; yet, they somehow ran themselves into a dead end. The Neanderthals are a continuous reminder to us of the need to remain open to change for the sake of new growth. The restlessness in the human spirit is not merely a prescription for survival, but a prerequisite for thriving. In building empires, hoping they will last forever, we pave the way for our own cultural disintegration.

Is There a European Archetype?

"Europe" is the name for a geographical region of the planet, and to many people that is its sole significance. To many Africans, however, it is the cradle of colonialism, and to many contemporary Muslims it is a harbinger of Christian imperialism. Some looking from afar admire European attempts at integration, especially through the various agencies of the European Union, largely unaware of the struggle going on within Europe itself to maintain that integration within the context of a formalized constitution.

In terms of ancestral grace, our long evolutionary history, and the epochal role of the Neanderthals within that story, I'd like to explore the archetypal role Europe (and its culture) has played in shaping planetary and human emergence. In their day, the evidence suggests that the Neanderthals exhibited a quality of power, domination, and mastery not immediately obvious in the other developments reviewed thus far. They set out to conquer, seeking a type of ultimate control! Admittedly they never seem to have extended this desire beyond what today we describe as the European landmass. Nonetheless, the desire for supremacy seems to have had universal targets in mind.

The resilience of the Neanderthals is often described in terms of adversarial weather conditions that they seem to have mastered and managed with great skill and practical wisdom. One begins to glimpse something of the *archetypal warrior,* the one who will stand up and resist every pernicious force. Phallic symbolism appropriately depicts the Neanderthal psyche and its desperate will to live. These features surface again — quite explicitly — about ten thousand years ago, as a new wave of patriarchy begins to unfold (see chapter 12 below), and of course are very much to the fore in the colonial conquests of the nineteenth and twentieth centuries.

In his writings the mythologist Joseph Campbell often bemoans the fact that the warrior archetype is weak in our time and, ironically, among males in particular. A great deal of power is projected outward, precisely because it is not integrated into our inner beings, which in turn may be related to our very poor understanding of creation and its story of inner meaning. We tend to view creation as an external object to be tamed and controlled, and disconnected from our archetypal rootedness, we project mindlessly, seeking power over, instead of attending to our weakened capacity for empowerment. And the phallic undercurrents are all too apparent in the projected sexualized and abusive hurts inflicted upon innocent people, particularly women and children.

Can the Neanderthals Inspire Us Today?

Today it is the Europeans more than any other cultural group who suffer from a deflated warrior archetype. Europe today carries a great deal of decline and death. Our birth rate has been in reverse for several decades. Our economy is lethargic, even when we reap abundance — but we have so little imagination and sense of generosity we can only convert it into wine-lakes and butter-mountains. The wearied bureaucracy of the European Union militates against creative concerted action on various monetary, social, and political issues. To resolve the 1998 war in Kosovo, we had to ask the U.S. army to assist us.

The warrior archetype flourishes elsewhere, particularly in the amazing resilience of the millions of poor people around our earth who hold nerve and survive, despite appalling conditions. This warrior-like resistance never hits headlines but surely must be among the greatest virtues of our time. Paradoxically, this resilience is often evoked to cope with the cruel suffering inflicted by power-hungry autocrats, not primarily from Europe but from within Africa, Asia, and Latin America itself. The proverbial pendulum has swung; the internalized oppression of the European colonists rears its ugly head, as the warrior archetype once more translates into excessive and dangerous projections. All told, we don't seem to have learned much from the Neanderthals, who for most of their time handled the power issue with a wisdom and ingenuity badly lacking in our time.

While many people regard Europe as progressive, wealthy, and powerful, many people within Europe itself do not share this experience. Weariness, apathy, and selfishness are rampant. Despite their distance from us in time, the Neanderthals can inspire us in a graced way. Positively, they were incredibly vigorous and proactive for at least a hundred thousand years. They brought humanity forward in evolutionary leaps and bounds. And then became so cocksure in their false arrogance that they ended up destroying themselves — which contemporary Europeans are also in great danger of doing.

Let us today learn from the wisdom and daring initiatives of our Neanderthal ancestors. Their ancestral blood flows in our veins, their ancient wisdom informs our minds, and their spiritual ingenuity is precisely what we need to regain some faith and trust in our diminished abilities.

Chapter 10

The Discovery of Language

Archaeologists are confident that both music and language were present in all prehistoric societies of Homo sapiens.

— STEVEN MITHEN

W HEN I VISITED the Cradle of Humanity Museum (Maropeng) in South Africa (*www.maropeng.co.za*), in January 2008, the commentary on the evolution of language indicated that humans used sign language as far back as 1.5 million years ago, and evolved verbal speech as early as two hundred thousand years ago. Once again, these dates stretch conventional dating, that of a hundred thousand years ago being the one most frequently cited for the origins of human speech.

Staying for now with the conventional date of a hundred thousand years ago, this is a remarkable timespan for those who judge progress by the two-thousand-year benchmark; or by the landmark of five thousand years ago when, allegedly, a civilized culture first evolved. This timespan of a hundred thousand years is quite short when viewed within the context of our 7 million years of human evolution. Even in terms of our status as *Homo,* a hundred thousand years covers less than 1 percent of our existence since the emergence of *Homo habilis* around 2.5 million years ago.

How then did we survive *without the use of verbal language* — for over 99 percent of our existence since the time of *Homo habilis?* This is a crucial question rarely entertained by researchers and scholars of human origins. And we cannot hope to offer a meaningful response without the illumination provided by the notion of ancestral grace.

For most of our earthly existence, we have not spoken verbally, yet we have communicated efficiently and creatively. And not merely have we survived; we have actually thrived. But how?

Proto-language

Scholars devote an enormous amount of research to language, its origins and development. Scant attention is paid to what might have preceded language, although proto-language is a subject of immense interest for scholars today. Animals and primates communicate. We assume that they do so entirely by the power of instinct, and in many contemporary cultures instinct has a negative moralistic connotation. But if instinct is imbued with ancestral grace, if instinct is another dimension of archetypal meaning, as Carl Jung suggested, we obviously need a more attentive analysis of these insights.

Scholars have hinted at what proto-language might have looked liked. Perhaps it mimicked animal sounds and bird-song. Or was it largely without sound, relying more on nonverbal gestures of hand, eye, and other bodily deportments. Perhaps, unknown to ourselves, we are actually geniuses in the art of nonverbal communication — and have been — not just for hundreds of years — but for millennia!

Others suggest multi-syllabic utterances, messages rather than words, that later became segmented into the structure of language as we know it today (Wray 2002). Anthropologists Leslie Aiello and Robin Dunbar (Dunbar 1997) view language as a successor to primate grooming, a form of social and bonding behavior no longer possible when groups of hominids became large and dispersed. Michael Corballis (2002) sees gesturing as a precursor to spoken language, noting that a great deal of our communication, even to this day, includes a vast range of nonverbal gestures.

A number of these theories coalesce in the groundbreaking insight of British scholar Steven Mithen (2005). Mithen traces evidence for the development of music in human history, suggesting that among the Neanderthals — and possibly further back into prehistoric

time — humans communicated mainly through the use of melodi-
ous music-like vocalizations which he names "Hmmmmm" (Holistic,
manipulative, multi-modal, musical, and mimetic):

> Neanderthals may not have had language but they did have
> "Hmmmmm. . . . " I have examined several functions of music-
> like vocalizations and argued that Homo habilis, Homo ergaster
> and Homo heidelbergensis would have employed these to vary-
> ing extents within their communication systems. Homo habilis
> most likely used vocalizations and body movements to express
> and induce emotions in a manner that far exceeded any mod-
> ern nonhuman primate but that was quite restricted in terms
> of modern humans, owing to the possession of a relatively ape-
> like vocal tract and limited muscular control. (Mithen 2005,
> 233–34)

Musicologist Steven Brown (2000) proposes that "musilanguage"
precedes human speaking by thousands of years, while Merlin Donald (1991) believes that mime belonged to our communication
abilities long before the spoken word evolved. All of this suggests
that our ancient ancestors not only communicated in what was probably a coherent and intelligible manner, but seem to have done so in
a joy-filled and sensuously enriching way.

Comparisons with modern humans are central to all research as
is the unwarranted assumption that we are more developed than
our ancient ancestors. Within the context of the present work, however, we also need to acknowledge that we may have lost distinctive
abilities as we became more sophisticated in our evolutionary development. For some time now, both psychotherapists and spiritual
mentors have observed that spoken language is quite limited in accessing inner wisdom. People often gain insight and potential for
new growth more rapidly by employing nonverbal strategies. When a
client cannot find words to express what is going on deep within, she
may often articulate insight and appropriate integration through art,
music, movement, meditation. It looks like the nonverbal is catching
up with us again. The ancestral grace of our deep past is coming to

our rescue as we approach new evolutionary thresholds, examples of which I offer in part 3 of this book.

Theories of Language

It seems to me that we have largely neglected the long phase in our evolutionary story when proto-language was to the fore; to our detriment, we underestimate its profound significance. Our ability to communicate — without words — is yet another reminder of a creatively endowed species, with potentials that rational scholarship in our time is reluctant to explore in a serious and comprehensive way.

I don't wish to downplay the significance of the spoken word and its emergence some hundred thousand years ago, whether because of some preprogrammed capacity, e.g., the innate propensity for grammar proposed by Noam Chomsky (1969; 2002); evolutionary forces leading to the development of the modern vocal tract, proposed by Philip Lieberman (2006) and several others; or the evolution of a new gene, FOXP2, explored by the geneticist Svanta Paabo of the Max Planck Institute in Leipzig, Germany. And true to Darwinian insight, a number of scholars, like Derek Bickerton (1990), Steven Pinker (1994), and Terence Deacon (1997) claim that the spoken word evolved through the pressure of natural selection. Despite this intense scholarly debate consensus seems nowhere on the horizon, nor are we throwing much light on the possible dynamics that initially drove us to develop the ability to speak.

Scholars of several disciplines endorse what to me seems a rather anthropocentric bias, namely, that we became fully human only when we learned to speak. Only then, it is suggested, could we use imagination, think symbolically, and relate intelligently with the rest of life. In other words, before the acquisition of language we were not much more advanced than primates or animals. Terence Deacon (1997) challenges this view, suggesting that language could have been only developed by a species that was already highly intelligent and capable of symbolic interaction with its environment. For Deacon, spoken language is not the beginning of an evolutionary process, but rather its culmination.

Of all the scholars exploring the meaning of language, David Abram offers on analysis most congruent with the thesis I explore in this book. Abram (1996) attributes great significance to our human integration with the natural world, the grounded context through which we grew in wisdom, grace, and creativity. In our convivial relationship with the natural world, for thousands of years, we were absorbing the sounds of nature: the singing of the birds, the whishing of wind in the trees, the gurgling of stream water, the banging of thunder, the bellowing of animals. Over a long period of time, these various sounds of nature penetrated our inner being and became ingrained in our inner soul. Then at a moment of evolutionary readiness (natural selection, perhaps), the sounds became human sound, first as proto-language, then as grunts and groans, and finally as spoken word. We learned to make human sound because of our assimilation of nature's capacity to make sound.

Language and Social Bonding

According to Robin Dunbar (1997), some 635 devices of human conversation relate to matters of social interaction, largely gossip, not to the exchange of technical information. Language has a primary function of bonding people in a whole range of relationships. Both Pinker and Bickerton disagree, seeing language serving a more technical function, dealing practically with the local environment and its demands upon our resources and ingenuity.

Derek Bickerton of the University of Hawaii is an oft-cited theorist in the literature on language acquisition. In the development of early language, he suggests two stages: *pidgins,* symbols used by chimpanzees, adopted by the earliest humans, and also used as the first words of infant children; *creoles,* describing the use of words with inflection and syntax. Bickerton (1990) believes we used words (without grammar) from a very early stage as a kind of primary representation system (PRS), focusing on hierarchical order and binary distinctions.

In Bickerton's analysis we detect many of the favored presuppositions of the scholarly world: rational logic, hierarchical ordering, binary differentiation, all of which enable humans to be in control of reality. Once again we need to ask: Was this desire for domination and control as central for our ancient ancestors as it is for us today? The evidence strongly suggests that it was not. The interactive convivial relationship worked in a very different fashion, one that requires us to keep our theories and postulations much more open and transparent to fresh insights, particularly those that can honor the graced vision of creativity and cooperation.

Robin Dunbar's theory of the social inspiration for language is much more congruent with the vision of the present work. In developing our capacity to relate more closely and intelligently, language began to unfold, perhaps along lines favored by natural selection. This connecting thread — our capacity for cooperative relating — underpins all our major evolutionary breakthroughs, as indeed it drives the whole process of cosmic and planetary evolution as well.

One area where the spoken word exploded into meaning was in ancient ritual practices. Having danced our religion for thousands of years and chanted our praises to the great enveloping mystery, we now began to voice our prayer in a more verbal way. Our spiritual development reached a new evolutionary threshold. We explore its significance in the next chapter.

Chapter 11

Pagan Spirituality

It has never been like this before, for evolution progresses moment by moment, and no other humans have stood where we stand today. This is our threshold and these are our times and only now has it become clear that our survival is dependent on our spiritual awakening. — JAN PHILLIPS

S EVERAL ALLUSIONS have already been made to an ancient sense of religious belief. Various scholarly texts of ethnography and paleontology suggest that our ancestors believed in a divine life force but exercised this belief in great fear and within a very primitive and barbaric context. In this analysis, projections abound, most of which are grossly inaccurate and seriously lacking in the liberating power of ancestral grace.

Two words encapsulate prehistoric religion: "pagan" and "spiritual." The Concise Oxford English Dictionary defines pagan as "heathen, unenlightened or irreligious person." Living a spiritual life (spirituality) is widely considered to be a consequence of following and practicing a formal religion. Formal religion is a development of the past five thousand years; therefore, spirituality is deemed to be impossible before that time. Time constriction seriously hampers our vision, and the inspiring riches of ancestral grace are once more destructively subverted.

Paganism Reinstated

Theologian Marc I. Wallace (2005) is one among many contemporary scholars seeking to retrieve and reclaim what we have so tragically dishonored in our rich cultural past. He argues that pagan people of ancient times (and modern neopagans as well) were *lovers of the heath,* deeply embedded in the land, which they understood to be an embodied expression of the divine in creation. As such, the earth was perceived as holy and sacred, always to be treated with love and respect. On this foundational belief rested an integrated faith, the envy of many spiritual seekers in our time.

What was transpiring throughout Paleolithic times (ca. 40,000–10,000 BP) is not easily discerned, but one aspect does seem to be fairly clear: *the love of the land.* The close partnership with nature, the ability to listen and respond in a discerning way to the exigencies of nature, was the saving grace for our ancestors throughout the epoch under consideration, and indeed for long before it. The earth's ability for birthing, nurturing, sustaining, healing is probably what prompted our ancient ancestors to envisage earth-life in divinely feminine terms. The archetype of the Goddess is not to be compared with the transcendent divine figures we know in the formal religions; rather it is an imminent embodied presence, empowering all that grows and flourishes from within the living earth itself (Reid-Bowen 2007).

The ancient Spirit-world also remains largely incomprehensible to the crude rationalism that governs a great deal of contemporary research. Cultural reductionism has taken a frightening toll on the history of spirituality. Long before formal religion ever evolved, about five thousand years ago, our ancestors danced and drummed, chanted and meditated, prayed and ritualized — all in tribute to the divine life force they intuitively knew to be loving yet awesome, near yet all-encompassing, benign and at times inexplicably capricious. When it comes to spirituality, our graced ancestors could embrace paradox to a degree largely unknown in the congealed religious world of our time.

Ritualizing the Spiritual

Ritual burials are known to have happened among the Neanderthals as far back as a hundred thousand years ago. This is the oldest verifiable evidence we have for what seems to have been quite an elaborate ritual, signifying a species that perceived human life as a journey with a destiny (not necessarily a notion of afterlife as we understand it today), determined by the guiding spiritual force that imbued all creation.

The capacity for ritual-making is a phenomenon of great age, and numerous scholars have examined its significance in human history. William James, Rudolf Otto, Aldous Huxley, and Gregory Bateson are among the many who identify ancient ritual as endowed with graced inspiration (see Rappaport 1999, 382ff.). Outside Europe, the oldest evidence we have for ritual is that of the python-based worship in the Ngamiland region of northwestern Botswana. Here in the summer of 2006, Sheila Coulson of the University of Oslo discovered a cave in the Tsodilo Hills containing thirteen thousand artifacts related to ancient rituals (see p. 46 above). Many of these were stones and spearheads, not manufactured by the local San people, but imported possibly from hundreds of miles away.

Coulson has dated her discoveries to some seventy thousand years ago, predating the Paleolithic caves by at least thirty thousand years. Much more important than the ancient dating is the apparent elegance and sophistication of the ritual enactment. Several stones exhibit patterns of indentation, probably tracing the design of the python's skin, especially when illuminated by sunlight or the nighttime fire. Coulson also suggests that the cave was probably used as an inner chamber, the sacred space of the shaman; when the shaman chanted or spoke within the chamber his voice may have been symbolically regarded as coming from the mouth of the python itself. Speculative though some of these ideas might be, they are congruent with that ancient creativity and sense of imagination which was probably far more prevalent among our ancestors than we have henceforth been prepared to concede.

From contemporary rites of passage we can glean the context in which ritual practices became popular. In general, we can say that we are dealing with threshold times and boundary places. And in both cases, the person and the natural world intersect and often overlap. Rituals evolved to mark the beginning and end of human life, and also the beginning and end of each season. Rituals were developed to negotiate and make sense of disruption and disorder, the unexpected occurrence of sickness in humans or storms in nature. Many such rituals were structured around reconciliation and healing, with the person and the surrounding environment always perceived as two different expressions of the one-life continuum. Dualistic divisions are largely unknown in pagan spirituality.

Enter the Great Mother

I have briefly outlined evidence for our capacity for ritual-making going back at least a hundred thousand years, with the more verifiable data focused on seventy thousand years ago. Our next substantial evidence is that of Ice Age art (detailed in chapter 6 above) and particularly the controversial findings related to the Great Earth Mother Goddess. Under review here is a long timespan, possibly from 40,000 to 10,000 BCE, when humans may have worshiped God as a great woman whose body was regarded as that of the earth itself. Scholars such as Marija Gimbutas, Riane Eisler, Merlin Stone, and Carol Christ opt for the factual truth of this assertion, while Cynthia Eller, Rosemary Radford Ruether, and Paul Reid-Bowen find such literalization unnecessary and potentially damaging for more serious research.[15]

Ice Age art exhibits a distinctive fascination with women and with female fertility. At the very least we can assert that the female was the central focus of a unique and prolonged discernment, and the massive surge of creative energy through art, music, and sculpture throughout this entire time is evidence of a culture of egalitarianism that we will probably never uncover in its full impact. I suspect something quite archetypal was happening during this time, a kind of spiritual flourishing more momentous than the formal religions of our time are capable of representing.

There have been few epochs in human history since Ice Age art in which the issue of the Great Goddess has not surfaced with an intensity that has evoked strong reaction and frequently outright condemnation from formal religions. This archetypal female figure in the spiritual background never seems to be too far away, and her persistence to be taken seriously is likely to catch up with us — perhaps sooner than we think. Even men can't escape her allurement. To quote Sam Keen:

> The Goddess since her historical dethronement has remained alive and well, and continues to exert power from deep in the hidden recesses of the human psyche. Granted she has been sentenced to remain in a kind of internal exile, under house arrest, but her power is obvious from the efforts spent to keep her imprisoned. (Keen 1989, 17)

The publication and popularity of Dan Brown's *The Da Vinci Code* in 2003 was widely proclaimed and denounced as a type of modern paganism. Focusing on the Great Earth Mother, the book became an intriguing and fascinating read for millions around the world. Reviewed at length, it was widely condemned for its factual errors and misleading ideas. But few seem to have discerned or grasped its subliminal, archetypal appeal: it was because of its central character, the *Great Earth Mother Goddess,* that millions of readers became hooked and fascinated. Timely evidence that the Goddess has not been dethroned, as Sam Keen intimates.

The contemporary fascination with the Goddess is not a regression to primitive paganism, nor is it merely a nostalgic desire for some utopian past. Neither can it be construed as feminists wishing to replace male divine models with female ones. We are witnessing something much more complex, with a timely sense of urgency. *Our need to be mothered in a more wholesome way* is at stake. And the mothering is not so much in the personal realm as in the domain of the transpersonal. It is our need to be held, nurtured, and embraced by the living earth itself that is to the fore. In the language of John's Gospel, it is an archetypal desire to be "born again," to reconnect in a more meaningful and coherent way with the great nourishing womb of cosmic and planetary life.

As intimated by contemporary writers like Alex Pirani (1991) and Jean Shinoda Bolen (2005), we are starving for mothering nourishment. Disillusioned and alienated by excessive rationalism and feeling overpowered and undermined by patriarchal dominance, we seek an alternative that will be more culturally empowering, spiritually liberating, embracing us in our vulnerability but also in our generativity. And increasingly, we realize this is possible only when we learn to relate with our cosmic and planetary creation, adopting something of the graced wisdom known to our ancient ancestors.

Earth Spirituality Today

The paradigm shift in contemporary spirituality has rightly been described as a cultural revolution (Tacey 2004). Reconnecting with deeper ancient wisdom features strongly. And above all else, spirituality is not just for persons, but rather for persons seeking to live in a more convivial and integrated way with the great cosmic and planetary life forces (see Clarke 2005). In the whole of creation we encounter most authentically the wholeness and goodness of God.

Joan Chittister states quite forthrightly this new orientation in the emerging spirituality: "There is a new question in the spiritual life; it is the spirituality of the spiritual life itself. Life here, and how we relate to it, rather than life to come and how we guarantee it for ourselves, has become the spiritual conundrum of our age" (1998, 1).

The battered earth cries out for justice, and thanks to ancestral grace we are beginning to respond as no doubt our pagan ancestors did. We are reconnected with the primordial womb of our begetting, knowing that without a healthy and wholesome earth our holiness (wholesomeness) is also in jeopardy. Whereas formerly spirituality was very much about *escape* from the surrounding creation — to save one's soul in an eternal realm beyond — we are now coming to understand the spiritual task as *engagement* with God's world, the co-creative sphere where authentic spiritual maturation can be truly realized.

Paradoxically, as we enter more deeply into the mystery that is creation, with something of that awe, wonder, and trepidation of our ancestors, we begin to rediscover a strangely familiar resonance between our spirit and the spirit of the living earth itself. We begin to reclaim a oneness that should never have been fractured. We begin to come home to dimensions of ourselves that intuitively feel familiar. We have been there before; in truth, we never totally abandoned that place.

Wisdom from Deep Within

Spirituality is not just a learned wisdom; it is an innate, natural endowment of the human psyche. We were born with it. We have always had it, ever since the time Lady Toumai began to explore the world of ancient Chad, in North Africa. How it was articulated down through those long aeons is obviously beyond our access today. For much of the twentieth century, we relied on currently extant indigenous peoples for hints and clues on how our ancestors lived and worshiped. At best, these provide partial insights. Thanks to more sophisticated archaeological research, abetted with more refined dating techniques, we can piece together some vital dimensions in the great jigsaw puzzle of our spiritual unfolding.

In this newly evolving sense of the sacred, many Christians react negatively, fearing a collapse into something cold and impersonal. It is not so much a lack of personhood as a different understanding, an ancient wisdom once again reclaiming its rightful place. Indoctrinated in dualistic binaries, we fear that a loss of the person automatically means we are dealing with an impersonal force. No, we are being asked to embrace a *transpersonal* archetype, incorporating all that makes sacred and fertile everything in creation, human persons included. This is what is so gracefully empowering about the notion of the Goddess.

Did our ancient ancestors of Paleolithic times know all this? Not at a conscious level (we think), but they knew it intuitively and subconsciously, probably to a degree that modern humans, so conditioned by rationalism and literalism, are incapable of internalizing. How they did grasp it — subconsciously and intuitively — can be gleaned from the human propensity for what is beyond literalism and rationalism, namely, the liberating power of the symbolic. In this realm, ancestral grace reaches a new depth, wonderfully illustrated by the achievements of Ice Age art, but correspondingly undermined by the rationalism that accompanied the rise of agriculture, the topic to which we now turn our attention.

Chapter 12

Agriculture and Its Discontents

*Agriculture introduced the concept of land ownership and also
resulted in food surpluses, which in turn created excess wealth,
which translated into power.... The agrarian revolution's creation of surplus wealth so reduced the status of hunters that
they resorted to conquest which in turn led to the downfall of
egalitarian societies and ultimately the defeat of the Goddess.*

— LEONARD SHLAIN

B Y TEN THOUSAND YEARS AGO, our ancestors had inhabited all
but the most inaccessible parts of planet earth. North and South
America had been reached from Siberia. Australia and New Guinea
were settled after significant sea-crossings, and all habitable parts of
continental Africa and Europe were occupied. Then independently,
and at different times in at least nine parts of the world, the domestication of crops and animals began in earnest. Starting in the Near East,
agriculture rapidly spread into what is now India, China, West and
East Africa, Central America, and the East Coast of the United States.

The earth's fertile potential had been discovered long before this
time, and it appears that women had been exploring the fruitfulness
of the earth for several millennia. Now a new impetus irrupted with
the extensive growing of crops and widespread domestication of animals. Why it happened at this precise time, and why it happened so
suddenly, are intriguing questions for which there is no clear answer.

Agriculture as an Axial Moment

Most bewildering of all was the rather sudden change in the social
and cultural complementarity of the sexes. A new male caste came to

85

the fore: aggressive, acquisitive, gregarious, militaristic. A deterioration in weather conditions may be one factor triggering the sense of panic and the compulsive need for control and dominance that began to ensue. Rather quickly the land was commodified and parceled out to greedy bidders. A new violent streak entered humanity. In a short time, it would give birth to warfare, a phenomenon largely unknown in any previous epoch of human evolution.

Population began to grow rapidly, causing further consternation and competition for resources. The proximity of domesticated animals and dense human populations led to the emergence of diseases never known before. Measles, tuberculosis, and smallpox spread from cattle to humans; influenza, whooping cough, and malaria spread from pigs, ducks, and chickens. Humans had made a massive evolutionary stride but paid a high price in the process.

The rise of agriculture about ten thousand years ago is hailed as one of evolution's greatest achievements and one of humanity's foremost discoveries. But it has a dark and destructive side that has not been duly acknowledged (see Shlain 1998, 33ff.). It gave birth to a new wave of human dominance that has prevailed to the present time. It gave birth to the patriarchal system that features in every form of contemporary governance, political and religious alike. And it is now a wearied system, losing credibility at a rapid rate. Yet thus far humanity has not dreamed a global alternative to this faltering institution.

According to Geoffrey Carr, agriculture turned out to be a mixed blessing. "Both modern and fossil evidence suggests that hunter-gatherers led longer, healthier and more leisured lives than did farmers until less than a century ago. But farmers have numbers on their side" (2005, 10). Ancestral grace, however, is not primarily about numbers; it is about relationships of a type that honor the complexity and interdependence of everything on earth. And it was the precarious twist in our human capacity for relating — especially to the land — that bedeviled an otherwise promising development.

The Rise of Anthropocentrism

One would have thought that agriculture would have given humans a new sense of their connection with the land as a living system, and undoubtedly it did to an extent that is difficult to determine with hindsight. Tragically, what is much more in evidence is the negative aftermath. The land came to be treated as a commodity, an object to be fought over and used to foment the patriarchal philosophy of divide and conquer. Power mongering came to the fore in ways previously unknown in human history.

Humans placed themselves at the head of the ruling pinnacle, to such a degree that they invented a divine overlord, the Great Sky God. From here on, agriculture becomes synonymous with domination and control. And a more disturbing corollary evolves: the sky-God inhabits the distance heavens, whereas the Great Goddess was perceived to inhabit the cosmic and planetary creation.

In the culture of the Goddess the land was deemed sacred, always to be treated with love and respect. Now with the triumph of patriarchy, the land progressively comes to be seen as a commodity, over which humans (i.e., males) have total ownership and control, validated by the patriarchal Holy One who also stands apart from, and rules over, the commodified land.

The hierarchical ordering becomes the monopoly of all truth. God at the top rules without advisor or rival. The heavens are inhabited with hierarchical layers of beings: archangels, angels, saints, martyrs, and so on. And the same pattern is presumed to prevail on earth with the king at the top of the pyramid and males to the fore in all forms of governance and control. The priority of the human, popularly known as anthropocentrism, is firmly established on earth and unquestioningly validated in heaven. Paul Reid-Bowen captures the sense of distortion when he writes: "It was only with the coming of patriarchy that the spiralling model was suppressed and ultimately supplanted by abstract linear models and eschatological narratives of specifically human progress" (2007, 119).

Creation becomes what humans wish to make of it. Earth is progressively objectified, culminating in the mechanistic science of seventeenth-century Europe. The final chapter is well encapsulated in the oft-quoted saying of Francis Bacon: "We must keep torturing nature 'til she reveals her last secrets to us." Objectified though the earth may now be, we detect in the background the haunting presence of the Great Goddess. Humans are now in charge — in a self-perpetuating myth that will haunt humanity from here on. Today the manicured, poisoned land screams back at us, as painfully and confusedly we strive to return the soil to its innate biophilic organicity.

Religious Validation

The agricultural revolution, intentionally or otherwise, changed the landscape of human perception and action. What previously was understood as one earth, organic and alive, functioned as a holarchical, interdependent organism. Now *hierarchy* replaced *holarchy*. We lost the sense of interconnectedness. The web of life became anthropocentric, a phallo-centric regime addicted to the allurement of power rather than the ancestral grace of mutual empowerment. Although in recent times biologists have reclaimed the notion of nested hierarchies at work in nature, the top-down ordering still dictates and informs our misguided engagement with creation.

Religion was largely co-opted into this new schema. Even in the more egalitarian view of the great Eastern religions the divine power is identified primarily with rulership from on high. I fully endorse the view that in their purity all religions affirm and enforce the deep spiritual aspirations of ancient times. Yet one cannot ignore the fact that the major religions we know today all evolved under the umbrella of the dominant patriarchal culture. Whatever their pristine source and purpose, the influence and conditioning of patriarchal validation rests heavily on all religions. Most disturbing of all, the religions inherited a great deal of the violence that characterizes patriarchy from its very origins.

And for all religions, material creation is suspect at best and at worst a gross distraction from the things of God, from the essential demands of the spiritual life. In many of the great religions — Hinduism, Buddhism, Christianity — holiness is judged by one's willingness to flee the world, renounce the world, even hate the world. While scholars argue that the concept of the world in use here (as in the Gospel of John) is quite complex, nonetheless it has left us with an ethical and spiritual ambivalence toward material creation. We have been told so often that we must not be at home on earth that we are left with a deep sense of spiritual alienation, which ancestral grace requires us to shed as we reclaim the graced wisdom of our deep past.

Agriculture and Ancestral Grace

The agricultural revolution did not deal well with ancestral grace. With humans at the helm, we inaugurated a cultural breakthrough, but at the price of substantial destruction of other life forms. Many contemporary commentators endorse the view of South African John M. Anderson (see du Toit and Mayson 2006, 25–47), that as cultural catalysts, we humans consistently exhibit violent oppression and leave behind us trails of mass destruction, often leading to extensive extinction of other life forms. This is certainly true of the early human explorers in Australia sixty thousand years ago and in North America twelve thousand years ago. I am not convinced that we have *always* been innately violent and destructive. As we reclaim our deeper, more ancient story, we are likely to encounter a species much more caring and responsible for all the other creatures with whom we shared the planet. This assertion in no way denies or belittles the fact that we too contribute to the paradox of creation and destruction that characterizes planetary life at every level.

It is all too easy to rationalize our present addiction to violence and destruction by projecting it onto an imaginary barbaric past. Whatever the precise facts about a postulated violent past (see my comments on man-the-hunter hypothesis, pp. 54–56 above), the violence we have known over the past ten thousand years — all too apparent in the brutalities of the twentieth century — is based on quite an explicit rationale that our dominant culture today simply does not wish to face or resolve. I refer to the patriarchal philosophy of *divide and conquer.*

This patriarchal addiction is the more manifest aspect of the rise of agriculture in its shadow (dark) expression. It is a brutal denial of much that had been unfolding over many previous epochs (e.g., the culture of the Great Goddess). Rather, it forced through a kind of rapid cultural maturity, for which I suspect there are few precedents in previous evolutionary eras. Axial ages tend to be ambiguous, with the great paradox of creation and destruction weaving a new breakthrough for creation and its inhabitants. Ancestral grace was overshadowed, but not disempowered.

The postagricultural epoch, with its various social and personal depravities (outlined briefly above), is probably best viewed in the league of the great extinctions. It is one of those regressive developments that on the large scale of ancestral grace does not make anthropocentric sense, but serves a deeper subliminal wisdom. It is the ambiguity and ambivalence we can expect in the downward curve of creation's great cycle of birth-death-rebirth. Creation has been through this cycle more often than we humans can ever hope to calculate. Without it, neither we, nor the magnificent planet we inhabit, would be here today.

For the human species, however, it raises predicaments almost too scary to contemplate. Most frightening of all is the prospect that we are — as Leakey and Lewin (1996) have so bluntly stated — *the sixth extinction*. We are the primary culprits in the mass destruction we evidence all around us. Increasingly, it looks as if it might have to be this way if we are ever to be brought to our senses in terms of the things we do wrongly, the ways in which we have ignored or disregarded the call of ancestral grace. In our grossly destructive behavior, we stand the best chance of destroying the primary cause of the destruction, namely, ourselves. A thought almost too grim to entertain!

In terms of the earth and its resources, ancestral grace will win out, as it has done so often in the past. And there is a slight chance that we will be there to share the experience. But if we are to be there, we will need to act urgently and with something of that global unanimity that characterized our earthly existence for several thousand years. In the power of ancestral grace all things are possible. Time alone will reveal the outcome!

Part Two

The Human as Christian

We no longer rely on the disembodied God...but engage with Christ as narrative, vision and imagination, passionately committed to creative growth and liberation. That appears to be what those who provided us with the narratives were doing in the first place. — LISA ISHERWOOD

Chapter 13

Jesus, Disciple of Ancestral Grace

*When Jesus appeared on the scene, the collective unconscious
of the age was fully prepared. His life tapped into the massive
psychic upheaval that was affecting numerous groups, not only
in Judaism but in the Mediterranean world generally. Something
seismic was about to happen, and Jesus stood at the epicenter.*
— WALTER WINK

ANCESTRAL GRACE names and celebrates the divine playfulness exhibited throughout the entire story of creation and specifically in
our human becoming over 7 million years. Christian faith acknowledges God's deep involvement in that story, yet it is a story deeply
flawed to such an extent that God had to send his own Son to rectify
the fundamental flaw. This puts God in a rather precarious double
bind: on the one hand it is a creation abundantly blessed by the divine creator, yet so deeply flawed that, allegedly, it requires an act of
divine rescue to save it from sinful destructability. One wonders who
has concocted the plot: *God or patriarchal humans?*

One also wonders why has it taken humans so long to see through
the fallacy and short-sightedness of the allegation of a fundamental
flaw. The prevailing myth begins with angels warring in heaven with
the predictable patriarchal outcome of winners and losers. Tough luck
on us humans: we become the progeny of the losers, the fallen angels
who contaminate not merely humans but *everything else in creation.*
This is the anthropocentrism that so bedevils religion generally: *patriarchal humans are the supreme species;* they dictate and determine
what happens to the rest of creation.

That perception — of humans lording it over the entire creation —
is certainly a flawed perception, one that is, indeed, deeply sinful in

the true biblical sense of *hamartia* (missing the mark). Now that we are relearning and reappropriating our true story of 7 million years, we need no longer rely on the fabricated narrative of patriarchy, a mere ten thousand years in age. We can begin to reclaim our true story and therefore a more authentic fidelity to our creative God.

For Christians, Jesus is the one who embodies primordially what it means to live by ancestral grace. But Jesus, too, has been distorted by patriarchy, and ironically he must himself be rescued from those professional Christians who try to convince the rest of us that they alone have the whole truth — a challenge aptly worded in the title of Carter Heyward's book: *Saving Jesus from Those Who Are Right* (Heyward 1999).

Creatures of Ancestral Grace

As indicated frequently in part 1, there is little evidence to substantiate a fundamental flaw in the human emergence of the past 7 million years. While we never got it fully right, we achieved an amazing feat, thanks to the prodigious blessings of ancestral grace. A great deal of the confusion seems to arise from the human failure to differentiate between a fundamental *paradox* and a fundamental *flaw*. The former belongs to the foundational story of all creation, human evolution included; the latter arises from our human inability to comprehend and discern the true meaning of the paradox.

From a patriarchal perspective, the decisive issue is that of domination, humanity's inordinate desire for absolute control, a feature of the patriarchal governance of the postagriculture era. *We cannot control paradox;* if we could we would have eliminated the very foundations of enduring mystery. As indicated in chapter 7, the cosmic paradox of creation-and-destruction is the driving force behind and within the recurring cycle of birth-death-rebirth, the elegant and complex dance through which creation thrives. Without this strange and baffling cycle of creation-and-destruction everything would come to nought; in fact, life as we know it today would simply not exist.

There is no flaw in this enterprise, and never has been. And for humanity, for most of our time on earth, we seem to have managed it with grace and maturity, until we began to set ourselves over against the living earth itself. When we turned the land into a commodity, about ten thousand years ago, we began to lose the plot. The ideology of divide and conquer came to the fore: lording it over the land, the people, the life process, especially death (which we have demonized in an extreme way), and finally the Godhead itself, by projecting the living God back into the fantasized world above the sky.

Inevitably, such a God had to be seen to be in charge. Therefore, he had to intervene, and in good patriarchal fashion did so, by sending a *male* representative. And to appease the angry God (the supreme patriarch) he had to suffer and die, as ruling males sometimes demanded in the feudal justice of the Middle Ages. Jesus now becomes integrated into the fundamental flaw, and his archetypal significance as the radical, radiant face of divinized humanity is subverted. But in the end truth endures, and today growing numbers of Christians seek a faith that is credible and real, one that honors our deeper story as beneficiaries of ancestral grace.

Rescuing Jesus from Patriarchy

In the present chapter, I want to see what Jesus might look like when we situate his presence and mission in the context of ancestral grace rather than within the patriarchal anthropocentrism of the past ten thousand years. Let's try to rescue Jesus from anthropocentric reductionism and ideological minimalism. As suggested in a previous work (O'Murchu 2005), we need to loosen the chains that have held Jesus incarcerated so that we can follow him more authentically as Christian disciples.

I wish to reclaim the Jesus of ancestral grace in a series of prayerful statements, perhaps as a litany of Christian liberation:

Blessed are we as cherished earthlings of God's wonderful creation.

Blessed are we whose incarnational humanity has been affirmed from the beginning of our evolutionary story.

Blessed are we who have been graced to embrace the unfolding paradox of creation in the unceasing process of birth-death-rebirth.

Blessed are we with creativity and an enormous capacity for innovation, contributing to the building up of God's reign on earth.

Blessed are we because we got it right for most of the time throughout our long history of 7 million years.

Blessed are we who are forgiven by our large-hearted God for the times when we got things badly wrong.

Blessed are we because in the fullness of time, Jesus evolves as the one who affirms and confirms all we have achieved in our evolutionary story.

Blessed are we because Jesus illuminates the archetype of humanity radiant in evolutionary maturity, confirming our past achievements and challenging us to future evolutionary growth.

Blessed are we as co-creators, called to build up on earth the New Reign of God, committed to right relating in the name of love and justice.

Blessed are we because amid huge risk and misunderstanding, Jesus dared to heal, forgive, liberate, and empower those trapped in oppression, poverty, and pain.

Blessed are we because Jesus shares our sufferings, affirms our hopes, and liberates our potential for future growth.

Blessed are we who have inherited open-ended parables, stories of a dangerously empowering memory of inclusive liberation.

Blessed are we as custodians of the open table, symbol of creation's abundant resources, from which no one is ever to be excluded.

Blessed are we because Jesus bridges the way to our next evolutionary leap, illustrated in the empowerment of his resurrected presence.

Blessed are we because Jesus models life as a Spirit-filled being, the evolutionary destiny to which we are all called.

Blessed are we as the body of Christ today, challenged never to betray the great story and to tell it afresh in each successive generation.

Blessed we are indeed with a tradition that is illuminating and inspiring. It is a grace for which we must be forever grateful. Yet it never leaves us off the hook. Rather it compels us to engage in a deeper and more enlightened way, to embrace the graced blessings of future evolutionary stages with something of that same wisdom and resilience with which we managed in the distant past. In this troubled turbulent world, things can be different — if only we take seriously the hope that radiates in the great story of our origins, affirmed and confirmed for Christians, in the life and example of Jesus.

Jesus as Archetypal Human

That graced humanity, ever old and ever new, is the heart and soul of Christian revelation. It is, at one and the same time, a humanity frail and fragile like we often experience in our daily lives, but also a human life stretched to the fullness of what it means to be human. This latter dimension is what scripture scholar Walter Wink (2002) describes as the archetype of the truly human:

> As bearer of the archetype of the human being, Jesus activates the numinous power that is capable of healing, transforming, or rebirthing those who surrender themselves to it. . . . Jesus shows us something of what it means to become human, but not enough to keep us from having to discover our own humanity. We must weave the story, and for each of us the story will be unique. (Wink 2002, 139, 257)

Jesus, in his life, death, and resurrection, confirms our human nature in all that had evolved up to that time, while also incarnating those deeper potentials we will gradually acquire as we evolve in our future growth and development. Anything Jesus did we can do also — when the evolutionary time is ripe for God to call forth in us those potentialities, already evidenced in the life and behavior of Jesus.

Ironically, what has distracted us from following Jesus in a more responsible evolutionary way is the emphasis we place upon his divinity. What makes him different from us is conceived as divine power and attributes, when in fact these are really qualities and potentialities belonging to future evolutionary unfolding. I am not denying the divinity of Jesus and its importance for millions of religious believers. As a social scientist, I am choosing not to address it because I feel it distracts — quite seriously — from the more important insights arising from the social and anthropological sciences.

When I review the magnificence and elegance of our human becoming — without in any way denying or ignoring the terrible mess we created at times — I have no doubt that a deeply spiritual life force is at work, in us and in all creation. I don't wish to control or analyze it in detail; I don't even wish to attribute traditional religious names to it. I want to allow the mystery to be the mystery, and hopefully enable myself, and others, through the embrace of ancestral grace to be drawn more deeply into this creative and empowering liberation.

It seems to me as a Christian that Jesus belongs to this deep ancient tradition, not just as the Son of God, but as the radiant icon of the divine immersed in the great story of human evolution. And it is not the divine aspects of that immersion that inspire and challenge me; much more immediate and much more awesome is the transformative power of the archetypal human exemplified and radiated in the life and ministry of Jesus (see chapter 15 below).

With this enlarged horizon of engagement, let's explore afresh some key dimensions of our inherited Christian story.

Chapter 14

The God Who Incarnates

All creatures are siblings from the same womb, the brood of one Mother of the universe who dwells in bright darkness. In her, as once literally in our own mother, we live and move and have our being. — ELIZABETH JOHNSON

RE-VISIONING JESUS in the larger context of creation and within the tapestry of our evolutionary story inevitably raises questions about God as creator and the role of the Holy Spirit in the grand scheme of things. These are weighty theological matters beyond my wisdom and expertise. However, some brief comments are necessary in the hope of honoring the wider concerns that may arise for the reader.

Let me briefly restate my purpose in writing this book: to illuminate our evolving human story, highlighting how our ancestors throughout a 7-million-year timespan, collaborated closely with the creative God, precisely by maintaining a close and convivial relationship with God's creation. Our ancient ancestors seem to be much more at home with the unity of all life, including the great paradox of creation and destruction, contrary to the dualistic categories so familiar to us: God vs. humanity, heaven vs. earth, spirit vs. matter, etc. Ancestral grace endowed people with the ability to entertain and respect paradox to a degree that seems largely absent in people of our time. Against that background, the ancients began to envision and articulate a sense of the great mystery, some elements of which I wish to highlight in this chapter.

The Divine as Spirit Power

First, I want to reflect on that dimension of the divine we call the "Holy Spirit." This seems to be the most ancient and primordial

99

understanding of the divine familiar to our prehistoric ancestors. One finds interesting parallels in the spirituality of contemporary indigenous peoples. That presence of the great mystery which endows, imbues, and enfolds the whole of creation was experienced as living Spirit. To the ancients, that Spirit was experienced as tangibly close and intimate yet simultaneously fierce, threatening, and awesome. Apparently, our ancestors felt no great need to resolve what to people of our time feels like a disturbing contradiction.

The stumbling block for many of our contemporaries is the perception that such devotion and religion are totally impersonal and therefore archaic and superficial compared with modern religious consciousness. Dualistic thinking may be the major obstacle here. If something is not obviously *personal,* as we currently define that term, then we assume it must be *impersonal.* We can best resolve this dualism with the notion of the *transpersonal,* a concept well known in our time but not favored in rational academic research. The transpersonal endorses much of what I have been exploring about ancestral grace in part 1: personhood, to be fully realized, can flourish only in a relational context that includes every aspect of creation, from the vast cosmos to the smallest dimensions of being.

The transpersonal asserts that persons cannot grow or flourish in human isolation. A truly fulfilling life can transpire only in the context of the entire creation. All that we are, all that we desire to be, is bequeathed to us from the cosmic creation through the interdependent interaction of all that constitutes the web of life. When African peoples, therefore, consider their ancestors to be inhabiting mountains, lakes, trees, or animals, it is crass to dismiss this perception as primitive animism. Something far more profound is being articulated, an insight best discerned through the notion of ancestral grace.

Typically the Holy Spirit has been imaged as a bird-like nebulous organism, who tends to get lost between the two patriarchal poles of archetypal father and king-like Son. The very sense of God that our ancient ancestors had known intimately and tangibly for several thousand years has been usurped and undermined. Later it was demonized as "primitive animism."

Today we experience a theological retrieval of the central role of the Holy Spirit in which animistic concepts can once more be honored. Theologians such as Marc Wallace (2005) seek to redeem the rich cosmic and spiritual meaning of metaphors like vivifying breath, healing wind, living water, purifying fire. As we deepen our sense of the sacred at work in creation these become liberating phrases that help us to understand and comprehend the magnificence of God creatively animating, sustaining, and empowering life at every level.

The Divine as Creator

In this sense the Holy Spirit becomes the oldest expression of the divine at work in creation. Foundational to all other articulations of ancestral grace is God's gracious presence as empowering Spirit. In terms of ancient human discernment, the primordial presence of the divine in our midst is not the patriarchal male (pro)creator, favored by all the great religions; the primal perception of the divine is that of a primordial, transpersonal holy energy that theologically has been named "Holy Spirit of God."

Where then does that leave the concept of an original creator? History and anthropology indicate that humans have always been fascinated by origins, and many of the great myths are about the divine foundations of creation. Those stories that belong to the post-agricultural era — associated with the classical Babylonian, Egyptian, Hebrew, Greek, and Latin cultures — tend to favor the priority of an *inseminating and sustaining male*, whereas the more ancient wisdom of Upper and Middle Paleolithic times favors the notion of *a great birthing mother*. In the long story of humankind's spiritual awakening, the prized place of a male creator seems to have been quite a recent development. That which dominates all the major religions of our time finds little support in the wisdom of ancestral grace.

In previous chapters I have alluded briefly to the culture of the Great Mother Goddess, a spiritual tradition that seems to have flourished across the humanly populated world of Paleolithic times, covering a timespan of some thirty thousand years. Perhaps this is the deep connection being reclaimed by the twelfth-century mystic

Meister Eckhart when he makes the bold claim that *birthing* should be considered to be the most generic activity of the divine in our midst. The ancient galaxies, the great planets (and many still awaiting to be discovered), the Milky Way, our home planet, and all living organisms from bacteria to humans, are the progeny of this *birthing* God(dess). Might not this be a pregnant metaphor long known to our ancient ancestors and now seeking to reclaim its legitimate place in a revitalized spirituality for our time?

Prior to the God who *rules, governs, saves, and redeems* is the God who *gives birth,* co-creating in and through the cosmic process in the vast array of life forms we evidence today. More accurately the creative process is that of *birth-death-rebirth,* with death as an integral dimension and not a kind of deviation or curse, as suggested by many of the great religions.

The Feminine Face of God

Birthing, as we know, is distinctively a female experience. The woman who nurtures life in the womb, brings that life to fulfillment in the act of giving birth, creating a bond between mother and child that rational discourse can never hope to analyze comprehensively. Amid pain and ecstasy, birthing is poetry par excellence, a moment of utter revelation in which the divine and the human cooperate in a supreme act of co-creation.

Idyllic and idealistic though these words may be, they probably captivate an aspect of ancestral grace long suppressed and now revisiting humanity with a timely vengeance. Did our ancient ancestors of Paleolithic times envisage the divine as a motherly figure? Currently we don't have the evidence to answer affirmatively. But we have inherited from that ancient epoch a tantalizing fascination with female fertility. It seems to have informed spiritual awakening over many thousand years, maturing in the rituals and accompanying artifacts discovered in the Ice Age caves of Paleolithic times.

If we want to honor what ancestral grace has bequeathed to us, we need to reappropriate the incarnational, embodied presence of God that seemed so real and engaging for our ancient ancestors. The epoch of the Great Goddess may well have marked a significant maturation of what was previously more inchoate and amorphous. Contrary to the frequent condemnations of self-righteous religionists in our time, ancestral grace flourishes in ways that defy and challenge many of our most cherished orthodoxies. And occasionally these same orthodoxies camouflage the deeper cultural and spiritual significance of prevailing icons and images that surface in the culture of formal religion. Relevant here is the role of Mary in Christian faith.

Of the numerous incarnations of the divine that adorn religions ancient and modern, significant female figures allure and bewilder us. All tend to be enigmatic, passionately real, and intimate, yet awesome, strange and paradoxical. For instance, in Christianity, one of the most enduring and culturally diffuse characterizations of Mary is that of the Black Madonna. Here we find represented the historical Mary of dark Palestinian skin color (see Johnson 2003). Yet most of the popular images of Mary depict a woman of European origin, often adorned with the trappings of Western royal accolade. This is the Mary of Western colonialism, marking a seriously disturbing betrayal of the true historical and scriptural Mary.

But the Black Madonna is not merely a corrective of Western idolatry. It signifies a great deal more, rooting Mary in the graced tradition of prehistoric times. We detect echoes of this historical grounding in the Inca culture of South America, which regards Mary as a divine embodiment of the fertility and creativity of God that in cosmic and planetary terms they encapsulate in the notion of the Pacha Mama. Parallels have been noted in many ancient cultures and in many extant indigenous groups. And pregnant links can be made with the other great religions, e.g., Kali in Hinduism, Tara in Buddhism.

The birthing power of the divine, exemplified in enduring archetypal *female* figures, has been consistently subverted by patriarchal religion. That which was so central to our spiritual evolution over many thousand years has been consciously suppressed throughout the postagricultural era. But archetypal energy will not lie dormant for long, and in our time the Great Mother archetype is becoming explosive once more.[16] Within the next few decades I suspect it will invade mainline theology and religion with some devastating but exciting consequences. It will be one more moment of pregnant birthing forth!

Jesus as a Model of Inspired Birthing

In creation's great story God incarnates. God empowers through embodied expression — first through the awakening of the Holy Spirit, and then through the birthing forth of the primordial Creator. That dimension of Holy Mystery which incarnates in and through the human we Christians identify in the mission and person of Jesus. In and through the human, Jesus brings to new expression and realization the impregnation of Holy Spirit and the birthing forth of the primordial Creator.

The Western addiction to exclusive male personifications of the divine in creation is beginning to unravel. It is no longer capable of honoring a truth that is deep and ancient. If the truth is ever to be retrieved, we need to embrace alternative ways of envisaging and conceptualizing the embodiment of the divine in creation. There is much to suggest that female-embodied modes of incarnation informed our ancestral history over several thousand years. The divine imbuing all things was perceived as a pregnant, birthing life force, inviting and challenging humans to become co-birthers in creation's great enterprise.

And Jesus, as faithful disciple of ancestral grace and as archetype of what is deeply human, brings together these strands for Christian life. Many contemporary scripture scholars consider Jesus to be a being in which Spirit-power radiated in a distinctively unique way. Even Jesus is accountable to the awakenings and urges of the Great Spirit (see Haight 1999, 163–68). And led by the Spirit, the earthly Jesus reconnects us to our deep ancient past, inspires us to be co-creators in the present (the mission of God's New Reign), and paves the way for our next evolutionary breakthrough.

And specifically in his earthly life, as well as in his archetypal significance, Jesus engages with the great co-birthing of God in creation. In the context of Christianity it is particularly about the co-birthing of the human (incarnation), a process happening simultaneously in the other great religions (see chapter 21 below). That incarnational dimension is not reserved to Jesus' thirty plus years living on this earth. It belongs to the entire 7 million years of human emergence, and to the thousands of years in which humans will unfold into the future, the topic that will engage us in the next chapter.

The co-birthing becomes most visible in Jesus' commitment to what the Gospels proclaim as "the Kingdom of God," often described by modern scholars as "the New Reign of God," that novel dispensation of global scope seeking to foster and maintain right relationships based on love, justice, compassion, and liberation. The vision of the New Reign of God will be outlined in chapter 17 below. I wish to conclude briefly the present chapter by reviewing one major strategy used by Jesus to break open the meaning of the Kingdom of God on earth. I am referring to Jesus the storyteller and the stories of dangerous memory we commonly call the parables.

Wisdom Has Set Her Table

Jesus proclaimed a wisdom that baffled and confused the people of his day. Contrary to expectation, he did not become the rabbi many had hoped he would be, nor did he turn out to be the reformer of Judaism some scholars still claim he was. When the disciples sought clarification regarding his vision of the Kingdom of God, and probably hoped for a clear-cut definition, they were given a response that must have deeply frustrated their desire for linear clarification: "The Kingdom of God may be compared to. . . . " And we are plunged into a parabolic narrative that often tore to shreds the conventional worldview of mainline Judaism.

Why did Jesus tell stories? Jesus seemed very much at home in the world of narrative and aphorism (proverb). Culturally it made sense in terms of his indigenous audience, believed to be agrarian folk, much more at home in the domestic reality of daily life rather than in formal wisdom or learning. A great deal of their culture was imbued in story and folklore.

If, however, Jesus also belongs to the archetypal realm, then we have to look deeper than just the immediate historical context. In fact the search for right context becomes a critical issue as it is for many Scripture scholars in our time. It seems to me that scholars like Elisabeth Schüssler Fiorenza, Elizabeth Johnson, and Denis Edwards have contributed significantly to this search for fuller and richer context. All three open up possible influences from, and connections with, the Wisdom literature of the Hebrew Scriptures, indicating this was probably a major (possibly primary) source inspiring and empowering Jesus as a prophetic storyteller.

Conventionally, we have sought to understand Jesus against the background of the great kings and prophets of the Old Testament. Here we detect something of a self-fulfilling prophesy: male scholars use male models congruent with a predominantly patriarchal culture. Of course, the same can happen with females, veering in another direction, and the scholars I cite above are well aware of this danger when they raise the possibility that Jesus modeled his life and ministry more consciously and explicitly on Wisdom literature. From that source he may well have borrowed those elements of storytelling, proverbial sayings, and the emphasis on the open common table as a focus for wisdom's inclusive and liberating empowerment.

The congruence is certainly noteworthy, but of greater consequence is the central personality in Wisdom literature: an alluring, charming woman who "was there when he created the world" (Prov. 8:30). This is Lady Wisdom, identified by some researchers as a personification of the Great Earth Mother. Now we detect a fascinating line of exploration opening up provocative possibilities for discernment and deeper truth. The pregnant Spirit, co-birthing with the Great Mother Creator, archetypally reawakening in the Wisdom Woman, co-birthing the new humanity in and through Jesus, and continuing to be manifest in various incarnational figures throughout time.

Jesus told stories that birthed forth the justice and love of God's New Reign. These are expansively disturbing stories stretching every local context toward the great story of creation itself, the primary site of God's in-breaking revelation, the homestead where humanity is called to grow into the fullness of life made possible in the power of ancestral grace.

Chapter 15

Jesus as an
Archetypal Human

Seize your moment — enflesh the Christ you profess to believe in.
— ROSEMARY RADFORD RUETHER

IN CHAPTER 13 I suggested that it is the humanity of Jesus, and not his divinity, that calls us to a deeper and more engaging discernment. Our preoccupation with the divinity of Jesus over the two thousand years of Christendom often seems to be fueled by an arrogant and patriarchal desire to declare every other faith system and all other believers to be heretics devoid of loyalty and faithful submission to God. In this self-defensive process, we have underestimated that which would really empower us all — including those we sought to overpower — namely, the radically liberating and empowering face of God incarnate. That is the *archetypal* humanity I now wish to describe at greater length.

Jungian psychology is our primary source for understanding the function and power of *archetypes*. For Jung, archetypes are active living dispositions, ideas in the Platonic sense, that perform and continually influence our thoughts, feelings, and actions, something akin to living organisms endowed with generative force. Theologian Paul Knitter offers the following useful resume:

Archetypes are predispositions towards the formation of images, a priori powers of representation, in-built stirrings or lures that, if we can feel and follow them, will lead us into the depths of what we are and where we are going. They might be called messages-in-code, which we must decode and bring to our conscious awareness. It is difficult to speak about what

107

these messages contain. Their general contents, Jung tells us,
have to do with light and darkness, death and rebirth, wholeness, sacrifice and redemption. He saw such archetypes as the
common seedbed of all religions. (Knitter 1995, 57)

We must not confuse archetypal living with the traditional notion of Christian perfection, vested primarily in an all-knowing,
all-powerful God. Realizing more fully the power of an archetype
does not make us more perfect, but it does lead in the direction
of greater wholeness. When we become more whole, a deeper integration begins to take place. This may lead to greater bliss and
happiness; it may also mean embracing more pain, anguish, struggle,
and at times the absolute depths of darkness and abandonment.
The mystics are the primary examples of this paradoxical combination of light and darkness, as described vividly by Dorothee Soelle
(2001).

Here we encounter what often disturbs and even bewilders conventional Christians. We assume that a holy, perfect, and divine Jesus
must always get it right, whereas an archetypal Jesus will at times
get it drastically wrong. From time to time, all humans get it wrong,
they make mistakes, even one entrusted with the archetype of the
deep human. Not surprisingly, therefore, we find contradictions in
the Christian Gospels: the Jesus of radical inclusiveness who informs
the disciples that they must exclude all except for those belonging to
the house of Israel (Matt. 10:5); the Jesus who expected the world to
end in his lifetime and was obviously mistaken in that belief (Matt.
10:23); the Jesus who at times is very inclusive of women but seems
to collude in the oppression and exclusion of the Syrophoenecian
woman (Mark 7:24ff.). To live authentically at an archetypal level is
not about getting it right, but rather about befriending our paradoxical humanity in a more grace-filled way. Even Jesus had to endure
that struggle, perhaps epitomized in the anguished, despairing cry
from the cross: "My God, my God, why have you forsaken me?"
(Matt. 27:47). (On this topic see Sullivan 2002.)

Reclaiming the Human Face of God

Christians are intrigued by the divinity of Jesus. It puzzles many, inspires others, baffles some, and for millions around the world it is the "power" through which they believe Jesus influences their lives. Safeguarding and promoting the divinity of Jesus holds high priority throughout the history of Christendom. While also seeking to honor the humanity of Jesus, clearly this aspect has never enjoyed the attention or affirmation with which we regard the divinity.

Several influences are at work here, foremost being a patriarchal preoccupation with power and privilege. Even the synoptic Gospels reveal the dilemma of Jesus trying to save himself from the patriarchal projections of the dominant culture. The followers persist in trying to make him a king, something Jesus rejects time and again. The history of Christendom repeats this error many times over.

At the root of the problem are the expectations of the Jewish people: if Jesus is a messianic representative of God, then he must emulate the king, understood to be the primary embodiment of the divine in the culture of the time. Kingship and divinity were deemed synonymous. The immanence of God in creation — in this case in the person of Jesus — stands little chance of recognition or acceptance, because the cultural expectation is that of a royal, divine figurehead, ruling from the heavens. The Immanuel of the Gospels belongs primarily to the heavenly realm; the incarnational, embodied presence is consistently obfuscated.

Walter Wink (2002) is one of many contemporary scripture scholars seeking to reclaim and rehabilitate Jesus as a primordial human being, revealing to us the way to become more God-like specifically in becoming more human. Being human is the heart and soul of the Christ consciousness, and only by embracing this in depth can we glimpse and grasp something of the divine significance of Jesus. Many years ago the Canadian theologian Gregory Baum stated it with poetic vividness: God is what happens to a person on the way to becoming human.

Being human is the gateway to access divine meaning. Indeed, ancestral grace thrives on the great story of humans being receptive and responsive to divine initiative over several million years. The humanity of Jesus is the key that unlocks the secrets of divinity, not the opposite, as we have believed for much of the Christian era. The mystery of God becomes transparent in the mystery of the human. In Wink's language, the human is an archetypal statement of divine empowerment. For Christians, Jesus serves as the primordial example of that radiant giftedness; for Christians, Jesus is the first disciple of ancestral grace.

Christian humanism is the human story embraced in all its paradox and transformed in its graced potential. The Jesus who cries out in utter despair, "My God, my God, why have you forsaken me?" (Mark 15:34), is the divine one engaged in the vagaries and vulnerabilities of the human condition. Even our absolute depths of despair belong to the human-divine Jesus.

And Jesus does not get rid of our despair as many Christians expect the divine Jesus to do. Rather in the transformed humanity, modeled by Jesus, we can embrace our despair and not be overwhelmed or destroyed by it. This breakthrough we often accomplish by putting our vulnerability at the service of others in helping them cope with weakness, pain, and suffering. In our woundedness we become more wholesome. In weakness is the paradoxical gift of fresh strength (see 2 Cor. 12:10).

The archetypal human is not programmed for perfection, but is graced for wholeness. And this wholeness must always honor the great paradox of creation itself: creation and destruction work hand in hand for the flourishing and enrichment of creation (see chapter 20 below). True redemption is not in "destroying death for ever" (1 Cor. 15:26; 2 Tim. 1:10; Rev. 21:4), but rather empowering us to embrace in a more enlightened (grace-filled) way the enduring paradox that characterizes everything in creation: the unceasing cycle of birth-death-rebirth.

Soulful Living

Archetypes may be understood as patterns of energy that knit together and sustain the cosmic fabric of creation (see Tarnas 2006,

37–61). Within that tapestry the human has a distinctive role, not one of control and domination, however, but perhaps something more akin to *soulful consciousness.*

Ours seems to be a unique way of understanding and comprehending, as creatures endowed with the capacity for self-reflexive consciousness (we can think about the fact that we can think). Under the influence of patriarchy we have often translated this as a superior wisdom entitling us to dominate and control everything else in creation. But that is not how we lived or behaved for most of the 7-million-year timespan, nor is our compulsion for control likely to be of much use to us if we want to live more meaningfully for the future.

Soulful wisdom, or consciousness, focuses on the ordinary rather than the extraordinary. We are well on the way to being people of soul when we opt for engagement rather than achievement, when we favor relationship rather than heroic separation, and when we are more at home with befriending rather than controlling. Soulful wisdom seeks to respect and cherish the earthiness of our being and our belonging to cosmic creation. Soulful living treasures the immanence of the holy (whole) rather than the glory and power of divine transcendence.

For Christians, Jesus grounds the soulful wisdom, liberating people from the crippling guilt of a religiosity in which they were always losers, inviting people beyond the allurements of man-made power and domination. To this end, Jesus confronts and denounces various systemic forces that prevailed in his time: social, political, economic, and religious. Declaring and embodying a New Reign of God, Jesus toppled conceptual hierarchies, declaring a new egalitarianism of equality, inclusiveness, liberation, and justice. It was so shockingly human and so humanly empowering that the powers-that-be panicked, and rather than attack the new dream they scapegoated the dreamer. They got rid of Jesus, but the dream continued.

Reclaiming the Dream

In fact, the dream has survived rather than flourished. Christians have not fared well in honoring the archetypal dream of Jesus. For one thing, we have over-spiritualized it, thus relegating it primarily to "holy" people with ambitions for salvific power and glory that have little to do with the prophetic, archetypal Christ figure. We have rationalized the rhetoric in Greek metaphysics and turned the living Christ into a respectable religious guru. The archetypal human, the embodiment of soulful consciousness, has been consistently undermined, domesticated, and dishonored.

Truth, however, has its own way of retrieving what has been subverted and, today, Jesus scholarship is facing deeper truth with increasing transparency and integrity. As more lay people enter the dialogue of theology and scripture, the ecclesiastical grip is being loosened and soulful wisdom percolates more freely. Jesus, as the human face of God in our midst, exerts deeper appeal and inspiration today. Not only are we challenged with the task of freshly discerning Gospel foundations, but we also experience pressing pastoral questions of how we witness to this Jesus in the church and world of our time.

It is the radiant face of the human Jesus that reconnects us with the liberating power of ancestral grace. Jesus is not just another individual person (divine or human) who appears just once on the landscape of human history. He signifies a great deal more than that. Jesus is the incarnational affirmation of the divine flourishing in the human species, not just in the Middle Eastern context of two thousand years ago, but in the planetary context over a timespan of some 7 million years. To that larger evolutionary context, we now turn our attention.

Chapter 16

Jesus in Evolutionary Context

We are all part of a great parade about which we know little, it seems. The essential Gospel has not been proclaimed very well. We prefer to doubt both Jesus' incarnation and our own. It is, frankly, just too much. — RICHARD ROHR

R ELIGIOUS BELIEVERS of all times and cultures have claimed that God has been fully at work in creation at every stage of its unfolding. It logically follows that God was fully involved in affirming our human evolution throughout the 7 million years of our species' existence. Moreover, in the transition from our primate condition to our present-day human status we must logically assume that the birthing, creative God affirmed and rejoiced in every breakthrough during that long, complex emergence of our evolving story.

Assuming all this — *which advocates of all religions do* — we face an urgent task of redefining the notion of "incarnation" as applied to humans. Christians claim that the incarnation of God in the human happens for the first time in and through Jesus of Nazareth. While other religions do not use the concept of incarnation (as we shall see in chapter 21), the actual reality is integral to their respective visions as well.

The Two-Thousand-Year Benchmark

Christians attribute an enormous significance to the date that initiates the Christian era, just over two thousand years ago. It is widely assumed — by Christians and others — that nothing of much significance happened before that time, while massive cultural progress has transpired since then. In the reflections that follow, I briefly outline

113

the stultifying ideology that has amassed around this time-frame. The consequences for religious belief are particularly disturbing.

Positively, I want to reclaim the notion of incarnation for that primordial time of 7 million years ago when God was fully engaged with our emergence as a newly evolving species. *This is where the incarnation of God in humanity begins.* The co-creative God of this pregnant moment was not looking down the time line and musing: "I'll create these human creatures now, but will then wait until Jesus of Nazareth is born — about 7 million years hence, and only then will I declare them capable of being saved." No! For the birthing God, what happened in ancient time was essentially and fundamentally good and had the full blessing and endorsement of ancestral grace.

For conventional Christians this raises a question: What then is the significance of Jesus and the events related to him two thousand years ago? In evolutionary terms, Jesus marks the *culmination and fulfillment* of a process, not its beginning or launching. In the life and ministry of Jesus we evidence an affirmation and celebration of everything humans had achieved throughout the 7-million-year story. In Jesus ancestral grace reaches a new threshold of elegance, growth, and fulfillment.

Rightly, therefore, some scholars suggest that we regard the two-thousand-year benchmark as an axial age, a maturation of all that has been growing, developing, and flourishing through the human species, now reaching a new critical threshold, while also inaugurating a new evolutionary phase, a novel breakthrough for humanity — one I will describe presently.

The human tendency to isolate the two-thousand-year landmark and literalize the life and ministry of Jesus within that time-frame is a disturbing example of patriarchal minimalism. To commandeer power and control it to our own advantage, we humans tend to reduce everything to a context that we can manage and make sense of in accordance with our rational capacities. We suffer from a terrible deprivation of intuition and imagination. Our chosen depiction of the divine life force, as Creator, Savior, and Holy Spirit, all end up congealed within time capsules that make sense to us humans, but clearly are not congruent with the creative expansiveness of ancestral grace.

Jesus in the Big Picture

We have been so conditioned and indoctrinated in the conventional paradigm of the small Jesus, it is not easy to adjust to the call of ancestral grace, which requires us to perceive and imagine in more expansive terms. This is where the material explored in part 1 is so crucial. It begins to illuminate the mystery within which we are held and portrays a divine co-creating in and with the human, which otherwise would elude our attention.

Several important consequences ensue. These I will briefly enumerate here and develop their significance in subsequent chapters:

+ Theologians need to embrace these new horizons and *redefine incarnation* accordingly. The Immanuel of the Gospels is fully embodied in our ancestral inheritance of 7 million years ago, initiating a process of growth toward that fullness of life exemplified in the life and ministry of Jesus — and also in the incarnational figures of the other great religions.

+ Humans, like all other aspects of divine birthing in creation, are characterized by the paradox of creation-and-destruction, subject to the dynamic cycle of birth-death-rebirth. This untidy process guarantees freedom and creativity; otherwise, everything would be predetermined and humans would be merely robots in the hands of a divine manipulator.

+ This untidy feature of human history has been poorly served by popular Christian notions like the doctrine of Original Sin and the depiction of humans as creatures who are fundamentally flawed. In the whole of God's creation there is a fundamental *paradox*, but not a fundamental *flaw*. Yes, humans are imperfect and incomplete, and always will be. It seems to me that the divine birther has no problem with our imperfect nature. *It is we ourselves who have invented this problem,* one that seriously hinders us from seeing the deeper spiritual meaning of our long evolutionary story.

+ If there is no fundamental flaw, then there is nothing from which we humans need to be rescued or redeemed. We don't need a

Savior or Redeemer, at least not in the terms espoused by atonement theories. Jesus did not come as some great divine rescuer. Rather, he came to bring to *fulfillment* that which we have achieved throughout our 7-million-year mission on earth.

♦ For most of our time on earth, we behaved as an innovative, creative species (see part 1 above). For most of that time, we got it right! As a creatively wise species we will always get it right rather than wrong, provided we remain close to the earth in which we are grounded and attuned to the cosmos to which we belong.

Over the past eight thousand years of patriarchal domination, we have not fared well. This has been one of our dark ages, and the massacre of 62 million civilians in the wars of the twentieth century amply verifies this. But eight thousand years is less than 1 percent of our entire story, and in all probability it is not the only time in which things went badly for humanity. Our God will forgive us for these cultural misadventures. The more urgent question is: *Will we forgive ourselves,* outgrow this dysfunctional way of behaving, and opt to become a cosmic-planetary species once more?

♦ The God who sees and embraces the big picture can cope with humanity's occasional lapses. Humanity itself, deluded by the myopic arrogance and short-sightedness of patriarchal governance, tends to get stuck every now and again. At the present time we also tend to project onto our ancient ancestors the deviant behaviors that characterize our time. This is another example of infantile rationality: "If we are as bad as this, our ancestors must have been much worse." Not much semblance of ancestral grace in that perception, and one assumes not much knowledge of our great story either.

♦ So for us Christians, Jesus is not about rescuing us, but about affirming and celebrating our graced achievements. What the Gospels call the "Kingdom of God" is first and foremost an affirmation of God's reign throughout all creation, forging the right relationships that make love and justice more transparent for all.

♦ Laterally, it is a call and challenge to our patriarchal culture to outgrow the power-games that undermine and damage our integrity.

This new celebratory challenge proved too much for the authorities in the time of Jesus; to get rid of the threat, they executed the prophet. And Christians went on to assert that his death was an act of divine rescue, when in fact the real rescue is in his life and not in his death.

• Jesus, as an icon of incarnational fulfillment, marks and celebrates a high point in our Christian evolutionary development. Teilhard de Chardin described it as our biological evolution reaching a new critical threshold, after which our story becomes one of psychic evolution rather than physical growth and development (see also pp. 218f.). Could it be that this is what the writer of John's Gospel was alluding to when Jesus speaks of his imminent departure (see John 16:5ff.) so that the Spirit-filled creature becomes the central focus, as humanity is invited to embrace its next evolutionary breakthrough — with the evolution of mind and spirit as central features.

• Following the same logic, could it be that the Resurrected Jesus serves as an exemplar of what all humans are destined to be in this new evolutionary cycle? Perhaps the powers of the Risen Jesus are not some extraordinary divine qualities that prove Jesus' divinity, but rather human characteristics we will all exhibit one day. In this case, I suggest we view the Resurrection as the jewel in the crown of a life radically lived rather than linking it explicitly with the Calvary death, as Christian theology has been doing — ever since the time of St. Paul.

Savoring the Enlarged Context

By situating the Christian story in this enlarged evolutionary context, not only are we rescuing ancestral grace from its narrow and stultifying confines; we are actually reclaiming a deeper, more engaging meaning for Jesus also. Christian culture has suffocated Jesus to a frightening degree. It began already in the apostolic era when the first followers tried to exalt Jesus as an earthly, powerful king.

It quickly became indoctrinated in Greek metaphysics with the rational desire for clarity and power. It became politically enculturated in the fourth century when Constantine adopted Christianity as the official religion of the Roman Empire. Amazingly, Christianity survived all those deviant enculturations, which, paradoxically, proves that it does embody archetypal truths and potentials that cannot be subverted by human manipulation.

One of the more prevailing suffocations of Jesus is that of clericalism, namely, that Jesus becomes embodied primarily — exclusively for much of Christendom — in male priesthood. Not until the late 1800s did we begin to break that controlling monopoly and, of course, it still prevails in denominations like the Catholic Church.[17] Priesthood itself is rapidly sinking into irrelevance and decadence, dying a rather painful death in various parts of the Christian world, and with its demise one of the most entrenched suffocations will be loosened. Jesus will be liberated to be the Christ of all people — irrespective of rank or status. Liberated as well, we hope, will be the archetypal human who embraces all people in love and equality throughout the long reign of ancestral grace.

Finally, this evolutionary portrayal of Jesus not only enlarges the human horizon of God's deep involvement with earthly creatures, but also invites us to reclaim in a more conscious way the context in which such human flourishing takes place. We belong beautifully to the clay from which we are formed. The Gospels rarely allude to this, but, it seems to me, we must henceforth work with the assumption that Jesus loved the creation which was, and is, so central to our human well-being. For Jesus, it was not just salvation in a life beyond; it was also growth in the fullness of life and grace in the here-and-now of an already graced creation. How we might begin to reintegrate that dimension into a revamped Christian story for our time is the topic of our next chapter.

Chapter 17

Humans at Home in God's Creation

Discipleship means that we live to give God glory by loving the world and everything in it. This is what God does in Christ; this is what we do as followers. — SALLIE MCFAGUE

FOR SOME DECADES NOW Christian spirituality has been recovering from the distortions and deviations of earlier times. A prevalent distortion was the notion that we should not take "the world" seriously, that as far as possible we should flee the world and look forward to an eternal reward outside and beyond this created realm.

Some attribute this anti-world spirituality to the dualistic thinking we inherited from classical Greek times. In the dualistic worldview everything is portrayed as opposing forces; hence the divisions, God vs. humankind, spirit vs. matter, soul vs. body, sacred vs. secular. Dualisms are inventions of our rational mind creating neat binary distinctions that in all probability have nothing to do with God. For the divine creator everything matters: spirit and matter, soul and body, sacred and secular.

Others attribute the negative spirituality to the rise of Jansenism in fifteenth-century Europe. Initiated mainly by a Flemish bishop, Cornelius Otto Jansen (1585–1638), to counter the perceived threat of liberal Jesuit teaching, the movement flourished in France throughout the eighteenth century despite it being outlawed by the Catholic Church in 1712. It endorsed the notion that humans are innately depraved, sinful, and destined for eternal damnation. Our only hope of becoming the beneficiaries of supernatural determinism, and thus attaining eternal life, is through rigorous devotion and daily penance.

119

Whatever the contributing causes, Christians of the twentieth century inherited a spiritual ambivalence toward the created order. Although many disagree with Lynn White (1967), who claims that this defective spiritual view has contributed directly and destructively to environmental degradation and ecological exploitation, few can deny that it has left Christians confused and ambivalent about the planet we inhabit and the cosmos to which we belong. In terms of the present work, it consistently prevents us from seeing the deeper and richer meaning of our own evolutionary unfolding.

Exile and Alienation

The spiritual literature of the past few centuries persistently portrays humans as sinful creatures, alienated and estranged from God, and therefore living in a state of spiritual exile. Here we encounter the dualism between the all-perfect God and the flawed human. While reconciliation is theoretically possible, it always remains something of an illusive realization.

Spiritual writers often base these reflections on the events recorded in the book of Exodus, which describes the expulsion of the Jewish people from the land of Israel and the pain of exile in the land of Egypt. I allude to the scriptural context in a previous work (O'Murchu 2000). Spiritual and scriptural commentators take great liberties in spiritualizing this notion of biblical exile. It becomes a metaphor to describe the gap between God and humanity, portraying our human inability and unwillingness to be reconciled with God because of the stubbornness of our wills and our attraction to sin and evil.

Other key words quickly enter the spiritual vocabulary, "alienation" and "estrangement" being to the fore. Frequently, the fundamental flaw, or Original Sin, is adopted as the primary culprit. The human is not meant to be at home in creation; indeed, creation itself is deemed to be flawed and sinful and can become a serious distraction from the things of God. Life, then, is perceived to be one long struggle to get things right with this insatiably demanding divine ruler. In the face of this challenge, some grow more fearful and guilt-ridden, although in our time increasing numbers of people have outgrown allegiance to this capricious, moralistic God.

A New Metaphor

The metaphor of exile and alienation is another tragic example of our misguided patriarchal religiosity, which tries to subdue and control people by inculcating fear and guilt. It worked for quite a long time, but now it is rapidly becoming a wearied rhetoric. As people become more adult and self-confident, they outgrow the kind of co-dependency generated by this spurious spirituality.

However, it has left a spiritual vacuum, filled by various contending placebos. Some of these are useful and worth cherishing (e.g., meditation, vegetarianism, holistic health strategies, rituals for empowering self and others, rediscovering the sacred in creation, commitment to justice-making), while others have been commodified to the benefit of spiritual charlatans (using spiritual resources to augment marketability and consumerism). Yet despite the valuable critique of scholars like Carrette and King (2005), few have actually succeeded in naming creative alternatives. Reappropriating old-time religion — the solution proffered by Carrette and King — is effectively yesterday's answer to today's problem. It simply does not work.

As I suggest in a previous work (O'Murchu 2000), we need a new metaphor to transcend the spiritual malaise of our time. I propose the metaphor of *homecoming,* and my central argument is that we need to come home, not to God, religion, or church, but to the creation to which we innately belong. Our exile, alienation, and estrangement are not from God, but from creation. With God everything is basically okay. Our spiritual *not-at-home-ness* has to do with our ambivalence and ambiguity toward God's creation.

The long journey involved in this homecoming has several dimensions. It involves coming home to where God first encounters us, not with the threat of judgment and punishment, but with the embrace of unconditional love. From God's point of view, that is expressed first and foremost in the cosmic and planetary creation. Long before

humans ever came to be, long before formal religion was ever conceived, God was birthing forth ancestral giftedness in the unfolding
of stars and galaxies, of planets and quasars, including the paradoxical cacophony of building up and tearing down (Jer. 1:10) as the web
of universal life unfolded.

Here is where we first encounter and come to know the embracing mystery of divine benevolence. Deprived of this awareness,
we inevitably short-circuit the meaning of God and inevitably we
misconstrue the meaning of God's creation.

At this juncture, alienation and estrangement began, and this is
what still perpetuates destruction and disintegration at every level. We
have not been exiled from God because of Original Sin, but because
of our ignorance of, and alienation from, our primordial home in
God's creation. And all the religion on earth will not redeem or save
us until we become reconciled with our cosmic-planetary God and
come home to where we truly belong as God's co-creative partners
in the cosmic-planetary enterprise.

Coming Home to Our Human Story

For many this sounds awesome and daunting, and it feels like such
a betrayal of conventional religion that many are at a loss on where
to begin. Thanks to many new insights from social and historical
sciences, we realize the appalling ignorance of our true evolutionary
story. We have ended up in an anthropocentric capsule that is all
but choking us to death. The story that ensues from what Dorothee
Soelle (2001) so often calls our spiritual and cultural imprisonment
is petrifying and unimaginably destructive.

This, and not the lack of religion, is the source of our deeply felt
alienation. It has nothing to do with God, who despite all our patriarchal silliness, still loves us unconditionally. God can do nothing to
salvage us from our alienation until we begin ourselves to undo the
suffocation that hems us in. We begin doing that when we choose to
reclaim our larger story of graced engagement — with life, with creation, and with God. Then our redemption can commence in a truly
salvific way.

The implications for Christian faith, and particularly for the notions of sin, salvation, and redemption, are formidable. Stephen Duffy articulates both the dilemma and its resolution in bold theological language when he writes: "Christology, not hamartiology, is the axis of soteriology. The significance of Christ does not derive from sin; it must be the other way round. Sin is situated against a graced horizon. It is less lost innocence than incompleteness" (Duffy 1993, 331).

The Kingdom Reenvisioned

Only when we first rectify our perception and understanding of human life do we stand any real chance of reclaiming our life in Jesus, as the Christ of our faith-allegiance. This is not about notional assent of faith nor is it simply about declaring Jesus as Lord. Indeed, any articulation of Christian faith centered around co-dependency on either earthly Christian authority or around some imperial construal of the historical Jesus will never satisfy our spiritual hunger. In a paraphrase of the Christian Gospel: "It is not those who say to me Lord, Lord, who will enter new life and embrace new possibilities!" (see Matt. 7:21). Christian faith is about a radically new way of relating and engaging — with the whole of cosmic, planetary, and human life. Nothing short of that, and nothing less than that! Essentially this is what the Gospels describe as "the Kingdom of God."

Jesus spoke frequently of a new "reign of God" taking shape under his instigation and serving as the inspiration for his words and deeds. Translated into English as the "Kingdom of God," and often described as "the New Reign of God" in current scholarship, the term refers to a very complex and profound phenomenon. In the original Greek text of the Gospels, the term is rendered as *basileia,* which is a feminine word, which in Jesus' original Aramaic language translates as *malkuta* (a feminine word), the written Hebrew version of which is *mamlaka* (also feminine). What initially seems to have been a term of strong feminine significance has obviously lost much of its pristine meaning in the process of translation. Has some of the richness of ancestral grace been once more undermined and corrupted?

There is a growing consensus among contemporary scripture scholars that the term "Kingdom of God," as used in the Gospels, has
nothing to do with earthly kingship and should more accurately be
described as "the companionship of empowerment," as suggested by
John Dominic Crossan (see also Borg 1998). In fact, it is the antithe-
sis of royal power as understood then and now (see Horsley 2003;
Crossan 2007). Jesus seems to have invoked royal language and imagery as a subversive strategy for the breakthrough he was seeking
to activate (see Herzog 1994; 2004). Appropriating the kingly context of his life and times, he kept turning it on its head, declaring
it moribund, while, in fidelity to ancestral grace, he inaugurated a
new "reign" in which empowerment rather than power would be the
central feature.

Most of the early Christians, particularly the twelve apostles, failed
to grasp the message. It was too original, provocative, and prophetic
for their conditioned minds. They had been heavily indoctrinated by
the reductionistic culture of patriarchy. The horizon of their desiring was hidebound by the cult of earthly kingship, and they could
not envisage transformation except within that earthly context: the
messianic liberator would have to be king-like! And what a massive
disappointment he proved to be when he did not fulfill their limited
expectations.

Two thousand years later, it would appear that little has changed.
Exalted christologies still flourish, and the transformed vision of a
new heaven and a new earth inaugurated by Jesus has yet to be
realized. The human species, still struggling to find its way through
the patriarchal maze, has not really taken Jesus seriously. Had we
done so, we would have reappropriated ancestral grace in ways
that would enrich our experience and liberate prophetic possibilities.
Walter Wink articulates the challenge in these words:

> As bearer of the archetype of the Human Being, Jesus activates
> the numinous power that is capable of healing, transforming, or
> rebirthing those who surrender themselves to it. As such, Jesus
> knew himself to be in the grip of a power greater than he. A

problem arises at just this point, however. When Jesus is worshiped as the sole bearer of the archetype of humanness, He is made a supernatural being. As such he loses his connection to the struggle to be human, and becomes a cult figure in a religion focused on his person (individual) rather than on the reality he bore. (Wink 2002, 256)

Healing and Empowerment

Commensality (the open, common table) and healing are two central features of the new vision of Jesus. In all probability, they also feature strongly in prehistoric times and may well have been the "rituals" through which our ancient ancestors experienced God's abundant grace in their lives.

The liberation Jesus proclaimed and activated was first and foremost a freedom from political oppression and stultifying religiosity, from the material and economic binds of those who usurped indigenous resources to their own benefit (mainly the Romans), and of those who perpetuated a cult of purity accompanied by legal details almost impossible to fulfill (mainly the Jews). Neither had much in common with the great tradition of blessing and grace we humans have known over the long aeons of our earthly existence.

Two thousand years later, the clarion Gospel call — "set my people free" — still echoes around the Christian world with a frightening shallowness. Where freedom has been implemented in the name of Christian faith it always has strings attached, many of which have been imperialistic and colonial. Within the body of the Christian churches themselves, women still battle for equality and justice. Christianity still clings to a past embedded in Roman power and Greek rationalism. For much of the reign of Christendom, the countercultural empowerment of the Kingdom has not been taken seriously, and in many situations it has been disturbingly subverted.

Creation and the Kingdom

Few Christian scholars have considered the worldview out of which
Jesus operated. Indeed, most assume that he accepted and endorsed
the three-tier hierarchical ordering of the universe consisting of upper
world (heavenly realm), this world, basically planet earth, and the
underworld (Hades). Assuredly, this was the prevailing worldview
of the time, but I wish to suggest that in proclaiming and embodying the New Reign of God, Jesus consciously sought to transcend
and transform that hierarchically governed set of perceptions (see
Crossan 2007).

The vision of the Kingdom is postulated on a worldview of
radical inclusiveness and egalitarianism. Nothing is excluded, particularly the surrounding creation from which we inherit the primary
paradigm of right relating. All the parable stories break open the
conventional paradigms based on differences and distinctions. We're
challenged to reclaim what we share in common (particularly the one
earth), rather than clinging on to what separates and divides us. And
it is not by accident that many of the parables relate to *the land,* its
usufruct, and the way landowners treat those who worked on the
land. Here as in the Covenant of the Hebrew Scriptures, the land
is a representative icon of the ever nourishing and sustaining God,
with echoes of the key role also attributed to the Great Earth Mother
Goddess (see pp. 81–83, 102–6 above).

By making the New Reign of God the heart and core of his mission,
Jesus was not merely activating a renewal program for the Jewish religion, nor was he consciously trying to invent a new religion (in all
probability). No, his dream, as John's Gospel illustrates with some
unfortunate patriarchal language, was to call humans to a radical realignment with the God at the heart of creation as a cosmic-planetary
organism. It was an awakening call, ever old and ever to embrace
afresh, in radical love, justice, and liberation. Beyond all human, social, and political ideologies, Jesus brought a dream of a new heaven
and new earth. As a Christian people, we still have not caught up
with that visionary cosmic Jesus.

Whether Christians begin with creation or with the vision of the New Reign of God matters little. Both lead to the same prodigious creativity and proclivity of the gifting God whose ancestral grace flourishes first and foremost in the creation we inhabit. More disturbing for conventional religionists of all persuasions is the Jesus who also sought to outgrow the long-established hegemony of patriarchal ordering. That was an even more daring enterprise, to which we now turn our attention.

Chapter 18

Jesus beyond Patriarchy

*Much of the confusion and cruelty that arises in the name of
religion is a result of the idolatry of the messenger instead of the
embrace of the message.* — V. V. RAMAN

WHEN CONSTANTINE, Roman emperor from 307 to 337, declared
Jesus to be the Pantocrator (ruler of the universe) in the Edict
of Milan in 313 CE, he was affirming a conviction we can trace back
to the earliest literary sources of Christianity. From a very early time,
Christian faith had been domesticated into an imperial dispensation
(see Crossan 2007). Jesus was depicted as the true representative of
the sky-God, ruling from on high in accordance with the views and
wishes of every earthly despot.

Gradually, we are beginning to discover that this marks a serious
departure from the Jesus of the Gospels, from the primordial story
incarnated archetypally in the historical Jesus, and from the radical
egalitarian vision of the New Reign of God. Perhaps more disturbing than anything else is the pruning that needs to happen within
the Scriptures themselves if we are to expose the false projections
and allow a more real Jesus to come forth. I refer to the Jesus who
never identified with patriarchal governance and tried to demolish its
hegemony in some highly subversive ways.

Dislocating Stories

The subversion of power is a central feature of numerous parable
stories. It is often the aspect that has been domesticated and even
anesthetized. We have made safe these disturbing, challenging stories
and have excessively spiritualized their meaning and message. During

128

much of the era of Christendom, we have kept the dangerous memory of Jesus well out of human reach.

I offer a brief commentary on one parable to illustrate my central concern. The story of the talents (Matt. 25:14–30) is often used to demonstrate how God rewards those with initiative and condemns the lazy, those who do not use the "talents" God gives them. Here we encounter an interpretation that not only dishonors the original context of the story but also conforms the prophetic dimension to the conventional requirements of capitalistic culture. A few contextual facts need to be highlighted:

- In the time of Jesus, a talent was a form of silver coinage, weighing between sixty and seventy pounds. One talent was equal to six thousand denarii, with one denarius being the average subsistence wage for a day's labor. In these terms, one talent was the equivalent of fifteen years' wages. The talent was a financial concept rather than a measure of currency. Five talents would amount to seventy-five years' wages, and two talents to more than thirty years' earnings. We are dealing with extraordinary sums of money to highlight an exaggerated hyperbole.

- Some commentators (e.g., Malina 1996; Rohrbaugh 1996) claim that the Jewish culture of Jesus espoused values more akin to socialism rather than to capitalism. It was considered alienating and destructive for one person or group to make massive profit to the exclusion of everybody else. To protect the social fabric of life it was considered irresponsible for people to accrue profits exceeding 12 percent of one's total wealth. And every seven years all debts were wiped out, thus lifting up those in danger of being excluded, in an attempt to bring everybody to a shared status of radical equality. While our contemporaries may admire the ingenuity and sense of initiative of the one with the five talents and the one with the two talents for doubling their money, it would have been considered grossly irresponsible to those hearing the story in its original context.

- When reading the parables we must always be alert to subversive, prophetic nuances. Literalism can be dangerously misleading. For example, the first two slaves are commended as good and trust-worthy. Furthermore, they are invited into the "joy of the master," with the promise of promotion: "I will put you in charge of many things." The cruel irony is that they are still slaves, and worse still they now collude in treating others in the condescending and dis-empowering way that they themselves have been treated. There is no "joy" in their newly acquired promotion. They are more deeply trapped than ever in the cycle of corruption and oppression.

- Burying the talent in the ground strikes us as strange at a first glance. Once again, we may be witnessing a clash of two cul-tures: the traditional agrarian culture of "use-value" (investing the money in the land) and the culture of "exchange value" (the capi-talistic practice of making money out of money). In this context, it may well be that burying the money in the ground is a metaphor for investing the money in the land. Even an option to bury money in the ground (in the literal sense) could be seen as quite responsible, thus ensuring that the money was not robbed or stolen.

- That the one with the single talent used the money to invest wisely in the land may underpin the challenge he throws at the landowner: "I knew you to be a hard man, reaping where you did not sow, and gathering where you did not winnow" (Matt. 25:24). These audacious words call to task the accountability of a harsh capital-istic hoarder. He is further described as one who sows where he does not reap (i.e., he exploits the resources) and gathers where he has not scattered (i.e., he hoards for selfish gain). The outsider sees through the sham and brutality of the corrupt landowner.

- To prove that the one with the single talent is right in his judgment, he is brutally treated for his whistle-blowing, for exposing the corruption and demanding accountability.

Disrupting Regimes of Normalcy

Viewed in its original context, the hero of the story is the one with the single talent, the one who does not collude with the corrupt system, and, like Jesus himself, he pays the ultimate price for speaking truth to power. With such empowering stories, Jesus consistently questions the underlying values, disrupts the regimes of normalcy, exposes the corruption, and shakes the foundations upon which patriarchy functions.

This covert subversiveness becomes even more potent in Jesus' challenges to the purity laws by which some are excluded and others included (e.g., the story of the good Samaritan in Luke 10:29–37; the Pharisee and the publican in Luke 18:9–14). In these narratives, Jesus blatantly breaks the laws of his own religion, yet never apologizes for doing so and never seems to offer a rationale or justification for his cultural and religious deviance.

Despite the overwhelming endorsement that scholars seek for the Jewishness of Jesus and the consistent desire to honor the Hebrew Scriptures as the basis for understanding the New Testament, it seems to me that Jesus disassociated himself from his Jewish roots over several fundamental issues. Might it be that Scripture scholars, generally coming from a religious background and often mandated in their work by a specific church or religion, project onto Jesus something of their own attachment to formal religion?

The Jesus we claim to be a loyal and faithful Jew, respectful of and abiding by his inherited traditions begins to look increasingly like a figment of the patriarchal imagination. This leaves the subversive Jesus largely undiscovered and, worse still, submerged in cultural layers of the very oppression from which Jesus sought to liberate all peoples.

Is Jesus Still a Dangerous Memory?

Over the centuries we have caricatured Jesus as a powerful, guru-type male, primarily identified with respectable middle-class clerics. We have over-spiritualized the incarnated face of God, undermined his soulful humanity, tamed his fiery prophetic challenge, and domesticated the subversive project of the New Reign of God almost beyond recognition.

The dangerous memory is no longer dangerous; in fact it has not been for several centuries. Ironically, it is Christendom itself that has instituted and maintained the domestication. Ecclesiastical power, glory, and imperialism have badly distorted the primordial archetypal vision. By legalizing and literalizing the subversive story, we have undermined the deeper meaning encapsulated in archetype, myth, symbol, and ritual.

Ancestral grace cannot accommodate this reified, well-rounded imperial Savior. He lacks the groundedness, struggle, and desire that guides humanity through the long aeons of evolutionary becoming. As a primordial male — up ahead of us or up above us — he feels more like someone who has abandoned the interpersonal and earthly solidarity that was so crucial to the unfolding of our species. As an interventionist, rescuing redeemer, he alienates rather than reassures us; instead of suffering with us, he becomes exalted as the one who suffers for us. He becomes the hero and we the passive victims.

The Jesus of the dangerous memory is above all else *an empowering liberator.* He stands in solidarity with our dreams and hopes, our struggles and confusions, at every stage of our evolutionary unfolding. He keeps before us the big picture of our ultimate destiny while never betraying the intimate details of daily struggle and growth. It sounds like he might be both too big and too intimate for the culture of petrified patriarchy.

Chapter 19

Being Human—Being Person

Relatedness is more vital than any consciousness and lies within it. A human being is first of all a being-in-relationship, then consciousness, then personal creativity.   — IVONE GEBARA

IN TERMS OF BEING INTEGRATED into the wider human culture, Christianity went through a process remarkably similar to the other major religions. Consciously or otherwise, it sought out what seemed like the most persuasive and credible cultural container through which it could sell its message to the wider world. Greek philosophy was burgeoning at the time, with a particular appeal to patriarchal systems, religious and otherwise. It offered clarity in its conceptual framework, a logical and rational way of dealing with knowledge (epistemology), a metaphysical worldview, and a hierarchical sense of order with strong appeal to the dominance and control so endemic to the politics of the time.[18]

Had Christianity adopted the Hebrew culture, things would have been very different. The sacredness of creation would be much more to the fore, with a stronger sense of the divine working through creation rather than inhabiting a distant heaven. The oneness of everything, rather than dualistic divisions, would occupy a more central place. Conceptual clarity would give way to unfolding processes, and a communal sense of organizing would be favored to that of hierarchical structures. And human personhood would be notably different — much more congruent with ancestral grace and capable of honoring the evolution of humanity over the 7-million-year story.

The Person in Aristotle

Human identity today is caught in the conflicting strain of two major ideologies. The first dominant position owes its origin largely to classical Greek culture. Plato and Aristotle bequeathed to us an understanding of the human person that has prevailed over the past twenty-five thousand years. To be authentically human we see ourselves as different from, and superior to, everything else in creation. Individuality, characterized by autonomy, self-reliance, independence, and rationality, constitutes the essence of human nature and the heart of human identity. *Each person stands alone in his or her uniqueness.* The ability to achieve and maintain a strong sense of separation and independence is, according to this model, the goal of all growth and development.

This is also the understanding espoused by political economy and legal jurisprudence. Humans are first and foremost atomistic creatures, always regarded in their individual uniqueness and assessed for their worth and value in terms of individual gift and talent. The survival of the fittest, although it has social and interpersonal dimensions, ultimately is based on each person displaying extra nerve and fortitude in making it for oneself.

Anthropologically, we adopt this view on the understanding that for much of our evolutionary development we humans were enmeshed in nature, and our coming into maturity required us to be clearly differentiated from everything else. Hence, the notion of *separateness* came to the fore. This is the basis for the severe alienation that humans experience today, especially in the so-called developed nations of the West. By delineating ourselves from nature and setting ourselves over nature, often with the blessing and validation of formal religion, we effectively cut ourselves off from the sustaining womb to which we intimately and integrally belong.

Our concept of autonomous personhood may well be the greatest delusion from which we humans suffer. It is alien to how we have understood ourselves for most of our 7 million years on this earth. It is largely, if not totally, the product of patriarchal times. It is another corollary of the compulsive need to have humans totally in charge.

The more we put ourselves in charge, the more estranged we become from the cosmic relational matrix to which everything in creation belongs.

An Alternative Paradigm

The other dominant view can be traced to more recent developments in the social sciences, but it also incorporates ancient insights from anthropology and paleontology. It is encapsulated in the statement: *I am at all times the sum of my relationships and that's what constitutes my identity.* Whereas the contemporary vocabulary of personhood is constructed around words like "autonomous," "atomistic," "self-reliant," "rational," the alternative paradigm is articulated with words like "relational," "interdependent," "holistic," "process," "intuitive."

Here we encounter two value systems that are not easily reconciled. The latter emphasizes the central role of relationality in giving birth to and sustaining individual entities, thus fostering the diversity within the primordial unity, while the former claims that only individual entities are real, and relationships are devised merely to enable such entities to survive and thrive.

These two understandings cannot be meshed or integrated. One is essentially false, because it is not congruent with how creation operates, while the other evolves out of the relational dynamics that sustain everything in creation. One belongs to cosmic processes; the other is a man-made fabrication, a caricature so widely accepted as being normative, and even divinely sanctioned, that it will not be easily challenged or changed.

For many peoples in Africa and Latin America and for various indigenous groups around the world, the relational paradigm provides the primordial understanding of what it means to be human. The robust individualism we take so much for granted is alien to, and alienating for, many of our contemporaries. The relational model is, in fact, the one we have known and appropriated for most of our history as a human species.

What Kind of Person Was Jesus?

Because early Christianity created such a close affinity with the thought and ideology of classical Greek culture, the individualistic construct of personhood infiltrated every aspect of Christian faith, including its application to the person of Jesus. It features in many of the early church councils, including those of Nicea and Chalcedon, and specifically in the formulation of the early christological doctrines. It is the philosophy of personhood widely adopted in contemporary Western cultures and in those strongly influenced by Western values. Indeed, all the major religions adopt it to one degree or another.

Christian apologists from the dawn of Christian times assumed that Jesus belonged to the world of autonomous personhood. Hence the desire of the apostles to exalt him on a throne like a kingly figure, something he always resists, according to the synoptic Gospels. In what must be one of the most persistent strains of ignorance in any religious tradition known to humankind, Christians never seem to have questioned this foundational assumption about the personhood of Jesus. We invoke much rhetoric about being molded in the image and likeness of God, but in truth we spend an enormous amount of energy molding God in our image and likeness, and we have done that with Jesus in an outlandish way. In the words of Richard Rohr, "Jesus came to make a confounding statement about *us,* and we have avoided that message by trying to make profound statements about *him* — statements about which we never all agree and never will agree, but merely argue" (Rohr 2004, 122).

One of the most transparent clues in the Gospels, one in which Jesus hints at a very different self-understanding, is in the response made to the disciples of John the Baptist in Luke 7:18–22. The disciples put the direct identity question to Jesus. Interestingly, he does not answer in what the church has proclaimed to be the great assertion of faith, allegedly spoken by Peter: "You are the Christ the Son of the Living God." Jesus does not give a direct response to the disciples of John the Baptist. In fact he gives a strangely bewildering answer: "Go and see what is happening . . . " (v. 22).

What seems to be happening is that Jesus is suggesting they go and look at his relational matrix, the context in which his life is lived out in liberating relatedness — what the Gospels name "the Kingdom of God" — a quality of engagement with his culture from which Jesus himself obtains his personal, individual identity. The Kingdom vision is an extension of the person of Jesus through which Jesus grows into a unique personal identity. The New Reign of God is Jesus' relational matrix in its largest and most inclusive sense. This is why Jesus always points his finger away from his individual self and toward the Kingdom that is the fullness of his relational self. In the words of Robert Funk:

> Jesus pointed to something he called God's domain, something he did not create, something he did not control. I want to discover what Jesus saw, or heard, or sensed that was so enchanting, so mesmerizing, so challenging that it held Jesus in its spell. And I do not want to be misled by what his followers did: instead of looking to see what he saw, his devoted disciples tended to stare at the pointing finger. Jesus himself should not be, must not be, the object of faith. That would be to repeat the idolatry of the first believers. (Funk 1996, 305)

Jesus belongs totally and unambiguously to the relational way of being human and should never have been imprisoned in the patriarchal construct of the autonomous self. This is the reductionism that in time created a voyeuristic preoccupation with the divinity of Jesus, and it became a gross distraction from the radically new way of being human that Jesus manifested to and for us. This enterprise of engaging with the liberative relational revelation of God in Jesus remains one of the biggest challenges of the Christian faith still awaiting an authentic response from the Christian people.

Chapter 20

Incarnation Embracing Paradox

Whenever evolution brings forth greater complexity, coopera-
tion, and interdependence, new challenges and dangers are born,
too.... Let us recall that the primary driver of evolutionary cre-
ativity is chaos. Paradoxically, from an evolutionary perspective,
bad news is often a good thing, a blessing in disguise.

— MICHAEL DOWD

FOR MANY CHRISTIANS, grace denotes the favor of God's love that
sends Jesus to rescue us from our sinfulness and bring us to the
fullness of life beyond this vale of tears. According to this interpretation, Jesus achieves this primarily through his death on the cross.
Salvation and redemption come through the cross. In his passion,
death, and resurrection Jesus rectifies the fundamental flaw that has
held humanity in bondage from the beginning of time.

In this context, grace is a divine gift given primarily (some claim
exclusively) through the historical Jesus of two thousand years ago.
It has nothing to do with ancestral grace, which is considered a kind
of theological gimmick or, worse still, a pagan fantasy. Before Jesus,
everybody is assumed to be in the darkness of sin. Only in Jesus is
liberty made possible and salvation guaranteed.

While this view is adopted by millions of Christians and to varying degrees affirmed in the worldview of other religions, it is based
on patriarchal distortions that went largely unchallenged until the
twentieth century. Thanks to a more critical and discerning evaluation of our Christian inheritance we are now empowered to address
the faulty namings, dualisms, and distortions that underpin the more
conventional understanding.

Naming Our Reality Afresh

According to the conventional worldview, civilization first begins about five thousand years ago, and the salvation of all, made possible in Christ, originates about two thousand years ago. There is a frightening short-sightedness in this overview. Humans select a few recent developments, which they believe they can comprehensively discern, and declare them to be of supreme value for all peoples of all times. Arrogance and idolatry flourish in this appropriation of knowledge and truth. And it is excessively dualistic, a feature inherited from the classical Greek culture of the time. Everything is assumed to work in adversarial binaries: earth vs. heaven, body vs. soul, matter vs. spirit. The Jesus who proclaims and embraces the vision of the Kingdom of God transcends all these misleading distortions and invites all Christians to do the same.

Several false namings are embedded in this analysis. While it strives to honor the creativity of God across time and culture, the God being envisaged is very much the product of anthropocentric projection. It is a God-concept that can be managed and controlled in a time-constricted frame and adorned with many of the trappings of the prevailing Greek and Roman cultures of the time. It fully endorses the notion that the king is the primary embodiment of divinity on earth. And the divisions and struggles that define and characterize patriarchal governance are adopted as the core dynamics of religious belief. To the fore is the battle to overcome the fundamentally flawed nature of creation itself.

Jesus never declared creation to be essentially flawed. Humans began to narrate the Jesus story in a manner that fundamentally betrays Jesus as a disciple of ancestral grace. Jesus engaged life in terms of a fundamental *paradox,* but not in terms of a fundamental *flaw.* This is a distinction of enormous importance, one that religion and theology scantly acknowledge.

The paradox describes the unfolding pattern of birth-death-rebirth as evidenced throughout creation over several billion years. The paradoxical mix of creation and destruction, more accurately of destruction as a precondition for new creation, characterizes all life, human included, at every stage of evolution. We see this process at work in the five great extinctions of the past 500 million years (see Donovan 1989; Leakey and Lewin 1996), but the pattern characterizes the evolutionary story from its origins, as comprehensively portrayed by Swimme and Berry (1992).

In proclaiming the Kingdom of God, Jesus was birthing afresh (more accurately, rebirthing) the dream of God for all creation: a new world order dedicated to the evolution of right relationships for the liberation and flourishing of all life. It involved the death of the prevailing system of patriarchal top-down ordering, along with the birth pangs of the emerging new, a process that involved intense suffering for Jesus throughout his entire life and culminating in his untimely death.

As I discussed in a previous work (O'Murchu 2005), Jesus did not come to rescue humans from anything. Rather, God in the coming of Jesus affirms, confirms, and brings to further fulfillment all we humans had achieved throughout our 7 million years of human evolution. And Jesus also points the way forward, particularly in that newly evolved way of being that Christians describe as Resurrection. This is not so much a supernatural miracle relevant only to Jesus; it is also an embodied expression of what all humans are called to become, as we further evolve into the open-ended future.

In 1939, the structuralist Claude Levi-Strauss confessed to what he felt was a major professional error in his career, namely, his liberal use of the word "primitive" to describe the behavior of ancient humans. Several factors led to this change of heart, primarily the increasing evidence indicating that our ancient ancestors were quite intelligent and sophisticated vis-à-vis their time and culture. It was also becoming clear that the allegation of being primitive was often based on a projection from the present onto the past, perhaps to distract from — or invalidate — the barbaric behavior of our own time.

While social-historical researchers refrain from using this term "primitive," it is still widely adopted in our understanding and interpretation of prehistoric behavior patterns. Even when the word is not used, it is generally assumed that human behavior improves over time, being more developed and advanced now than in previous times. The widespread violence of the twentieth century should leave us in little doubt about the naivety of such a perception.

Any attempt, therefore, to exonerate our ancestors and to argue that their behavior was, at times, much more congruent with their cultural context than ours is today, tends to be countered with ridicule and hostility. People like myself, who tend to view prehistoric culture in a more benign way, are often dismissed as false idealists stuck in a kind of infantilism, utopianism, hankering for a golden age in the past. The self-righteousness of our time, despite various signs to the contrary, arrogantly exalts the present, while often harshly judging and dismissing the past.

Jesus Embracing Paradox

Jesus embraced the paradox of life at every level. In his own being and person he lived out the daily becoming of birth-death-rebirth. Archetypally, he did so in terms of the dying and rising of all creation; as a historical being he knew its exigencies in his daily life. Anthropocentric projections like *omnipotence* or *omniscience,* therefore, undermine rather than enforce the integrity and authenticity of Jesus. These attributions turn Jesus into an idol of patriarchal projections.

The strong focus on Jesus' divinity also results in distortions. It becomes the justification for anthropocentric self-inflation and power-mongering and seriously distracts from the immediacy of God's revelation in Jesus, namely, the human face of God radiating in our world. It is the humanity of Jesus, and not the divinity, that humans have badly neglected. As a result we have misconstrued aspects of the Jesus story, both from an archetypal and historical perspective.

The notion of ancestral grace invites us to reclaim the graced presence of God in the midst of creation. In nature and the created world, our ancestors worshiped and honored God for several millennia. We have disconnected Jesus from that great story, setting him up on a pedestal that fails to honor either his divinity or his humanity. The consequences for graced humanity are particularly serious.

The Christian scriptures exhibit contradictions, often embraced zealously by those who wish to ridicule the Christian faith and seek to undermine its integrity. What often is attacked are the allusions to the *mistakes* that Jesus occasionally made, and also those made by the writers of the Gospels. It is human to make mistakes; that is another dimension of life's paradox. Anyone deeply embedded in such life, including Jesus, will make mistakes. That fact confirms rather than undermines the authenticity and realness of Jesus.

Christian salvation is not about a divine intervention to set something right that had been flawed from the start; it is rather a confirmation of something that has prevailed from the very beginning, namely, that paradox which infuses every aspect of God's creation. By working with the paradox in a more enlightened and grace-filled way, we bring creation to greater fulfillment, to greater wholeness and flourishing. Our desire to sort out the mess for once and forever is not of God, nor of Jesus. It is another consequence of our petrified humanity, misleadingly preoccupied with power and dominance and failing to honor the creativity and vulnerability so central to the Jesus we confess to follow as a Christian people.

Instead the call to serve in the New Reign of God, inaugurated in and through Jesus, is an invitation to humility and service, to befriend the innate paradox of God's creation and work with it in a more informed and responsible way. Jesus offers a model and invites us to embrace the task as co-creators. Jesus does not try to get rid of life's contradictions and inconsistencies, nor does he try to rush the evolutionary process to some premature end. He embraces ambiguity, uncertainty, messiness, the struggles of his people in daily life. He imparts a wisdom to engage more creatively, not simply an escape route to redemption in this life, or utopia in a life to come.

Humans Embracing the Paradox

How to imitate Jesus, how to espouse a Christian praxis that learns to live with the paradox rather than get rid of it, is one of the most formidable challenges facing Christians today. The influence of classical Greek culture still haunts us as we continue to live out of an outdated dualistic worldview. Accordingly, we adopt binary think-ing to conceptualize so many aspects of life. And we generate false utopias that will never deliver true or enduring freedom.

To befriend the paradox in a more informed and empowering way requires of us a much more explicit commitment to one of the se-riously neglected Christian virtues, namely, *justice-making*. All the Christian churches have much to say about justice, but often fail to deliver in a way that compels credibility. Justice is frequently re-served to persons and their personal rights. Just regard for creation at large, for those right relationships that enable us to live con-vivially in a more wholesome and fertile earth, is where Christian rhetoric often falls short. Christian teaching on justice also fails to promote a more righteous way of living and relating within institu-tions whose allegiance to patriarchal values makes them essentially unjust themselves.

A more integrated program for justice has to be multidisciplinary at a conceptual level and engage all the major institutions that im-pact upon people and the planet we inhabit. Justice reserved to the sacred sphere of religion, but failing to engage the prevailing po-litical, economic, and social values, is inherently contradictory, and also a serious betrayal of the New Reign of God envisaged by Jesus. Gospel-based justice embraces life in its God-given totality. Without this more grounded redress all the rhetoric about love sounds shal-low and empty. Love and justice are complementary Christian (and human) values.

A stronger focus on justice, and work for right relating at every level of God's creation, helps to keep Christians centered on the evolv-ing paradoxical world where our creative God continues to reveal the birthing power of Holy Mystery. That same focus keeps us faithful to the dream of the Kingdom enunciated and fulfilled in the Christian Gospels.

This is quite a different stance from the passivity of the past, awaiting some heavenly realm where all will be well while grossly neglecting the heaven that has infused everything in creation, the sacredness our ancestors honored, the graced engagement we're called to embrace afresh each day of our lives.

Chapter 21

Christian Incarnation
and Other Religions

We constitute a common humanity on this planet, indeed a community, despite all the differences in religion and culture. We need a Christology that will confirm the importance of a common humanity, a human community in a common habitat.

— ROGER HAIGHT

THE COMING OF JESUS in our spiritualized human story marks two moments in what Grace Jantzen (1998) calls the process of "natality" (translated as "becoming" or "flourishing"). The first moment was, and is, one of affirmation — more accurately, confirmation — of all that humans achieved as co-creators with God over a 7-million-year period. The second moment is marked by a new evolutionary threshold indicating the way forward for future human growth and development, primarily in the realm of mind and spirit.

Incarnation basically means God entering fully and identifying with human embodiment. God did that in our species for the first time 7 million years ago. Unambiguously, without reserve or regret, the divine became manifest in creation in a totally new way, namely, in human form.

Parallels in Other Faiths

The celebration of this incarnation is assumed by Christians to be their unique prerogative. We consider *incarnation* to be exclusive to our faith. In a desire to be more inclusive, Christian theologians consider the incarnation of God in Jesus to be exemplary among, and

144

prescriptive for, all religions. Difference rather than commonality is emphasized. To state it with a tinge of fundamental bluntness: we have an embodied presence of God that they don't have, at least not as explicitly and completely as ours!

If the coming of God in Jesus belongs to an axial age characterized by the awakening of a new consciousness (an idea initially floated by Karl Jaspers in the twentieth century), then presumably it is axial (transformative) for all humanity and not just for Christians. Working from this starting point, we readily see that all the major religions articulate the concept of *incarnation*. It is hard to imagine that we could have overlooked the evidence for so long. Perhaps this is an indication of the lethal power of religious ideology, generating and sustaining a kind of dogmatic certainty that ultimately undermines rather than enhances the search for truth.

Hinduism, the oldest of today's major religions, has consistently highlighted the importance of *avatars*. Formally describing various appearances of the God Vishnu, Hinduism cherishes the memory of nine outstanding avatars, the earlier versions being partly human, partly animal, suggesting an integration of the human, the animal, and the larger creation. The better-known figures are those of Rama, Krishna, and the Buddha (the ninth and final avatar). A tenth, Kalkin, is postulated to appear at the end of the age, to redeem the troubled world and restore harmony. Christian scholars emphasize the fact that the avatar primarily denotes the descent of the divine into the world rather than the precise embodiment emphasized in Christianity. Again, one wonders if the exclusive claim to truth is really the issue being emphasized.

In all versions of Buddhism, particularly in the Mahayana tradition, Bodhisattvas hold an honored place. These are humans deemed to have attained the essence of bodhi but renounce entry into nirvana in order to help other beings on the journey. Compassion is considered to be the outstanding virtue of this holy person; scripture scholar Marcus Borg (1994; 2003) suggests it is also a dominant feature in the life of Jesus. While Buddhism does not adopt a notion of divinity comparable to other theistic religions, nonetheless the Bodhisattva characterizes a sense of transcendence made more real and tangible through these incarnation-type figures.

In the Muslim faith *prophets* are among the most emulated and empowering figures. A large number have been recognized but seven hold special prominence, namely, Adam, Seth, Enoch, Abraham, Moses, David, and Jesus, with Muhammad as the final prophet after whom there are no more. The mission of the prophets variously described as messengers (*rusul*) or ambassadors (*mursalun*), is to call the people to greater fidelity in allegiance to the one God.

Similar to the Islamic prophet, and often compared with the Hindu Brahman (holy man), is the guru in Sikhism. There have been ten outstanding gurus, beginning with Guru Nanak, the founder of Sikhism. The divine presence inhabits such individuals in a distinctive way. Although still subject to the law of karma like other humans, they do not accumulate any more karma. Acquisition of holy wisdom and insight for liberation are best obtained by attending closely to the teachings of the gurus.

One wonders how we could have missed and ignored the parallels for so long. Moving beyond the formal religions we know today are various similar articulations of the embodied presence of God in the religious beliefs of indigenous peoples. Many of these have been studied and need not be enumerated here. I do however wish to note two further incarnational namings of a more global nature, namely, the *diviner* in various African religions and the *shaman* (or shamanness) in many prehistoric faiths. Perhaps figures of *mystical* significance should be also included in the list as Smart and Konstantine (1991) suggest. Occasionally, these archetypal figures are reappropriated in contemporary "new age" movements with the risk of misrepresenting and undermining their profound historical and cultural significance.

Commonalities Rather Than Differences

The commonalities are striking, and have not been reviewed in a way that would unlock a more liberating truth. A type of Christian arrogance consistently gets in the way. The Christian Jesus, it is argued, is really God and not just a representative of God. Jesus is historically real, whereas many of these other parallel figures are mythological or merely symbolic. There is objective verification for who and what Jesus was, far in excess of the secondary nature of the source material for these other figures.

All these arguments favor differences over commonalities, and the desire to protect the uniqueness of Jesus' divinity is often motivated by a subtle, subconscious desire to validate Christian (Western?) power. The notion of ancestral grace seeks to name, reclaim, and celebrate something much more foundational that unites us across the vast story of our human existence, namely, the power of the divine at work in the transformation of our evolving humanity — a feature largely ignored by all the religions, including Christianity.

Is there not a common criterion that could be employed at the service of a more creative discernment, namely, the common humanity we all share under God? Is there not then an obvious, yet profound, wisdom in each religion adopting remarkable human beings perceived to serve as models for the embodiment of that transcendent power we name divinity? Indeed, a growing number of Christian scholars seem to be moving in this same direction. While not wishing to deny the divinity of Jesus, scholarly focus throughout the twentieth century veered more toward prioritizing the humanity of Jesus. It is the human aspect that has been largely neglected in Christendom, an element that needs to be reclaimed and prioritized if we are to duly honor the challenge of living according to the vision of the Kingdom of God and making it more real in our world.

All religions, therefore, focus on human beings who because of their distinctive attributes — especially, their greater transparency to divine mystery (grace) — embody more explicitly the divine in our midst. Nor is there any elitism in this notion, because consistently the message is that, potentially, all humans can attain this level of divine-human integration. And the authenticity of such enlightened beings, in all cases, depends on their ability to inspire and empower others to live in a more faithful and spiritually fulfilling way.

History has abundantly furnished us with graced incarnational beings who mirror and reflect the divine greatness to which we are all called. If the truth were to be fully honored, there were many, not just an outstanding few. Incarnation is not a single phenomenon, but like creation itself is effusive and prodigious in expression and articulation.[19]

Spiritual literature of the past and present is redolent with such inspiring incarnational people, with one notable tragic element, the widespread exclusion of outstanding female figures. This alone should make us suspicious of the exclusiveness that all the religions propagate to one degree or another. All are influenced by the corrosive impact of patriarchal imperial power, probably the single greatest threat to the liberating dynamism of ancestral grace.

Jesus among the Religions

The Jesus of ancestral grace transcends many of our favored boundaries and distinctions. The one humanity within a flourishing unity of planet and cosmos is the goal of the New Reign of God, the central vision of the Christian Scriptures. At this level, humans across cultures and religions share a common enterprise: commitment to building a world of right relationships beyond all the destructive distinctions and divisions that have wrought so much pain and suffering for humans and for the earth we inhabit.

The opening quote from Roger Haight echoes the challenge posed by Hans Küng (1998) some years ago when he invited all the religions to unite in addressing the serious ecological and ethical problems facing the earth community today, and in this process forge a new impetus for multi-faith dialogue and harmony. For the greater part the invitation has fallen on deaf ears.

Although a number of Christian scholars have promoted multi-faith dialogue for some years, this seems to be largely a Christian endeavor with limited cooperation or enthusiasm from other faiths. Undoubtedly, a suspicion of Christianity's colonial history still lingers; Christians are widely perceived as colonizers of other traditions with a tendency to manipulate and undermine other faiths and cultures. And the Christian scholarly endeavor does not seem to have penetrated deeply into the religious world in general. Rather than overtly committed to deeper dialogue, most rank-and-file believers seem to be happy with a strategy of "live and let live." A strange mixture of fear, inhibition, apathy, and indifference seems to hamper our enthusiasm for religious dialogue.

Through Religion and Beyond

Perhaps ancestral grace in our time is inviting us to honor and embrace a diversity of perspectives. Of central importance is the call to outgrow patriarchal power, which can tolerate only one dominant and domineering truth, and which, unknowingly or otherwise, perpetuates a cult of divide and conquer. Commonalities are subverted and undermined; differences are cherished and propagated. Not surprisingly, therefore, formal religion ends up abetting resentment and violence, frequently contradicting the most basic tenets of religious belief.

The notion of ancestral grace seeks to begin where God begins in time, with the story of creation itself. Creation is one, but thrives on diversity. Creation forms a seamless web, yet can also embrace a quality of paradox that often defies human rationality. Why can't religion and spirituality aspire to those same ideals? Why can't our spiritual engagement be one that honors God's graced foundations to our entire existence?

Our Christian story needs to be released from its cultural bondage of patriarchal conditioning and its constricted time frame of two thousand years. Reclaiming common strands with the other great religions is a first step toward this enlarged horizon. But not enough for an appreciation of grace. That leads us beyond all religion into the great spiritual exploration that is the story of creation itself.

Chapter 22

Jesus as Ritual Maker

Humanity is a species that lives and can only live in terms of meanings it itself must invent. — ROY A. RAPPAPORT

J ESUS LIVED IN A WORLD of signs and wonders, one not easily appreciated within the rational context of formal scholarship. For the greater part it seems to have been an agrarian culture, with the land perceived as God's great gift to the people. The land itself was sacred, and people readily read the signs of nature to discern a vast range of meanings, including weather prospects and the time of day.

People relied heavily on the land for food and sustenance. And they looked to their ecological surroundings for potions and herbs to address illness and help maintain a healthy lifestyle. All too easily, we describe such people as primitive and backward. In terms of convivial, ecological sustainability they were far more grounded in nature and living in a more wholesome way than millions in the sophisticated world of our time.

How Jesus reflected that culture with its customs and norms is a debate that will continue for many years to come. For much of the two thousand years of Christendom, the divinity of Jesus has been a major obstacle to this research. Typically, Jesus was portrayed as superior and external to this narrow primitive world. His words were over-spiritualized and any deed transcending normal behavior was deemed either as evidence for the miraculous or proof of supernatural power.

A Culture of Ritual

We have seriously underestimated and even undermined the capacity of Jesus as a ritual-maker. Because of their closeness to nature, people in the time of Jesus exhibited gifts and abilities that in our time are often dismissed as magic, witchcraft, or rare examples of special giftedness. People had a celebratory sense of the seasons and lived convivially with the cycle of birth-death-rebirth at every level of creation. Life transitions (birth, maturation, death) were marked with often elaborate rituals. Many rituals of healing and reconciliation were practiced. Later generations came to describe them as miracles, thus projecting them onto a supernatural plane and depriving humans of a spiritual resource they had known for thousands of years.

And the shadow side of this development also flourished in the time of Jesus. Men had far greater access to ritual enactment than women. Rituals involving bloodshed and sacrifice, with blood deemed to be the primary life substance, became distorted amid a plethora of rules regarding ritual purity, or became commercialized through exclusive clerical access to temple ceremonies. The Greek dualistic influence began to drive a wedge between the sacred and the secular. The Hebraic sense of unity and universal harmony was progressively suppressed.

In the life and praxis of Jesus, ritual-making features strongly. John Dominic Crossan (1991) claims that commensality and healing are the central features in the ministry of Jesus. For some scholars they are considered quite secondary. Sharing the open common table may well be the most daring and original activity of the historical Jesus. According to the prevailing Jewish norms, one brought to the table only those deemed worthy according to the rules and customs of the time. For instance, a woman menstruating would not share table with her family, because she was deemed ritually impure.[20] Yet to the common open table Jesus invites prostitutes, sinners, tax-collectors. Everybody is welcome; everybody is fully accepted and included.

In the practice of the open table, Jesus is performing a food ritual, the significance of which has been largely subverted in our time, first because food is widely regarded as a commodity rather than as a life-giving gift. Second, its formal ritualization has been monopolized in the religious practice known as Eucharist, with priests playing the primary ritualistic role. While ancestral grace considers all food sacred and the communal sharing of food a special moment for realizing the closeness of God, contemporary culture has totally despiritualized food, while formal eucharistic celebrations have so spiritualized it that only select people can gain full access. The witness of Jesus to open commensality denounces both subversions and evokes new possibilities in which all people are empowered to be active ritual-makers.

The healing ministry of Jesus needs to be reclaimed in a similar way. Illness in the time and culture of Jesus was much more a social-systemic condition than that defined by the modern medicalization of the human body. In the contemporary paradigm, illness is a physical defect in a machine-like body. Medicine and science try to provide the necessary knowledge and resources for remedial intervention, usually through medication or surgery. In earlier times, sickness indicated a breakdown or dysfunction in the connective web of life. The individual body always belongs to a larger embodied force whether understood in familial, social, national, planetary, or cosmic terms. Living healthily meant living in a wholesome way with all those other embodied presences that are perceived to constitute the web of life.

When Jesus is confronted by crippled, blind, or possessed people, the course of action described in the Gospels is not just about rectifying an illness, but also about reconnecting with the relational matrix of universal life. In some cases people were crippled with internalized guilt, considering themselves cursed because of some wrong deed in the past or an affliction brought on by the ill will of others. The complex story of the Gerasene demoniac (Mark 5:1–20) is a case in point. Described by Ched Myers (1988, 192) as "exorcism as political repudiation," the story very much belongs to the regime of Roman oppression and the desired freedom from bondage. Even the language used reinforces this interpretation: the Greek word used for herd, *agele* is usually used to describe, not a group of pigs, but a band of military recruits; the reference to *legion* suggests a strong link to the Roman imperial context. Some commentators also attribute symbolic significance to the location: the region of the Gerasenes was close to the city of Tiberias, capital for Herod Antipas. Herod had to coerce Jews to populate the city because it was considered unclean, having been constructed on the site of a graveyard (see Myers 1988, 190–94; Horsley 2003, 98–103).

In striving to honor divine initiative, we can actually undermine the rich contextual fabric in which Gospel-based healing is often located. In this case, we are also likely to overlook the rich interweaving of ritual and symbolism in the healing narratives, suggesting that these stories are not merely about individual recovery of health, but much more about *empowerment toward reintegration* into the recovery of earth-based citizenship at every level. Healing, therefore, involved realigning the context (in this case, the wider cultural context) to facilitate a more wholesome flow of life energy, through which human illness could be resolved and people could once more begin to enjoy something of the graced fullness of earthly and cosmic life.

Another example is that of leprosy, with a meaning very different from our time. In Gospel terms it describes a patchy skin condition, a flaking of the skin. It was not a life-threatening illness, nor was it contagious. It carried, however, an enormous social stigma, condemning the person not just to social exclusion but making him or her the object of moralistic, religious judgment, by which a person felt impure in God's eyes and an object of derision in the human sphere. According to Pilch (2000, 51), the problem was not contagion, but pollution. Healing, therefore, may not necessarily involve curing, something that could possibly have been obtained by better hygiene. The real task for the healer was the breaking down of the cruel social and religious castigation upheld by the culture of the time.

Healing rituals also involved — as in many indigenous cultures today — the invocation of altered states of consciousness (ASC), in which trance-induced techniques help to unravel, or at least loosen up, the congealed patterns causing the internal breakdown manifested in external symptoms (see Davies 1995). Such rituals may involve the use of clay, water, fire, light, touch, and, of course, words. These may also invoke emotional or hysterical reaction, which in sensationalized journalism earn more attention than they deserve. But from the perspective of the recipient, perhaps the key to the breakthrough is the intuitive awareness that one is no longer trapped in the dark hole of excessive guilt, rejection, and exclusion.

Commenting on the healing ministry of Jesus, Davies writes: "Jesus reframed his clients' presumed sinful condition as a condition of forgiveness and encouraged their metanoia" (1995, 145). To depict such conversion as some type of miraculous deed initiated through Jesus' divine power misses the rich cultural and transpersonal significance. It leads to assessments of the Gospel evidence in which these ritual acts become either *erga* (deeds) or *seimei* (signs), descriptions employed in Christian rhetoric to prove the divinity of Jesus. In all probability Jesus, faithful to ancestral grace, intended such ritualizations as acts of liberation from a complex range of cultural oppressions, while also serving as spiritual awakenings for all of us to the as yet unrealized potentials that we all possess.

Ritualization in Word

Scripture scholars John Dominic Crossan (1991) and Steven Davies (1995) situate the miracle ministry of Jesus within the vision of the Kingdom of God; the parable stories depict what the call to the Kingdom means in practice. Gospel speech is essentially ritualized word. The parables are stories that radically reframe context and meaning. They disturb the comfortable conventional wisdom and open up horizons of new vision and possibility. They portray another world where hope can flourish anew.

This gives us another aperture in which to view and understand Jesus, not as an imperial ruler or a dogmatic teacher, but as a prophetic subversive portraying ancestral grace with new vigor and vitality. Perhaps, then, as scholars like Elisabeth Schüssler Fiorenza (1994; 2001), Elizabeth Johnson (1992; 2003), and Denis Edwards (1995) suggest, Jesus should be contextualized within the Wisdom tradition of the Hebrew Scriptures rather than within the more patriarchal context of king, prophet, or male warrior. Wisdom literature abounds with aphorisms, proverbs, and stories. Was Jesus drawing on this background when he opted for subversive speech through parables and storytelling? Would it not then be more congruent to depict Jesus prioritizing women, since at the heart of Wisdom literature we detect an alluring woman called Lady Wisdom?

The more we literalize the Scriptures, the greater the danger of betraying alternative interpretative possibilities, much more illuminating for Christian faith and meaning. Christianity today has become extremely verbose. We need to reclaim the silence and the transverbal, those many gestures and responses illustrating Jesus the ritual-maker, the one for whom metaphor, symbol, story, and ritualization are all important to empower the people of his own day, but also those among us who seek to follow in his footsteps today.

Ritual in Our Time

One of the most serious deprivations in contemporary human life is the suppression of ritual-making. In psychological terms it should be described as a repression rather than a suppression. Inherent to the human spirit, ever since we first evolved in the dim and distant past, is a spirit of playfulness. It subsequently became manifest in game-playing, dance, music, art, and other recreational activities. And this playful spirit is key to many elaborate rituals developed by humans over several millennia.

Today ritual has become relegated to the reified realm of formal religion and specialists, called liturgists, clerics, or parish administrators. Ritual is deemed to be a holy act incorporating specific rubrics and a quality of participation that has to be regulated and controlled by a higher religious authority. By limiting the privilege to the select few, even when the intention has been to create real participation, we have robbed the many of one of life's most liberating and empowering skills.

Of course, this is not the full story, and hence my use of the word "repression" above. Because the capacity for ritual-making is so innate to humans, it cannot be suppressed. When a culture or religion tries to regulate it in a narrow and controlling way, all we achieve is driving it underground. This is where repressed energies begin to smolder and eventually create cultural time-bombs. Today we see the repressed capacity for ritual-making surfacing in the dark sinister arts and in a vast range of cultural articulations through music, drug-cultural, and other unconventional social practices.

A modern disco presents a good case study of ritual in the grip of repression. People are carried away by loud, jolting, chaotic music. A sense of ecstasy is further enhanced by the consumption of alcohol or, more frequently, a range of mood-altering drugs. Inhibition is easily overcome, even to the extent of at times feeling out of the body. For that brief but fleeting time, life seems wonderful. Indeed, for many young people, their sense of being able to cope with life is dependent on the lift-up of the weekly disco.

A more disturbing sphere of repressed ritual is in the modern arts, with their strong nihilistic flavor, depicted several years ago in a quip attributed to the playwright Samuel Beckett: "I have nothing to say, and I'm saying it." As most modern art galleries illustrate, the contemporary artist is stuck in the cultural breakdown of meaning and seems unable to act as a catalyst for the wider cultural release of hope and meaning. A great deal of popular literature has succumbed to a similar plight (see O'Murchu 2007).

The human capacity for ritual is actually flourishing, but in a dangerously confusing and counterproductive way. Where the deprivation is most serious is in the realm of religion and spirituality because, ideally, this is where ritual achieves its most liberating and empowering potential. Perhaps a better appreciation of ritual-making in the foundational sources of our Christian faith might inspire and challenge Christians today to attend to this serious displacement of our time. Without this dimension, our Christian faith remains seriously defective.

Chapter 23

Wholesome Holiness—
Incarnational Spirituality

The middle-class status of most academics has not been con-
ducive to seeing a socio-political dimension in the Jesus tra-
ditions.... The social location of scholarship means that we
often miss things in the text that the experience of poverty,
marginality, patriarchy, or oppression might have led us to see.

— MARCUS J. BORG

A MONG CHRISTIAN SCRIPTURE SCHOLARS it is widely assumed
that Jesus was an ardent religious believer. He was born into
a conventional Jewish family, and so a religious ethos would have
permeated every feature of daily life. The Gospels suggest that his
youth was marked by prevailing Jewish rites such as circumcision,
the presentation in the temple, the bar-mitzvah (coming of age as
an adolescent), and attending major annual festivals at the temple in
Jerusalem.

Scholars detect sufficient evidence in the Gospel texts to assert that
Jesus prayed and fasted, worshiped at the synagogue,[21] lived by the
moral guidelines of his Jewish faith, and attended the major religious festivals with the people of his time. Consistently, he has been
portrayed as a loyal Jew, faithful to all his religion required of him.

Jesus: Religious or Spiritual?

Some years ago, scripture scholar Thomas Sheehan (1986) made the
bold, provocative claim that Jesus was basically anti-religion, even
to the extent of wishing to dispense with religion entirely. This is

quite untypical of scripture scholars, most of whom are perceived to be strong faith-believers themselves, mandated by particular denominations and accountable to those who selected and supported their scholarship. Scripture scholars, like theologians, tend to be born out of a culture of formal religion, and inevitably have a vested interest in defending and promoting that inherited subculture.

Subconsciously, such scholars will approach the Jesus story from within the context of formal religion. Similarly, in the case of Hinduism, Buddhism, and Islam, the leaders, although birthing something quite new, belong to an inheritance that is overtly religious. However new the reformed vision may be, it matures into structures of worship, creedal formulas and ethical norms, three features common to all the formal religions we know today.

But was Jesus really religious? Was he a good, faithful Jew in terms of prevailing norms and expectations? A cursory glance at the Gospels suggests that while he may have drawn on ideas from his religious tradition, he so expanded the inherited wisdom that he often left the central tenets virtually unrecognizable in terms of the prevailing norms. A few examples spring to mind:

- *Ritual purity:* Some scholars argue that this was not a central feature of the Jewish religion at the time of Jesus. It is clearly and unambiguously emphasized in the books of Leviticus and Deuteronomy. Many of the miracle stories, and some parables, highlight Jesus' disagreement with these legal impositions, and not just his disregard, but at times his total abhorrence.

- *Sabbath rest:* There are many examples in the Gospels where Jesus openly transgressed the regulations surrounding Sabbath observance.

- *Forgiveness of sin:* This was deemed to be a prerogative of the Jewish priesthood, and it could be mediated only after the person earned forgiveness by the fulfillment of specific temple requirements.

- *Interaction with women:* Jesus defied the social and religious norms of the time by close and frequent consort with women, with the growing likelihood (according to recent scholarship) that his primary disciples may have been a group of women of whom Mary Magdalene is the best known example.

◆ *Strained relationship* with his mother and probably with his immediate family — most likely because of his divergence from standard social and religious expectations.

◆ *Cleansing the temple:* William R. Herzog (1994; 2005) suggests that the cleansing of the temple was not merely a denunciation of the money-changers for extortion and exploitation of the poor, but a prophetic gesture declaring the temple itself to be redundant. In proclaiming the New Reign of God, the old reign, with the temple as a central symbol, was no longer relevant or necessary.

◆ *Undermining kingship:* In the time of Jesus, the king was the primary representative of God on earth, and those purporting to be of messianic status were expected to behave in a kingly way. Jesus openly ridiculed this notion and totally disassociated himself from it, confusing and annoying those who invested in his dream and vision.

Christian Spirituality and Ancestral Grace

Our desire for a neat conceptual framework of the historical Jesus arises from a human need for proof and rational verification. This may never bring us into contact with the living spirit of Jesus, the heart of true religion. On the contrary, it is the Jesus who embraces ancestral grace, with the inevitable untidiness and evolutionary trial-and-error that characterize the great story of creation and humanity alike, who is likely to evoke a credible response of faith in our time. The Jesus who was, and is, immersed in the ups-and-downs of daily existence is the one who truly breaks open our hearts to the compassion and liberation of new life.

The contemporary scholar Marcus Borg (2003) provides a useful overview to enlighten our search for an authentic Christian spirituality, one that honors the vision of ancestral grace but also grounds our search for meaning in the contemporary world. Borg identifies five central features in the life and ministry of Jesus: *a Jewish mystic, a wisdom teacher, a healer, a social prophet, a movement initiator*. Together they provide a kind of mosaic, empowering landmarks for contemporary Christians seeking to develop an incarnational spirituality.

First, Jesus as a mystic. Mystics throughout the ages are characterized by an immediacy of access to God. They are afire with the living spirit of holy mystery, which they see radiated in every aspect of life, including the depths of pain and struggle. Moreover, as Dorothee Soelle (2001) powerfully demonstrates, true mysticism engages us in resistance of all that militates against growth toward wholeness at every level of life. Incarnational spirituality, like ancestral grace, is that combination of divine intoxication with a passionate commitment to realizing right relationships of love and justice at every level of God's creation.

Second, Jesus as a wisdom teacher. The wisdom of the mystic, contrary to so many movements in our time, is not that of rational knowledge in which every truth has to be objectively verified. Incarnational wisdom adopts narrative and proverb to surface poetic and paradoxical meanings. Trust rather than doctrinal dogma is evoked. We inhabit a wise and intelligent creation, which can teach us many things, provided we align our energies with those of the inspiring Spirit, who infuses and informs everything in creation's evolving story, including the great paradox of birth-death-rebirth.

Third, Jesus, a healer. This is often confused with being a miracle-worker using some rare supernatural power. Anything Jesus did in terms of making people whole, we can do also. It is the transformation that takes place — within and without — as we learn to relate rightly across the entire spectrum of our cosmic, earthly, and human existence.

Fourth, Jesus as a social prophet. Walter Brueggemann (1978; 1986) describes the prophetic as the ability to speak truth to power and thus activate an alternative consciousness to that of conventional imperial wisdom and domination. It involves unmasking the false powers that inhibit our ability to see deeply and hinder us from behaving in liberating freedom. The prophetic stance is central to justice-making, a risky undertaking that can, as in the case of Jesus, incur much suffering and an untimely death.

Fifth, Jesus as a movement initiator. William Cavanaugh (1998), analyzing the Christian struggle in Latin America in the closing decades of the twentieth century, observes that while the media highlight individuals being tortured and executed, the real threat to the power-addicted status quo was not individuals but social movements. Individuals were punished in the hope of disempowering the liberation movements that they represented.

Against the cultural background of the present work, I wish to add a sixth feature: *Jesus as a non-Caucasian.* I recall the first time I visited a church in Africa, with a white European Jesus hanging on a cross at the back of the main altar. What a contradiction! Even after the collapse of Western colonialism, European idolatry reigns in parts of Africa. In terms of ethnic origin, Jesus would have resembled a contemporary Palestinian person, with a dark-colored skin much closer to the African pigmentation that marks our common origins. I suggest we change the prevailing images of Jesus, not simply out of respect for the past and the particular context of the historical Jesus, but also out of respect for the cultural context within which we reenvision the notion of incarnation. Then perhaps we stand a better chance of embracing and realizing the future so elegantly articulated by the African writer Albert Luthuli (quoted by du Toit and Mayson 2006, 20):

> Somewhere ahead there beckons a civilization which will take its place in the parade of God's history with other great human syntheses: Chinese, Egyptian, Jewish, European. It will not necessarily be all black, but it will be African.

From Orthodoxy to Orthopraxy

Faith in Jesus is not about notional assent to a set of doctrines and rules. It is primarily about a relationship, in which the incarnational body of God in our world grows and flourishes into that fullness of life, a new "reign" in which all are invited as active agents. It is not for those sitting on the fence, waiting for church, temple, or mosque to engrace us for a salvation hereafter. Nor is it some enterprise that elevates humans to a redemptive level above everything else in creation. It is a vision embracing the far-flung horizons of time and space, the cosmic and planetary landscape that becomes "the new earth and the new heaven" for all those committed to the co-creative task of building up God's Kingdom on earth.

Jesus was grounded in the ancestral grace that sustained and empowered humans over thousands of years. He, along with other incarnational figures of historical times, helped bring to fuller realization the fulfillment of God's dream for humanity. That is also the dream of the earth and of the whole matrix of cosmic creation.

The Jesus of ancestral grace was badly suffocated by patriarchal conditioning, channeled through Greek metaphysics and Roman imperialism. Now as we read our tradition with a more informed and enlightened wisdom, there is no fear of our losing sight of Jesus, a major preoccupation for fundamentalist Christians. Rather, we are more inspired and challenged by the lure of the visionary Galilean who set ablaze the New Reign of God, a new fire upon the earth, awakening once more the potential to become what we were always destined to be: creatures abundantly blessed in the power of ancestral grace.

In this new vision the holy translates into *wholesomeness,* and incarnation embraces all that the spirit awakens in the unfolding of the human, past, present, and future. In evolutionary terms we stand today on a new threshold, one characterized by the proverbial mixture of promise and peril. Lynne McTaggart (2007, 195) expresses the challenge in vivid terms: "We will have to reframe our understanding of our own biology in more miraculous terms," precisely what the cell biologist Bruce Lipton (2005) has attempted with such impressive evidence. Perhaps it would be more accurate to suggest that evolution will do that for us, throwing out yet another formidable challenge requiring all the graced resources at our disposal. Some of the onerous and urgent implications will be reviewed in part 3 of this book.

Part Three

The Human Lured
toward the Future

The historical mission of our times is to reinvent the human — at the species level, with critical reflection, within the community of life systems. — THOMAS BERRY

Chapter 24

The Grace of Evolutionary Becoming

To pass the test before us, we humans must demonstrate the intelligence and the moral maturity to liberate ourselves from the addictions of empire and to use our gifts wisely in the service of the whole. — DAVID C. KORTEN

W E'RE AN EVOLUTIONARY SPECIES, graced with a story full of elegance and paradox. Today, we have arrived at a crossroad, a place that is both promising and perilous, a juncture where the old and the new intermingle afresh. Our experience is old in the sense that we have been through massive crises before and we survived them; new, in the sense that each crisis involves adjustments that demand a great deal of versatility and creativity. At each such moment we encounter breakdown and breakthrough, the recurring paradoxical cycle of birth-death-rebirth. This time, too, we will have to die; otherwise, the breakthrough to the next evolutionary leap will not be possible.

Conditioned as we are by patriarchal norms of governance and commercialized lifestyles (what David Korten calls "the addictions of Empire"), we tend to measure everything in terms of our desire for control and management. But in a time of massive evolutionary change, many things are out of our control. Trust and not control is the great virtue needed by humanity today.

True to our deep mystical rootedness, we must risk all in order to free ourselves to flow with what is beckoning us forth. The regime of patriarchy has left us with few landmarks that are credible or trustworthy. We will create the necessary landmarks as we journey forth in risk and trust. It is reassuring to know that we have negotiated such transitions before, in fact many times in our long evolutionary history. The past is a valuable resource, providing guidance and illumination for the way ahead.

The future beckons forth. Are we free and creative enough to say the big "Yes" that echoes across our great history? If we are to honor the future as our graced ancestors honored the deep past we need to become daring visionaries with big vision:

- We need to think big and dream laterally.

- We need to flow with what is emerging now toward its fuller realization in the future life that God will make possible for us. Above all, we must not repeat patterns of behavior and ways of living that have outlived their usefulness.

- We need to trust the lure of the future to make all things new.

- We need to cultivate skills to keep us focused on what is unfolding now and for the future, messy and untidy though it will often be.

Beyond the Limits of Old

Two time boundaries are particularly significant for the culture of empire, first the two-thousand-year benchmark and, second, the time scale of the past five thousand years. Two thousand years ago marks the beginning of the Christian era. For a range of historical reasons this date has also become the benchmark for various features of global existence today. Even for the two-thirds of humanity who have never subscribed to Christian faith or culture, this time construct carries spatial, historical, and cultural significance. Although the Chinese people observe a different sense of historical time, in day-to-day interactions among themselves and for the purposes of international trade and commerce, the Chinese also follow the cultural dictates of the two-thousand-year timespan.

The five-thousand-year benchmark is a great deal more subtle but at a cultural level more influential than even the two-thousand-year mark. With the development of writing in the Sumerian culture and the initial construction of cities in the Middle East, so-called *modern civilization* comes into being. Today, every major text in every discipline traces the origins of civilization to approximately five thousand years ago. By implication, everything transpiring before that time, the elaborate and creative unfolding of ancestral grace over several million years, is all dismissed as uncivilized, primitive, barbaric, prelogical, etc. In the scholarly and academic worlds, research related to the pre-five-thousand-year time tends to be considered superficial, spurious, and unreliable.

The emphasis on the five-thousand-year limit is further reinforced by the development of classical Greek thought and the emphasis on logic and rationality. In the words of Thomas Berry: "Civilization was regarded as essentially a vast effort at liberating the human from the limitations of nature" (2006, 82). Before five thousand years ago, humans were deemed to be lacking in rationality, overidentified with nature and its processes. The ego had not matured into that fullness of humanity that postclassical Greek culture considered to be the defining feature of adult responsible people. And the "maturity" of everything else in creation was judged by the status of the human.

Enter Evolution

Evolutionary perspectives inform many disciplines in our time, or so it seems. When we look closer the impressive rhetoric provides a gloss beneath which evolutionary meaning is often stymied and suppressed. This is particularly so in patriarchal cultures, exhibiting an inordinate desire for order and control, focusing very much on the here and now, on the preservation and promotion of the empire. They embrace the recent past only to the extent that it reinforces the desire for dominance and control. Talk about life evolving, and particularly following processes beyond human interference and control, is intolerable for the patriarchal mind-set.

As the patriarchal culture of our time begins to decline and disintegrate, the desire and search for meaning requires us to reclaim larger contexts for emergence and unfolding. Evolution reenters the landscape. The horizons begin to stretch. Becoming — and not just being — demands our discerning attention.

It gradually begins to dawn on us that we have been living a stulti-fying existence in a stifling reductionism. The great story of creation spans several billion years, while the human story spans a time range of some 7 million years. And our expanded sense of research and knowledge confirms our suspicions that meaning is deeper and more ancient than the era of civilization or the Christian benchmark of the past two thousand years.

Human Emergence

For some 7 million years we have been unfolding as human crea-tures. The creative life force of God and creation has been with us throughout that entire time. We have been graced at every stage of the journey. As indicated in part 1, we got it right most of the time. We are not the flawed species propagated in the theories and doc-trines of formal religion. Certainly not perfect, but most definitely creative! And our creativity is the dimension that has not been duly acknowledged.

Faced with the demise of our current patriarchal scaffolding, we plunge deeper in our search for meaning. Ancestral grace has taught us to do that, and we have done it many times in our great story. Our current crisis may be the initial motivation for this perusal, but as we enter into the unfolding mystery we quickly realize that this is wisdom that needs to be reappropriated for its own innate value and not just as a resource to help us make sense of our current crisis.

We will continue to evolve: otherwise we become extinct. We don't and we can't control the direction of our evolutionary becoming, not simply because it is in the hands of a power greater than ourselves (the religious viewpoint), but because we always evolve in conjunction with the unfolding of other planetary and cosmic developments (co-evolution). Nothing in creation evolves in isolation. Everything co-evolves in a process governed and guided by the inherent wisdom of the evolutionary process (see Zimmer 2002, esp. 198ff.).

According to conventional scientific wisdom, the evolving pro-cess was best described by the great biologist Charles Darwin, who outlines three main dynamics: genetic mutation, conscious choice, and natural selection. The dimension that has attracted the greatest publicity and scholarly attention is that of *natural selection:* under evolutionary pressure, nature selects, adopting the strategy of favoring the strong and eliminating the weak. On the face of it, it looks very much like that, and quite understandably, patriarchal consciousness favors such a win-lose strategy.

Despite its commonsense veracity and its endorsement by scholars of various disciplines, the Darwinian approach has never been totally satisfying. It is not so much a case of its being wrong, but rather inadequate. It is too simplistic for a complex universe exhibiting an evolutionary process of birth-death-rebirth.[22] Darwin and his contemporary disciples provide a useful starting point. Even on a purely biological level many of his insights have had to be reworked thanks to the advances in modern genetics.

And new scientific breakthroughs in the concluding decades of the twentieth century have required an even deeper critique of the Darwinian synthesis. These have already been noted in part 1 and at this juncture require just a brief mention. First, and very much to the fore, is the dominant operational mode of cosmic and planetary life following the three principles identified by Swimme and Berry (1992) as differentiation, interiority (autopoiesis), and communion, or by Charles Jenks (in Rose and Rose 2000, 31) as nature, nurture, and self-organization. These ideas coalesce into the notion of *lifelines* as described vividly by Steven Rose:

> Lifelines then are not embedded in genes: their existence implies homeodynamics. Their four dimensions are autopoietically constructed through the interplay of physical forces, the intrinsic chemistry of lipids and proteins, the self-organizing and stabilizing properties of complex metabolic webs, and the specificity of genes which permit the elasticity of ontogeny. The organism is both the weaver and the pattern it weaves, the choreographer and the danced that is danced. (1997, 171)[23]

In a word, life at every level, including the human, is a complex, interactive, open-ended system, informationally guided from within (see Lipton 2005), and lured forth by larger sustaining life forces (explored in chapter 30 below).

Second, I once more draw the reader's attention to the pioneering work of Lynn Margulis (1998) on the theory of *symbiogenesis* (a concept originally developed by Konstantin Mereschkowsky in 1926), corroborated in the insightful analysis of the Australian scientist John Stewart (2000), and in the pioneering work of the American writer Michael Dowd (2007). These scholars highlight and seek to reclaim the primordial role of cooperation in the evolution of life. While numerous factors force us to question this perception — we see competition and conflict all around us — Margulis, Stewart, and Dowd alert us to our tendency to judge reality primarily by external, observable criteria, thus often missing the richly complex infrastructure, frequently revealing a very different scenario.

Co-creating the Future

There is no doubt about the fact that we humans have a future, and paradoxically a desired future is more likely to ensue when we abandon our rational efforts to a higher and wiser power. I am not referring to God or religion, although I appreciate that for many people, these come into the reckoning, and not always to our advantage (see Harris 2005). I am referring to the web of life in its full cosmic and planetary grandeur. Our future destiny is in the evolving wisdom of these larger organisms. The more we appropriate behaviors congruent with this embracing wisdom, the better our chances of living or dying with dignity.

Living or dying? Is the future as precarious as that? Most readers are likely to ask: Is it as futile and uncertain as that? This is not an easy discernment for those of us conditioned by patriarchal rationality. We have been indoctrinated into thinking that we are the superior species, with a resilience and longevity far in excess of any other being who shares the planet with us and, indeed, more enduring than the earth itself. That is the great delusion that feeds and sustains so much of our alienation.

As we evolve into the future that beckons us forth, these are some of the choices that will become inescapable:

1. *Continue as we are.* For a range of reasons, this is unlikely to be a viable option. The information explosion is catapulting us into being new creatures where mind-stuff is becoming more central to our experience than biological advancement. As Teilhard de Chardin intimated in the early part of the twentieth century, our biological evolution has reached a high point of development, beyond which we can't evolve much further. We are at a new evolutionary threshold. It is also unlikely that we will advance in the long term if we keep wrecking the material creation as we are currently doing, and that leads to a second option.

2. *Become extinct.* Grim and scary though this scenario may be, we do need to give it our focused attention. Already in the early 1960s, Rachel Carson predicted a precarious future for the human race, and the scientist Martin Rees (2004) has added his voice in recent times, giving us no more than a 50 percent chance of making it through. Most pessimistic of all is the declaration of Richard Leakey and Roger Lewin (1996) that we are in fact the Sixth Great Extinction, and we ourselves as the primary victims, metaphorically described by Peter Ward (1995) as an "asteroid." Obviously we won't choose to go extinct — *consciously!* But unknowingly, because of the way we are exploiting and damaging the sustaining web of life, already we may have opted for species suicide.

3. *Metamorphose into another species.* This is certainly an evolutionary option, one that is known in previous epochs of evolutionary becoming. It is not as common, however, as the birth-death-rebirth scenario, in which the prevailing species becomes largely or totally extinct. In most cases the significant breakthroughs of previous times were generated by species that seemed to be *totally* new. This is the discontinuity that academic scholars find so hard to fathom. It seems so wild and bizarre, totally baffling for human rationality. It is gratifying to see scholars like Neils Eldredge and the late Stephen J. Gould opting out

of their scholarly denial and attempting to befriend this disturbing fact; I am alluding to their theory of *punctuated equilibrium* (Eldredge and Gould 1972).

4. *Embrace transformation proactively.* This is the optimistic but unlikely scenario. It requires a massive conversion of humans, in which we let go of our power and domination and become the servant species to the great evolutionary story. It requires a spiritual revolution through which we opt to become co-creators with the creative Spirit of God, aligning our human desires and aspirations to those of the creative universe and ceasing to act in accordance with the perverse power games we have been playing over the past ten thousand years. This option will involve a good deal of suffering, but ultimately of a liberating type, a kind of dying in order to be reborn again.

Adapting to a New Way of Being

If the future is to be exciting and promising for us humans, it will be in our ability to engage and befriend the larger creation in its future growth and development. We must learn to co-evolve according to the dictates of a wisdom different from, and bigger than, ours. That is our surest path to salvation and new life.

As already indicated that requires a conversion far in excess of what any of the religions ask of us. And these are some of the dispositions that will help to make a difference:

+ Abandon our addiction to power and domination. Learn to be humble and reground ourselves in the clay from which we are beautifully formed.

+ Embrace the convivial web of life and rejoice in the interdependence that makes everything grow and flourish.

+ Learn the wisdom and skills to befriend complexity along with the chaos that inevitably ensues.

- Trust the great story of creation and the co-creative life force that births and sustains divine transformation; be vigilant for the lure of the future.

- Honor the dynamic of death in the grand scheme of things. Become hospice carers striving to ensure that everything dies gracefully and with dignity.

- Develop the skills of the midwife to facilitate the coming to birth of what evolution is bringing forth at this time.

- Cultivate a spirituality, big and inclusive enough to heal the terrible fragmentation of patriarchal times and embrace the rich diversity on which creation, and everything in it, thrives.

- Create networks (Tarlow 2002), fluid, creative, and flexible, to replace the permanently failing organizations (Meyer and Zucker 1989) that dominate the landscape of our time.

- Invest energy wisely in options more likely to augment new possibilities for the future rather than in maintaining institutions and structures that no longer serve the fullness of life (see Wheatley 1992; Phillips 2006).

- Develop a wholesome discipline imbued with a nourishing mixture of stillness and engagement in the work of justice.

Some readers are likely to react to the absence of the God word, while others may object to my inclusion of the notion of the divine. Others will be quick to label my list as typically "new age." Yes, I am attempting to describe something that is at once very new, and yet very old. Beyond all the differences and distinctions that are deemed so central to patriarchal ordering (and validated in nearly all formal religion), I want to highlight what unites us rather than what divides us; what we hold in common rather than what differentiates; what is primordial and enduring rather than fabricated and fragmentary.

In line with the American philosopher Jason Hill (2000), I want to transcend the reductionistic tribalism that has become so endemic and destructive to our culture. Or in more liberating spiritual terms, I want to endorse the nonduality so central to oriental mysticism (see Panikkar 1993). Nothing is lost within this synthesis, except the power that disempowers.

Finally, it is not so much a question of faith, and what we can believe in. In a world engulfed with anomie and despair, with a future often looking so grim and hopeless that we can't even talk about it, my desire is to awaken fresh hope so that people can begin to dream afresh, think bigger, pray laterally, and honor the promise of ancestral grace that has sustained us over so many millennia.

Chapter 25

Technology and the Protean Self

I would argue that contemporary concerns for the post/human are but the latest in an enduring fascination between humans and their own inventions, material and imaginary, and that the persistence of fantastic and monstrous creatures from earliest myth, religion and literature through to many forms of popular culture today testifies to the continuity of such enquiry into the implications of creative human endeavor. — ELAINE GRAHAM

A DETERIORATING STATE OF HEALTH was a vivid reminder to Jeremy that old age was catching up to him. It was a prospect he did not cherish. The conversation about pacemakers he found particularly disturbing — mechanical devices implanted in the chest to regulate heart beat. He was encountering a strangely unfamiliar world, one he could no longer take in his stride as he did in bygone days.

When Jeremy was first advised to have a pacemaker in 1985, he was none too happy and conjured up every conceivable argument to resist. What eventually persuaded him was the unreasonable risk he was taking with life and the prospect of an untimely death before reaching his seventieth birthday.

Jeremy died in 2002 at the ripe age of eighty-six years — which brings us to an interesting philosophical dilemma: If Jeremy had followed "the course of nature" and had not chosen the pacemaker, he may have died much sooner; someone of a religious persuasion might suggest that he would have died in accordance with God's plan for him. In choosing the pacemaker, therefore, he actually extended his life span, thanks to modern medical technology. In this case, are humans in danger of playing God?

175

In this scenario, the pacemaker radically altered the course of Jeremy's life. In a sense, it became an integral dimension of his evolving identity. Not only did it prolong his life, but it contributed to all the other experiences that molded and formed his character right up to the time of his death. In a sense, he became a type of new person, thanks to the introduction of a technical device that altered his life history. This is what contemporary scholars call the "posthuman," for which others have adopted the notion of the "cyborg."[24]

Mechanizing the Human

Over the past four hundred years, the mechanization of life has been a major preoccupation for humans, particularly for scientists. Technologically, it has advanced our capacity to live more creatively and productively, and in the richer countries we enjoy the immense benefits of this achievement. It also has a dark side, becoming even more ominous in our time.

Only the rich and powerful nations really benefit from this accomplishment, one that is often accompanied by violence, exploitation, poor work satisfaction, commodification, and perhaps most disturbing of all the use of technology to kill and maim human life as well as to pollute and exploit our planetary home. Arguably, the shift to mechanization was to relieve human labor of drudgery and make more space for recreation and joy. There is little evidence of that outcome, even in the richer parts of planet earth.

With the evolution of computerization in the latter half of the twentieth century, the focus shifted to the possible mechanization of the human brain itself. With machines far outpacing human computational skills, people began to wonder if one day the machine would take over from the human brain. The search for artificial intelligence (AI) was launched. The love affair with the machine took on a new significance, one that to many felt scary and dangerous.

Almost on a daily basis we get glimpses into a rapidly approaching future in which many daily experiences will be governed by the world of virtual reality. Visionaries like Michio Kaku (1998), Jaron Lanier (2005), and Terence McKenna (1999) highlight future modes of engagement with our living world. Even our modes of communication are likely to change significantly (Humphreys and Messaris 2006; Tarlow 2002).

Artificial Intelligence (AI)

The notion that the intelligence created through computerized technology might catch up with, and even outpace, human intelligence has been the subject of intense study in recent decades. As computers have become more effective for speed and performance, we can see their ability to achieve computational skills far in excess of human intelligence. Moreover, we know that the neural activity in our brains is devoted mainly to maintaining life-support functions rather than processing information. In the information explosion of recent decades the intelligence generated by our computers has outpaced human ability on various levels.

Scholars continue to evolve more refined and sophisticated capacities for our information machines. Kurzweil (2005, 266ff.) outlines some of the processes being employed: more expert systems to simulate the human capacity for decision-making, Bayesian nets, Markov models, neural nets, genetic algorithms, and the development of computer programs using recursive searching. As human intelligence advances the capabilities of machines, ironically the machines themselves adopt behaviors one time considered to be unique to human intelligence.

AI began to develop after World War II with the British mathematician Alan Turing, deemed to be one of the pioneering geniuses. The dream and hope that these intelligent machines would catch up with humans is far from realized and is now considered an unlikely achievement. While computers are able to exceed humans considerably in terms of computational skills, humans adopt other capacities, e.g., emotion, imagination, intuition, etc., in behavior and decision-making, which put humans in a different league from the achievements of intelligent machines. AI is not really a threat to human integrity, but the prospect of humans themselves being mechanically programmed is an issue of enormous import for our time.

Altering Human Behavior

This is the topic explored by the inventor and futurist Ray Kurzweil in his mammoth work *The Singularity Is Near* (2005). Kurzweil reviews not just how machines might develop brains, but far more importantly how the intelligence of machines can be used to evoke unprecedented potentials in the human brain. Reprogramming of human intelligence for the future is now at the cutting edge of science and technology.

In this process *nanobots* will be crucial. These are microchips that are invisible to the human eye, potentially capable of carrying massive quantities of information. They can be inserted into many different organisms, much like a pacemaker can be inserted to help regulate the human heart.

Nanobots, for example, can be inserted into the neurons of the human brain, thus modifying significantly the way humans act, think, and generally behave. Kurzweil claims that the strategy to do so is already well advanced, and he prognosticates that it will be an approved procedure by the year 2045 CE. At that stage — midway through the present century — reprogrammed humans will surpass the conventional wisdom *Homo sapiens* has known for over a hundred thousand years. We will be into a new, exciting, and dangerous world!

Posthuman, Protean, or Transhuman?

This new type of human being is currently being described as the "posthuman," the subject of numerous books in recent years (see Badmington 2000; Graham 2002; Hayles 1999; Kaku 1998). All these authors acknowledge the risks and dangers that lie ahead, particularly if these new possibilities end up in the wrong hands. Nonetheless, all agree that such developments are inevitable and moreover are congruent with the evolutionary dynamics we have known throughout the ages. Hybrids, cybernetic fusions, emergent relations, blurred boundaries, partnerships of unlikely allies, feature in every major wave of evolutionary unfolding and in hindsight tend to be to the advantage of newly emerging species.

Related to these reflections is the concept of *the protean self,* popularized by the American psychiatrist Robert J. Lifton (1999), although widely in vogue since the 1970s (see Becker 1971; Kennedy 1974). Instead of a clear-cut fixed identity, a type of multiple personality characterizes many people in our time, with the added ability to morph into a range of differing identities as complex demands arise. A sense of fluidity and flexibility characterizes the protean personality, illustrated vividly in the dexterity of eye and hand with which teenagers play computer games.

It is not so much a case of developing new skills to cope with the rapidly changing environment. Rather the evolving environment is evoking new potentialities, redefining the very essence of what it means to be human. This is co-evolution at work, evoking the wisdom and skill needed to engage the emerging breakthroughs. Although I do not fully agree with Tarlow (2002, x, 235ff.) that this effort is "human-driven," it certainly is not a case of humans being totally at the mercy of forces over which they have no control. Paradoxically, humans are cooperating with the dynamics of this new emergence, because under the guiding wisdom of ancestral grace that is what we have consistently done through the long aeons of evolutionary change.

Evolution carries an innate wisdom that the human psyche knows all too well. Unfortunately, the major institutions of our patriarchal era are not well aligned with that wisdom. The addiction toward control seriously gets in the way. Instead, therefore, of supporting what is emerging, most major institutions of our time extensively denounce and resist the protean outlook.[25] Cornel du Toit (du Toit and Mayson 2006, 49–73) of the Research Institute for Theology and Religion in Pretoria, South Africa, makes a compelling case for the liberating potential of contemporary technology, which assumes attributes analogous to those of omnipresence, omnipotence, omniscience and eternal life, which were once ascribed exclusively to God's incommunicable attributes. While many fear the onset of a new atheism, du Toit envisages a purification of oppressive religiosity, with humans reclaiming a new and creative spirituality that will enhance

rather than diminish authentic faith. This strange new partnership —
religion and technology — is one of several hybrids that characterize our new evolutionary moment. The prevalence and frequency of
such hybrid moments and their evolutionary potential is captured by
Elaine Graham when she notes:

> Human beings have always co-evolved with their environments,
> tools and technologies. By that I mean that to be human is al-
> ready to be in a web of relationships, where our humanity can
> only be articulated — realized — in and through our environ-
> ment, our tools, our artifacts, and the networks of human and
> non-human life around us. It also means that we do not need
> to be afraid of our complicity with technologies or fear our hy-
> bridity or assume that proper knowledge of and access to God
> can only come through a withdrawal from these activities of
> world-building. (Graham 2004, 25)

This is virgin territory for theology and spirituality. Following the
line of enquiry adopted by Ilia Delio (2003; 2008), technology in our
time serves as a primary means for organizing knowledge, thus ad-
vancing the evolutionary complexity we evidence today. In a word,
all indications are that this movement is of God and not the fruit of
some deviant or demonic force. It is a brave new world that theologians have scarcely begun to explore (see also Hefner 2003; Jackelen
2002).

Transpersonal Wisdom

If we could access the mood of humans in ancient times, we would
probably encounter reactions to rapid and drastic change very similar
to our reactions today. Incredulity in the face of change, moral denunciation of its unfolding, procrastinations for future generations, and
strong resistance to the change-shifters would have been widespread.
Yet in all such cases, or certainly in most, hindsight indicates that
the culture shifts were, first, necessary; second, timely and beneficial;
and, finally, crucial to the course of evolution's future.

Instead, therefore, of the term "posthuman," bedeviled by dualistic distinctions between the good past and the less-good future, I would favor the notion of "transhuman" (as used by Julian Huxley in 1957), describing humans in the throes of evolutionary transformation, challenged to outgrow a cherished, and possibly still useful, past, and invited to embrace a strange and risky future for which there may be little or no precedent.

Just as the concept of the "transpersonal" (see p. 100 above) revolutionizes our understanding of personhood, so the notions of the "transhuman" or the "protean" can be eminently appropriate for this new evolutionary moment. In former times we adopted the notion of the person as an autonomous entity above and beyond all other organisms, an inherited Aristotelian view heavily endorsed by patriarchy, Western colonialism, and modern economics. Increasingly we favor an understanding in which authentic personhood can be realized only through interdependent relationships with all other life forms, earth and cosmos included.

Concepts like the "transpersonal," the "transhuman," the "protean" encourage us to move beyond our dogmatic imperial personalism that veers toward domination, exploitation, violence, and the exploitation of everything else in creation for our use and benefit. Most challenging of all, the idea of the protean transhuman invites us to reconsider the possible virtues of our mechanized world and to work more diligently for a discourse with technology that involves greater scientific accountability, political transparency, and interdisciplinary dialogue to elaborate an informed ethical code to ensure that such future developments are used in creative and responsible ways.

The Shadow Side

Undoubtedly, the great fear is that the mastery of these new skills and the control of the technology making them possible will end up in the wrong hands, with outcomes that could reap untold havoc for humanity as well as for other organisms inhabiting planet earth. The breakthrough could easily become a nightmare. Many of us are only too well aware of the destructive desires of those who release worms, viruses, and other lethal mechanisms into the communication networks; this is small stuff compared to deliberately infecting the workings of the human brain.

Obviously we look to our respective *governments* to put ethical and protective measures in place, knowing all too well that much of this new information and power transcends the control of national jurisdictions. In our globalized world, corporations often outwit nation states (individually and collectively), thus leaving ordinary citizens at the mercy of dangerous and destructive forces. Will governments be capable of meeting this challenge? Dare I suggest that it depends as much on us, ordinary citizens, as it does on our respective governments and legislators.

Those who govern us, and the values they adopt, tend to reflect the consciousness of the masses. We tend to get the governments we deserve. The consciousness required for a more creative and constructive future is a joint cultural responsibility. It calls on all of us to become more aware and informed, more astute and enlightened. I am not alluding to more intellectual competence, valuable though that will be. What will be needed more than anything else is an attitudinal shift and expansion of consciousness that will sensitize us all to the momentous breakthroughs of this evolutionary moment.

Conclusion

For over thirty years, I have publicly supported Teilhard's suggestion that our species is on the brink of a new evolutionary breakthrough. Consistently, I have regarded the information explosion as a major component of this breakthrough. I see two processes that now need to coalesce to see the whole thing through:

1. a technological dimension of the type Kurzweil describes, which will make us not automatons but rather creatures imbued with new protean wisdom thanks to the contribution that intelligent machines can make to our evolutionary unfolding (see also Gardner 2007);

2. a mystical dimension, empowering us to discern and discriminate between wisdom that will enhance growth and flourishing as distinct from that which could wreak untold havoc on our species and the earth itself. Kurzweil makes no illusion to this second dimension, and this I regard as the major weakness of an otherwise timely and impressive work.

Despite all the negative press and the havoc that has been wreaked on our planetary home, the technological breakthroughs of the recent past and the present time are not alien to our evolutionary growth. They too can be seen as a dimension of ancestral grace, with precedents in our prehistoric past. How to use the technology in a wise and informed way is the great challenge of this time, one that engages every citizen of every country on earth. This is a quantum leap that must not be left in the hands of the governing few with the majority acting as passive onlookers. A concerted effort involving all humanity is necessary to produce a wholesome outcome.

Chapter 26

Toward Bioregional Networking

Every few hundred years in Western history there occurs a sharp transformation. Within a few short decades, society — its world-view, its basic values, its social and political structures, its arts, its key institutions — rearranges itself, and the people born then cannot even imagine a world in which their grandparents lived and into which their own parents were born. We are currently living through such a transformation. — PETER DRUCKER

ON JANUARY 30, 2005, the people of Iraq went to the polls to elect their first democratic government in over half a century. Similar to what happened in South Africa in April 2004 after the end of apartheid, we witnessed long queues at polling booths and people relishing this moment with joy and enthusiasm. Both events were hailed as a triumph for freedom and justice, ushering in a new dawn for people held for far too long under the yoke of oppression.

The tragic events that followed in Iraq highlighted how premature the euphoria was. Even some began to wonder if things were not actually better under the regime of Saddam Hussein. The new, so-called democratic dispensation, backed by the United States and Britain, seemed largely powerless in the face of the forces of violence and destruction. Declaring Iraq to be a democratic country, exercising democratic governance was one thing; translating that into the daily reality of such a complex culture was a much more formidable task.

The Dwindling Nation State

The dismal failure of democratic governance in Iraq vividly illustrates the limits of so-called democracy across the modern world. Basically

184

democracy is a functional political and economic arrangement designed to uphold and promote a patriarchal dispensation. Central to this arrangement is the institution of the nation state. Conceptualized initially by Aristotle, the nation state was first recognized as a formal structure of political governance at the peace of Westphalia in 1648. Most nation states have resulted from violence, the conquered territories of victors, in the cruel war for dominance and control.

Many African countries became nation states only in the 1950s and 1960s, while the subsections of the USSR appropriated this status only in the 1990s. Some countries, e.g., Israel, claim that the nation state is a direct endowment from God and by implication needs to be managed as the ruling patriarchal God governs and controls the rest of creation. The truth, however, is that the nation state is a very recent phenomenon, one with numerous dysfunctional ingredients, a strategy for governance that neither empowers nor liberates people. (For a more comprehensive critique, see Berry 2006, 75–86.)

In the globalized culture of modern times, the nation state has lost a great deal of its credibility and meaning. Today, it is *transnational corporations* that rule the world, not individual states. An oft-quoted statistic leaves little doubt about where the real power rests: in the year 2000 CE, of the hundred richest economies on earth, fifty-two were corporations (forty-eight were nation states), which controlled far more wealth than most individual countries. The McDonald's food chain has a larger annual budget than any country in Africa, with the possible exception of South Africa. Moreover, when corporations patent an acquired product or set a copyright on a commodity, e.g., vanilla from Madagascar, they do so with the full approval of the World Trade Organization (WTO) and consequently do not have to obtain permission from their own country nor the country from which they have literally robbed the raw material. In this scenario, individual countries have little or no power over their own destiny and their own resources.

And where does that leave humans as citizens of individual countries? Much more disenfranchised than we actually think! Some fifty patents have been taken out on indigenous peoples around the world, using human tissue and blood. The distribution of goods on international markets leaves many of us in the dark regarding the circumstances in which goods are produced and marketed. Fortunately, as more people become aware of the exploitation and injustices of employees in poorer countries, corporations are being forced into taking action. It is noteworthy that this is happening thanks, not to national initiatives, but to international agencies seeking justice for oppressed peoples. Once again, all we see on the part of the nation state is grim failure.

Politically, we live at a time when people feel disenfranchised, apathy is widespread, and cynicism abounds. The nation state has lost virtually all semblance of just and empowering governance. It retains a measure of credibility thanks to a few countries — United States, Great Britain, India, Brazil, China — that still claim to act as nation states but in effect behave like superpowers, backed by trade arrangements that favor their superiority.

In these countries, every few years people vote governments into power but really have little or no say about what happens in the intervening periods. The major decisions affecting people's lives will not be made from within these "superpowers" with people's interests at stake. They will be dictated by international market forces (controlled by corporations), and those in governance have become very adept at convincing the gullible electorate that the decisions are coming from within a country when in fact they are totally dictated by forces from outside. In the UK it is called political spin; in truth it should be called a pack of lies!

The reader will have noticed, I expect, that money and political gerrymandering have become totally intertwined. Money is primarily in the hands of corporations who shift massive sums across the planet on a daily basis, to evade tax and increase profitability.

Beyond the Nation State

The nation state has outlived its usefulness. Evolution is calling forth something quite different in our time. In fact for several years now, theorists have been considering alternative political and financial structures, ones much closer to the people on the ground, ones that are ecologically sustainable and humanly empowering. The wisdom is already in place; what is still lacking is the mobilization of consciousness necessary to make the paradigm shift.

What is being called forth at this time? Basically a set of structures that will be more *organic* (honoring the aliveness of everything in creation), *holarchical* (supporting the relational web of life), *collaborative* (endorsing cooperation rather than competition), and *empowering* (calling forth the mutual giftedness of all creatures). This requires of humanity a closer convivial connection with the living earth itself, the type of relationship that has graced and sustained us over previous millennia. At a local level this will be better served by the *bioregion* than by something akin to the nation state.

"Bioregionalism" suggests other ways of envisaging regional variation within the one earth, a construct small enough to facilitate familiarity and complex enough to honor diversity. The roots of bioregionalism go back to the 1930s when Frederic Clements and Victor Shelford developed the biome system of classification. *Biomes* refer to natural habitats such as grasslands, deserts, rainforests, and coniferous forests shaped by climate. Particular soils, vegetation, and animal life have developed in each climate region in accordance with rainfall, temperature, and weather patterns.

The bioregion may be described as both a geographical terrain and a terrain of consciousness. It is a new and different way of conceptualizing the human relationship with the earth and its resources. We invoke an alternative mode of relating based on a new way of thinking, facilitating a rehabilitation of genuine human desire. Kirkpatrick Sale (1991, 50ff.) identifies four central features of this new orientation:

Scale: Global socio-economic abstractions and intangibles give way to the here and now, the seen and the felt, the real and the known.

Economy: The cycle of production and exchange is determined primarily by the quality and quantity of local resources.

Polity: "A bioregional polity would seek the diffusion of power, the decentralization of institutions, with nothing done at a higher level than necessary, and all authority flowing upward incrementally from the smallest political unit to the largest." (Sale 1991, 94)

Society: Models of governance follow cellular principles in which families operate within neighborhoods, neighborhoods within communities, communities within cities, etc. Cooperation rather than competition, collaboration rather than conflicting interests, become the guiding norms. (See O'Murchu 2007.)

Global Governance

"Think globally, act locally" became an inspiring slogan during the closing decades of the twentieth century. Globalization also flourished, especially in trade and commerce, and despite its many negative features, outlined above, it needs to be viewed as a movement right for its time, the fuller maturation of the global village envisaged by Marshall McLuhan and others in the 1960s. The global consciousness that characterizes life today is here to stay. The tribalistic enclosure of individual nations, religions, tribes, and ideologies is breaking apart, causing widespread dislocation, much confusion, and violent reaction in many parts of our troubled world. Beyond all the impressive rhetoric of a new world order, disorder and chaos rule the roost at the present time. A new global strategy is urgently needed.

Along with a new political entity to facilitate empowering governance at the local level, namely, the bioregion, we also need a global structure to guide the global emergence that has become so rapid and complex in recent decades. Intuitively, we in the human community foresaw this development, and I suspect this was the deep subconscious rationale that led to the creation of the United Nations in the wake of World War II. We knew that we would shortly need a mechanism for global governance to engage more creatively with our emerging globalized world.

For some years now the UN itself has struggled to honor its own deep vision. Ironically, but not surprisingly, it is the central place attributed to nation states in the power structure of the UN that has seriously undermined its vision and potential. The UN is held for ransom precisely because of the ideology of the nation state. Over the years, that translated into the world's superpowers, namely, the United States and the USSR, dominating and controlling every initiative coming from the UN. Today, the United States is the major force of negative interference, with a whip hand holding the financial resources needed to keep the UN in being.

Despite the stranglehold of major nation powers, the UN has honored much of its founding vision, advocating the networking dynamic for much of the late twentieth century. Central to this strategy is the notion of the *nongovernmental organization* (NGO). NGOs have enjoyed major achievements in local initiatives, empowering those committed to more sustainable and just ways of living. Many NGOs have been subverted by national governments that readily foresaw their empowering potential and felt threatened by it. And within this subversion, many of the great achievements of NGOs have never obtained the publicity they deserve.

The NGO fosters a culture of networking, the desired alternative to the top-heavy bureaucracy that disempowers people and robs individual countries of much-needed financial resources. Applying the networking philosophy to work and money we note two imaginative proposals, likely to feature strongly when bioregional governance comes to the fore. The first relates to alternative economic models and the second to an alternative work ethic.

Bernard Lietaer (2001) provides a comprehensive overview of a range of alternative economic strategies that have been tried and tested in various countries across the world. He offers a number of inspiring examples in which complementary currencies operate. Not only are these empowering for people in a range of local circumstances but they also provide timely alternatives to a global economy becoming more jittery, unstable, and unreliable in the face of growing global instability.

Closely related is the notion of an alternative work ethic to supersede the destructive impact of equating the earning of money with the human need (and right) to work. For some years now, social activists and economists have been exploring alternative models. Among these, perhaps, the most imaginative and revolutionary is the notion of separating work from the living wage, requiring the nation state to pay a basic wage to every citizen over the age of eighteen. This notion sounds so idealistic and far-fetched that many people dismiss it before considering its radical ramifications. Contrary to popular expectation, research conclusively shows that this strategy would save Western nations millions of dollars annually. Bureaucratically, it is a relatively simple process to administer, and therefore enables a government to reduce significantly the top-heavy administrative machinery needed for the current system. In greater detail the scheme goes like this:

- Every citizen over the age of eighteen is paid a basic wage that guarantees a good quality of life in terms of access to basic needs, education, health-care, etc.

- Those in formal employment pay taxes to the tune of at least 60 percent, but they also obtain the basic wage.

- Voluntary work, rather than paid employment, becomes the norm, as all citizens are challenged — primarily through a revamped educational system — to contribute to the welfare of life environmentally, culturally, and personally.

Class distinctions would break down. Poverty would be eliminated in time. Unemployment, and its terrible stigma, would cease. People would learn to take pride in their achievements and would be happier in themselves. A much more harmonious culture would ensue, where needs and desires are met in a more responsible way.[26]

Would the system work? Researchers acknowledge that it would require an enormous amount of good will and huge numbers to transcend the greed and acquisitiveness that drives the current system.

That, in turn, would depend on the quality and quantity of education to make the perceptual and attitudinal shift without which the change is unlikely to happen.

When the Time Is Ripe...

It is all too easy to mount criticism of this visionary resolution and all too easy to dismiss it in a sinister and cynical way. *But evolution itself may resolve the dilemma for us.* As the prevailing model of a job-for-life — that is, work related to wage-earning — breaks down, we will be forced to look at alternatives, and patching up the existing system is unlikely to provide creative resolutions.

This is a paradigm shift with all the trauma and utopia that such transitions entail. The new reality will be different from the old, so new in fact as to be virtually unrecognizable — exactly what the philosopher Alfred N. Whitehead had in mind when he wrote: "It is the business of the future to be dangerous.... The major advances in civilization are processes that all but wreck the societies in which they occur."

As indicated by historical analysts like Michael Mann (1986) and Roland Wright (2004), our current civilization is proving to be more and more of a "trap" and a "cage" for growing sectors of the human population. The cultural model of *civilization* that has served us for the past five thousand years (more accurately for the past eight thousand years) is postulated primarily on imperial power. It still holds reality together for those that have the power, but for the millions that don't, cynicism, disillusionment, and alienation are heading for epidemic proportions. And the unprecedented violence of recent decades is just one of the deeply disturbing consequences.

The culture of civilized imperialism tried to convince us that ultimately humans are in charge of creation, and in the last analysis we alone can determine creation's desired outcomes. Intuitively most humans know otherwise, but the indoctrination of civilized imperialism inhibits people from honoring their deeper aspirations, often leaving people too scared to think and dream alternatives. *Our long historical story indicates that the alternatives will mature when the consciousness is ready to receive them!* Ultimately this is our enduring hope. The evolutionary goals of life win out in the end, thanks to the power of ancestral grace that always has guided the process of evolutionary emergence.

The death throes of our time are manifest particularly in what is transpiring within our major social, religious, political, and economic institutions. With greater rapidity and frequency they are becoming "permanently failing organizations" (Meyer and Zucker 1989), what another specialist calls "epics of entropy" (Maier 2006, 76), increasingly failing to deliver on anything of significance for humanity or the suffering earth itself. And from within the chaotic landscape we see emerging a new set of structures, *networks,* a revival of the NGO concept proposed by the United Nations in the mid-twentieth century. The networking concept honors the bioregional dynamic, small and fluid, flexible and creative, empowering for people and planet alike (see also Hawken 2007).

But the major institutions will neither entertain nor accept the concept. As has happened frequently throughout the twentieth century, the NGOs have been subverted or co-opted. Governments fueled by civilized imperialism read the threat, but probably not in its full truth. The network is not just an adjunct for the major institution; *it is an alternative to it!* The structural alternatives are already well known and briefly highlighted in this chapter.

What is needed is greater coherence in the collective consciousness to bring the new structures to the fore. I suspect the old order has not yet bottomed out sufficiently for this new endeavor to come to maturity. Hopefully, as more people become aware of the axial moment of peril and promise in which we are living, we will mobilize the creative consciousness to beget an alternative future.

Chapter 27

Embracing the Adult

We must consciously will the further stages of evolutionary process. While we were unknowingly carried through the evolutionary process in former centuries, the time has come in which we must in some sense guide and energize the process ourselves.

— THOMAS BERRY

THE SCIENTIFIC LITERATURE indicates that throughout prehistoric times, our ancient ancestors were of small stature, with males consistently more robust than females. Popular depictions tend to reveal hobbit-like or pygmy-type creatures. The Neanderthals are considered to be the first humans closely representing present-day peoples in size and stature, giving Europeans another cultural edge over the other inhabitants with whom we share the planet.

Size is only one among a number of factors whereby we deduce that our ancient ancestors were not really adult, in the normal sense of the word. We presume they were not as intelligent and rational as we are, nor would they have been industrious like modern working people. Their dependency on nature for basic survival tends to be interpreted as parallel to the kind of dependency on parents exhibited by children. That our ancestors were more childlike than adult then became a perception that remains largely unexamined to the present time.

For the patriarchal culture of the postagricultural era, dealing creatively with the adult is problematic on several levels. With the strong emphasis on obedience to higher authority, class distinctions flourished, particularly in terms of rulers and those over whom they ruled: masters and slaves, lords and servants, those who gave orders and those who were expected to obey them. Hierarchical structure and patriarchal governance invokes a quality of co-dependency that makes adult relating difficult and problematic.

The Adult in Creation

Hierarchy also disconnects the person from the relational matrix of the wider creation. It begets an anthropocentric view in which humans alone are of ultimate importance. The close connection with nature that has nourished and sustained us over many millennia is ignored and dismissed.

It is widely assumed that prior to a few thousand years ago we humans were so immersed in nature that we were unable to distance ourselves to appropriate the distinctiveness of being truly human. Why did we have to differentiate in order to become more fully human? The answer is in fact quite simple: the dominant patriarchal consciousness required us to differentiate so that we could dominate and control everything in the material, objective universe. This is the great delusion of patriarchal consciousness.

As we learn to understand afresh the deeper meaning of the creation that surrounds us, we are also confronted with the alienation we have incurred because of our ignorance and arrogance. Our deep immersion in creation did not deprive us of being adult. It both allowed and empowered us to be adult in a more integrated way. Long before the Lone Ranger became our primary model, we knew ourselves as relational beings who became our fuller selves through the quality of our relating: with nature, with other creatures, with the enveloping mystery, and with each other.

Assuredly we did not always get it right, nor do integrated adults feel a compulsive need to get it right consistently. The adult in the true sense of the word can live with limitations and failures, one's own and those of others. This is a quality of grace that comes from being close to creation and to the natural order. It is also important to assert once more: *we did get it right most of the time,* precisely because we remained closely aligned to the gift of ancestral grace.

The Adult and the Inner Child

Moore and Gillette (1990) make a profound and disturbing observation on the widespread failure to integrate the inner child in cultures where the values of patriarchy tend to dominate. In such cultures, even talk of the inner child is dismissed as childish. From a young age, males are catapulted into being brave and productive; females are expected to know their place as childbearers and homemakers. The hero in such a culture is the one who makes it to the top — consistently a male.

According to Moore and Gillette, such high achievers tend to be men who have not integrated their inner child. They are distinctly uncomfortable with the inner child and subconsciously project this discomfort. Ironically, they do so by requiring others to behave and act like children, because such men cannot tolerate adults around them. Because the inner child has not been integrated, neither has mature adulthood been achieved. Their fear of the external adult is in fact a lack of an internal sense of being adult themselves.

The inner child is an archetype of playfulness and spontaneity. It is much easier to realize this archetype in a natural environment where people playfully engage with nature's creativity, and their lives are often directed by seasonal flow and rhythm. In such an environment, the type most familiar to us throughout the long aeons of our evolution, the inner child stands a much better chance of maturing, bringing with it the accompanying propensity to awaken a more integrated sense of adulthood.

Much of the addictive behavior that characterizes life today, especially in our Western cultures, arises from a deep sense of frustration for not achieving the basic fulfillment of one's humanity. Intuitively we know something is amiss, and we feel the deep chasm of this longing. Compensations abound: shopping, lurid entertainment, drugs, gambling, etc. And in a culture compulsively addicted to quick solutions, we seek to resolve our alienations with an immediacy and wholeness that are in conflict with the developmental dynamics of healthy human growth. We expect in an instant what needs time and takes time.

Paradoxically, the increase in addictions is in fact a cry for recognition, a hunger to become what life desires us all to become, adult people who can take our place and play our role as proactive architects of a better world, the challenge expressed in the opening quotation from Thomas Berry (2000). Few today achieve this goal with a worthwhile sense of joy or achievement. Forces are stacked against us, the very ones we ourselves have invented in our highly functional "un-natural" way of living. It is a way of being human that is proving to be highly destructive. A new orientation is urgently needed.

Beyond the Preoccupation with the Child

The needs of the child hold a central place in all modern societies. We think of education primarily in terms of children and young people. Adults are considered to be fully formed persons, whereas youth are still growing and developing. Developmental psychology adumbrates at great length the various life stages through which we all need to negotiate our growth in maturity, yet the insights are rarely applied to the adult population and their respective needs.[27] While some opportunities are provided in professional training, the development of the whole person is grossly neglected, especially among adults.

And yet there is a growing awareness of the need for educational strategies and programs that honor and foster adult development. Many third-level institutes seek to promote adult learning; finance and funding seem to be a continual source of frustration. Lifelong learning through personal initiative has increased enormously in the past twenty years, thanks particularly to the opportunities provided by the World Wide Web. More information is more readily available, more widely accessible. The distinction between the few who, one time, had access to information and the many who had not is rapidly breaking down.

As indicated in chapter 25, the information explosion more than anything else has changed human perception and understanding. With more information circulating, human curiosity is heightened. As people become more aware they also tend to become more empowered. And more seize the opportunity for self-empowerment. Paradoxically, the outcome is not merely the widely publicized entrepreneurial economic hit-man, but the evolution of a new wave of cooperative endeavor brilliantly described by Tarlow (2002) as a new tribal myth with many features of classical aboriginal culture. The adult-as-adult begins to come into its own. Adult learning becomes a science requiring its own opus operandi.

Being Adult for the Future

In a previous work (O'Murchu 2007, 133–36), I outlined some of the principles being adopted by institutions and agencies seeking to promote adult learning. What is probably most revolutionary in this approach is the radical sense of equality being embraced and endorsed: both teacher and student are jointly responsible for the task of learning. The hierarchical privilege of the teacher, the one who has information or knowledge to impart, is no longer seen as useful or relevant. Even where there is an "expert" with information to impart, in the sphere of adult learning the method of communication adopted is that of mutual relating of adult to adult.

Utilizing life experience as an integral dimension of learning is a central challenge of the adult approach. The adult will spontaneously relate all new information to this experience. When the experience is illuminated, endorsed, or challenged, then the motivation for learning is enhanced enormously.

In the co-learning relationship, both the quality and quantity of information will need to be congruent to the needs and expectations of the recipient. How wisdom is applied to concrete life circumstances is central to adult learning. Theoretical considerations are relevant, but in adult learning greater effort is employed to root theory in practice.

Empowerment is meant to be the goal of all education, but in adult learning it tends to become much more focused. This may involve some painful moments, requiring one to unlearn patterns of knowledge or behaviors that are now seen to be inappropriate or codependent. The more informed adult, as adult, will also seek greater mutual participation in all life projects, a desire open to conflict and misunderstanding when others are not bringing that same quality of development to life situations. Such maturity and adult self-reliance are still considered deviant and even dangerous in many institutional settings.

Learning and Transformation

Edmund O'Sullivan (2002) describes the new adult-centered education as a process of *transformative learning*. It is not just about learning in a new way; it is much more akin to a conversion experience of embracing larger horizons of understanding which, in turn, activate a shift in consciousness. In our time this will frequently involve a reclaiming of our essential identity as cosmic and planetary beings, called to a convivial sharing of earth's resources with all the other creatures with whom we share the home planet.

Ecologically we will find ourselves called to live in much more organic and sustainable ways, with a keener realization that our treatment of the earth is in direct correlation with how we treat ourselves and all those we hold dear in the web of life. Daily interactions, with the food we eat, the air we breathe, the soil we cultivate, the waste we recycle, all take on added meaning as expressions of how we feel called to relate in more caring and responsible ways.

Transformative learning is innately spiritual, without necessarily being religious in a formal sense of the word. For growing numbers of people this spiritual awakening is foundationally cosmic and planetary, as illustrated vividly by Primack and Abrams (2006). The God of formal religion is regarded as small, functional, sectarian, excessively anthropocentric, and the basis for much of the irrational violence in today's world; see the informed critique of Harris (2005).

The awakening spirituality is much more globally focused, mystically inspired, and justice orientated.[28] It baffles and confuses many people in formal churches or religious systems. The vision is too big for institutional contextualization. What kind of cultural containers it will eventually adopt is a challenge for spiritual seekers of the future, rather than for mainline churches or religions.

This is fertile territory for adult dialogue, a mutual enterprise for which neither side is probably yet ready. The spiritual seekers themselves have not yet created a cohesive critical threshold from which they can articulate with clarity and conviction what they are about. Those from the churches and religions are petrified by what they are likely to lose and opt to blame others rather than seek to dialogue with them.

Transformative adult learning thrives on one central set of values, namely, *a countercultural, cosmic-planetary network for cooperative flourishing.* In this bold cosmic vision we seek to honor the primacy of the cosmic creation as God's primary revelation to us and as the primordial source sustaining and nourishing everything in being. The cosmic-planetary ecosystem thrives on cooperation, not on competition. It is in co-evolving as interdependent creatures, supported by more organic systems and processes, politically, economically, socially, and religiously that we humans will realize our fullest potential. Ambitious though this dream might be, it is probably the only one that will see humanity through our next evolutionary leap.

As adult people we seem to have little choice other than to think big, imaginatively, and courageously. And the ensuing consciousness will also require us to act differently — this time in a way much more likely to honor the time-honored imperatives of ancestral grace.

Chapter 28

Learning to Relate Laterally

One can discern in evolution a repeating pattern in which aggressive competition leads to the threat of extinction, which is often avoided by the formation of cooperative alliances.

— ELIZABET SAHTOURIS

C ONTEMPORARY PHILOSOPHERS struggle between the sense of personal autonomy deemed to be normative for our Western lifestyle and the various voices of our age suggesting that more relational ways of being are more congenial to growth and development. The Jamaican-American philosopher Jason Hill (2000) states it in much more provocative terms. He claims that our Western conditioning has enslaved us all to various forms of *tribalism:* around religion, ethnicity, nationhood. We define our identity over and against everybody else.

For Hill the challenge of our time is to outgrow those restricted ways of being and personal identity and appropriate the status of being a cosmopolitan, in which we learn to transcend race, religion, and even nationality as we begin to reclaim one universal citizenship within planet earth and the cosmos we share together. Conversely, Tarlow describes the challenge as the reappropriation of the tribal nomad, faced with the challenge to become "more nomadic, imaginative, tribal and intuitive" (2002, 241).

Commonalities and Differences

Undoubtedly Hill meets with the accusations of being unreal, utopian, and even anarchic. In fact, he is stating a profound truth, exactly the one known to our ancestors over the epochs of human becoming. Prior to the agricultural revolution around ten thousand years ago, we knew none of the distinctions we consider so essential to our contemporary existence. We lived within the womb of the one earth, as one people, serving the one life. Differences of custom and spirituality obtained, but never to the detriment of a common vision that proved far more unifying and empowering.

All that changed with the advent of agriculture. As we divided up the land, we also pitched tribes and groups against each other, as ruling male castes came to the fore. Some became wealthier than others and some more powerful than others. Rivalries of various types ensued and conflict of a more global scale evolved, thus laying the foundations of warfare and the commodification of the land as an object that could be conquered.

The philosophy of divide and conquer has been with us for some ten thousand years. We take it so much for granted — and it has been extensively validated religiously and politically — that we assume that that is how it always was and always will be. In fact, it is a very recent development in our long evolutionary history, and in recent decades it has been showing many signs of dysfunctionality and disintegration.

Some philosophers claim that it was a stage we had to go through to rescue the ego from the enmeshment of primitive times. It is widely assumed that in former times humans had no real identity apart from nature itself. We were just another face of nature. We were undifferentiated and it was deemed important that we should differentiate. This translated into setting ourselves over against nature and often beyond it. Thus we lost the context that had nourished and sustained us over some 7 million years. Instead of bringing us freedom and autonomy our differentiated state actually enslaved us in a new way. The independent observer in effect became the lonely tyrant.

The Identity Question

Several issues need clarification if this confused and confusing search is to be resolved meaningfully. Like all other creatures that inhabit planet earth, we belong to the earth in every sense. We are born out of the earth, nourished from its womb all the days of our lives, and sustained meaningfully by its evolutionary orientation for growth and development.

The felt need to escape or transcend our earthiness is a misguided philosophical and religious aspiration. It is born out of a defective cosmology, itself a by-product of patriarchal consciousness. For the culture of patriarchy, the sky-God is eminently important as the ultimate power that validates all power on earth. And the reward for those who obey the powerful ones is the promise of ultimate happiness with the sky-God.[29] Life on earth is essentially unfulfilling; only in the hereafter can true happiness be attained.

Classical Greek philosophy reinforces this alienation by emphasizing individual uniqueness. Persons are considered unique by virtue of their individuality. Every person is different and separate from every other, also separate from the earth and the cosmos, and, because of the alienation of life on earth, separate from God. One notes the strong emphasis on *separation, difference, aloneness,* begetting a distinctive emphasis on *individual autonomy.*

This is a mode of identity we never even dream of questioning. The whole Western edifice of politics, economy, and religion rests on this foundation. Robust individualism is thought to mirror the robust ruling God who is best served by our competitive, self-righteous cultures, which eliminate the weak (sinful) and advance the strong (virtuous). Any notion that this individualism might be questioned, never mind declared bankrupt, evokes huge resistance. So much is invested in this misguided sense of identity.

The foundational problem is neither political nor economic. Although bolstered by religion, it is of cultural rather than religious origin. And although validated over some ten thousand years (less than 5 percent of our time on earth), it is quite a recent phenomenon. Elizabet Sahtouris (1998) names it well: something akin to the adolescent phase of our species development, in which we have been behaving largely like belligerent adolescents. Clearly the call of our time — the graced future beckoning us forth — is to grow up as more wholesome adults, reclaiming a more creative role as planetary-cosmic creatures.

Viewed on a large global scale this mode of identity makes eminent sense. That is how we lived and thrived for most of our time on earth, *relational creatures* relating in a more interdependent and integral way with the life forces of cosmos and earth. We were never enmeshed in nature; we lived in a convivial way with the natural world, giving and receiving reciprocally. We constructed our identity — subconsciously for the greater part — from within the relational matrix that upholds everything in creation. Our capacity for relating is our greatest survival skill; we have not handled it well over the past ten thousand years.

We are now at a new evolutionary moment, in which archetypal wisdom rises up to confront, challenge, and redirect us on our way. Deep within us we recognize this wisdom, individually and collectively. We have been there before — in fact for most of our evolutionary story of some 7 million years. In evolutionary terms we don't regress; evolution always moves forward, bringing with it the cumulative wisdom of earlier times. At each evolutionary stage we recapitulate, as each fetus does in terms of our animal ancestry. We bring with us the archetypal resources of the past to empower us for the journey forth. In our time, this process is manifest particularly in rediscovering that we are *primed essentially for relating*. It is in reclaiming our capacity for relating that breakthrough rather than breakdown will become our future destiny.

Relational Dislocation

Conflicting ideologies invade the relational landscape of our time. Our dominant institutions still cling to a strange alliance between Darwinian science and conventional religion. According to the Darwinian view, humans forever battle it out, at the mercy of selfish genes, seeking their own perpetuation under the battle mast of the survival of the fittest. At the end of the day there seems to be more losers than winners. Religion essentially makes the same claim. In this vale of tears, in a creation fundamentally flawed, we each eke out our salvation amid struggle and pain. Assuredly we can, and must, love our neighbor, but in the final hour of reckoning each of us will stand alone before God and must render an account for our individual immortal souls.

This deeply distorted spirituality, prone to beget internal and external monsters, is manifest uniquely in our time in the phenomenon of the suicide bomber. And among the world religions, despite widespread protests to the contrary, Islam embodies this violent streak more integrally than any other major religion (see the informed critique of Harris 2005). This is a reenactment of the old heroic cult, with the martyr as the archetypal embodiment of true heroism. And, of course, the best heroes are always males.

It is in destroying one's life that one finds a true and lasting identity — and always in a world beyond. And for the mythic hero it is not merely a personal achievement. He also becomes the liberator for all those he can bring to paradise with him, while also in an ideological sense bringing freedom for the oppressed here on earth.

In the contemporary world we see a double reaction to this weird and fascinating ideology. People of poorer circumstance, especially in Muslim cultures, become more intrigued and fascinated by the cult of martyrdom and the individual heroism it invokes. And since the events of September 11, 2001, this trend has certainly increased in popularity. But much more widespread is the alternative reaction: the millions around our world fed up with all the "battling," weary of all the self-aggrandizement, desiring something much more intimate and connected, and recklessly embracing it on a universal scale.

The primary manifestation of this alternative intimacy is the ease with which people connect and bond on a psychosexual level. Not many years ago, sexual behavior was reserved for marriage, or at least for relationships considered to be more permanent, perhaps lifelong. And the widespread assumption is that such relationships would be heterosexual in composition. Within a short number of years, that conventional paradigm has all but collapsed. We are quick to judge and assess the causes, but frequently we judge superficially. This is not merely the fruit of a new wave of hedonism with promiscuity run rife. No, this is primarily a massive cultural reaction to the cult of individualism, the demolition of the *separate individual*. Relationality, and not separation, is back with a vengeance.

Relating Laterally

Relationships in the future are likely to be characterized by breadth rather than depth. Distinctions in the name of nationality, religion, or ethnicity will give way to a new multi-culturalism — the new tribalism Tarlow (2002) alludes to, already widely adopted by young people throughout the world. An exclusive job for life, confined to one or a few geographical locations, has already given way to a highly fluid (nomadic) job market, spanning diverse cultures and work practices. Spiritual seekers these days rarely adhere to one dominant system of belief and are markedly uneasy with sectarianism of any type. Political governance, still adopting political party strategies, has lost a great deal of credibility; at the present time there are no clear alternatives, but it is clear that more and more people are growing weary and disillusioned with the power games frequently played out in the political arena.

A more lateral mode of relating has become largely accepted in the areas outlined above. In the interpersonal realm, in the sphere of intimate behavior, there is a persistent sense of denial and rationalization with regard to the changing landscape. The institution of marriage is unlikely to survive this transformation. Psychosexual intimacy will not revert to the exclusive realm of the heterosexual married couple. Gay, lesbian, and transgendered lifestyles will continue to enter the mainstream of our daily lives. At some stage in the not too distant future, governments will have to address these difficult challenges and develop social strategies and cultural mores to accommodate these new developments.

Currently, governments often abdicate their responsibilities, passing the buck to the churches and religions. But those carry little or no credibility when it comes to substantial issues. And it is no longer responsible for church or state to be playing out the old dualistic divisions between the sacred and the secular. In a world of lateral relationships, dualistic modeling is exposed for the fallacy it has always been. Everything in creation operates out of a convivial interdependence of both-and, not a dualistic divide of either-or.

As I indicated in a previous work (O'Murchu 2007), nobody at this moment in time can predict the future shape of significant relationships, and some undoubtedly would prefer that the issue was not cast in the bare relief I outline above. I do so as an appeal for honesty and transparency. In every age, meaningful relationships can be negotiated only through healthy and transparent communication. My hope is that these reflections will activate an adult, open conversation on a matter of crucial significance for all who want to live in a fulfilled and fruitful way for the future.

Chapter 29

Apocalyptic Cataclysm
or Eschatological Breakthrough?

Sometimes those of us who live by hope and promise fail to
appreciate how alluring cosmic pessimism can be. For it often
seems more rational to embrace an absurdist view of the uni-
verse than to remain steadfast in hope, especially when there are
so many happenings within our evolving universe that, taken in
isolation, seem to warrant a tragic interpretation.

— JOHN F. HAUGHT

FACED WITH THE DAUNTING personal, interpersonal, and cultural
challenges outlined above, we demonstrate a number of predictable reactions. *Denial* is probably the most widespread and
potentially the most destructive for people and planet alike. Denial
can translate into a self-survival strategy, whereby I think only of me
and my own; alternatively, it can beget a kind of reckless frivolity
in which serious thought and action is largely suspended. And between those extremes is the daily grind known to millions in our
troubled world: they strive to survive from one day to the next and
that absorbs all their time and energy.

An unfortunate consequence of the culture of denial is the tendency to belittle or ridicule those of us who explore and articulate
alternative worldviews. Understandably we are often seen as wealthy
Westerners who have the luxury to philosophize all day long. This
is an unfortunate perception and in fact grossly inaccurate. As indicated in chapter 25 above, in this era of mass information, millions
around our world know what is going on, and often their frustration

is exacerbated by the fact that they can do nothing about the cruel injustices that have them where they are. Moreover, indigenous peoples in many parts of planet earth have operated out of enlarged cosmic visions for millennia; in the power of ancestral grace they were engaging with the "new cosmology" light years before we "educated" Westerners came on the scene.

A Lurid Fascination

Now with the frightening impact of global warming, global terrorism, and the breakdown of traditional communities, millions live in the daily grip of fear, uncertainty, and a very precarious future. Transitions of this nature are not new to our species; we have been there many times before — and survived. We have no way of accessing the precise skills we used to come through previous transitional times, but there is much evidence to suggest that our convivial relationship with the living earth and a more integrated spirituality were among our primarily resources for survival. Unfortunately, that ancient wisdom is not as extensively available to us today, and it is often undermined and demonized by religion in particular. Inevitably what ensues in troubled times is a culture of cataclysmic doom in which "false prophets" like to speculate in wild and bizarre ways about the dark and dangerous future that will befall us all. And these prophets of doom tend to show up specifically in the religious and political domains. A disturbing example is that of the late U.S. president Ronald Reagan, who at a dinner in 1971 told the California legislator James Mills that everything was in place for the battle of Armageddon and the second coming of Christ. To assist in the preparations the president had invited a number of reputable religious adherents to attend National Security Council briefings, including the American evangelist Jerry Falwell.

This type of religious fervor is sometimes consoling for people at the mercy of cruel persecution but offers little empowerment or hope for a more promising future; to the contrary it can all too easily inculcate a dangerous and deluding regression. Tragically the trend still continues in popular religiosity, with loud-mouthed preachers instilling guilt and fear in gullible listeners.

The Movement for the Restoration of the Ten Commandments is a Ugandan cult that whipped up quite a frenzy during the 1990s. As the millennium year 2000 CE approached, the movement declared with increasing nerve and certainty that the world was coming to an end, a final day of reckoning in which all would be called to render an account before the judgment seat of God. When the doomsday forecast did not transpire more than a thousand members committed mass suicide.

A Kenyan cult known as the House of Yahweh predicted the end of the world on September 13, 2006, having also erroneously hailed the apocalyptic doom for the millennial year 2000. When it failed to transpire on the specified date, the cult leader, Yisrael Hawkins, rationalized the situation by declaring a prolonged time for conversion and preparation for the doom that eventually would befall the human race.

Since early Christian times, millennial fantasies have haunted the human imagination, often condemning us to a type of infantile gullibility. As a species of the past few thousand years we seem to live in a perpetual state of dissatisfaction with the here and now. We are forever longing for a future utopia in some distant heavenly realm. Ironically, an incarnational religion like Christianity seems particularly prone to such bizarre predilections.

The Christian scriptures frequently allude to a future age inaugurated through cataclysmic conditions, marking the destruction of what currently prevails as a new and better world comes into being. It is unclear if this new world is totally outside and beyond the present creation, or whether it translates into something dramatically new and wholesome within the existing reality.

Intense persecution, and possibly impoverished living conditions, seem to be major contributory factors to this cultic fascination. Envisaging the present world order as hopelessly flawed, humans are encouraged to stake their hopes on the totally beyond, often described in graphic, triumphalistic imagery as we find in the Book of Revelation at the conclusion of the New Testament. The break-in of a new world order was taken seriously (literally?) by St. Paul. Indeed a number of Gospel citations suggest that Jesus also espoused a belief in a dramatic end to the existing order.

With the wisdom of hindsight, we can understand more easily why such fantasies would have arisen. It is much more difficult to comprehend why people are so easily lured to follow such prognostications — often to the point of death by suicide. The suicide bomber of the early twenty-first century sincerely believes that these acts of immolation contribute to a more God-like world, while also procuring a high reward in heaven for the bomber himself or herself and for the bomber's immediate family. It is particularly disturbing to see people in Western nations, which pride themselves in solid education and good living conditions, being brainwashed to follow disgruntled gurus with such potentially destructive philosophies of life.

The Apocalyptic Mind-Set

Some features of what I call the apocalyptic mind-set are easily discernible. Others are more subtle and require more skilled discernment:

- It is very much a male preoccupation, reflecting subtle aspects of the patriarchal will to power (see Crossan 2007).

- It subscribes to a God-image that is distant, harsh, and judgmental, quite alien to incarnational faith.

- It is very anthropocentric, with a strong tendency to infantalize the masses.

- It works on a strategy of inculcating passivity and irrational fear.

- It spawns heavily on notions of redemptive suffering; one must suffer to gain release, freedom, and salvation.

- It flourishes mainly among poor and oppressed peoples, but can also prevail among rich people with a poorly developed capacity for critical and reflective thought.

- It is based on a very negative view of the cosmos and planet earth, a worldview deprived of a sense of universal meaning and purpose.

- It thrives on a narrow, reductionistic sense of history, leaving little or no room for evolutionary perspectives.

- It thrives on a spirituality of escape rather than one of engagement.

Positively, many scholars are at pains to point out that in early Christian times, and for some time before, apocalyptic narrative and imagery provided the spiritual bulwark that sustained many people through the trauma and oppression of religious and political persecution.

John Dominic Crossan (2007, 77ff.) provides an informed and useful overview of apocalyptic sentiment in early Christian times. He goes on to describe the eschatological outlook as the more authentic core of Christian belief and its commitment to a culture of enduring hope: "A full-service eschatology . . . is not about humanity's evacuation from a destroyed earth to a heavenly alternative, but about physical, feral, and social life in a transfigured world on a transformed earth" (Crossan 2007, 81).

The Eschatological Outlook

For many fundamentalist Christians, the New Testament is inundated with submissiveness and fear before a judgmental God. They largely ignore the more foundational strand of a future-oriented faith, with a distinctive sense of hope that defies all hopelessness. This is broadly known as the eschatological outlook. Suffering takes on quite a different meaning, not redemptive for its own sake, perceived to be an integral part of a final cataclysmic event, but as the consequence of a commitment to bring about a better world in the face of the current oppression and despair. We suffer not because of some innate value in the suffering itself, but because of our efforts to help rid the world of meaningless violence and oppression.

The emphasis here is on a better future offering more realistic hope. It acknowledges, however tentatively, an evolutionary perspective to history and creation, in which everything moves toward a final goal of achievement and fulfillment. It favors this outcome on the basis that the Judeo-Christian God is a God who always fulfills the promise of new life and a better future. Integral to this view of Christian history is what John F. Haught (1993; 2000; 2003) describes as *the lure of the future* (see below p. 221). The God who promises new life and hope consistently makes possible for us the prospect of greater meaning up ahead. We look forward in hope, and that hope will not fail us.

Christian scholars have long debated the role of humans in the realization of this more hope-filled prospect. Those of a more fundamentalist persuasion claim that this is an initiative of God to which humans contribute nothing. We receive it in faith and trust as passive recipients richly blessed. In line with the vision of the present work, I favor the co-creative option. Together with God, we build up creation, realizing ever more fully the eschatological fulfillment God desires for everything and everybody in creation. Clearly, and tragically, that is not how most humans see themselves or their role in the contemporary world.

We lack an eschatological outlook for several reasons. We have not been spiritually prepared for a more interactive understanding of faith and our engagement with it. We also suffer badly from a petrified sense of time and history, forever waiting for a "promised messiah" to rescue and redeem us from our earthly plight. *The mess from which we seek to escape is the one we have created for ourselves through our ignorance and lack of an eschatological vision.* We invest little hope in the past and less in the future. We are stuck in a functional here-and-now with little sense of what has brought us to this point or of the future that lures us forth.

In the prevailing understanding of life, objectivity and certainty are postulated on the records of the past. But our sense of the past is atrophied and congealed. As indicated previously, we are imprisoned in the narrow functional worlds dictated by the two benchmarks of two thousand years and five thousand years. We invoke the notion of *revealed truth* to identify where we have come from and to guide us for the future. But it is a narrow, constricted sense of revelation that breeds pessimism and irrational fear. It thrives on the apocalyptic rather than the eschatological. It will not sustain us for a meaningful future.

Eschatology is a much more generic concept. It seeks to honor the flow of time through the cycle of past-present-future. It adopts a bigger picture that honors evolutionary emergence. It suggests that the future is not a total unknown that we wait for. Evolution yields to various future possibilities as life unfolds in greater complexity. One does not even have to postulate God as the source of this future hope; it is an imprint of the cosmic process itself, described in the scientific literature as *autopoiesis,* or the capacity for self-organization.

Religious hope, therefore, is not mere utopia, nor is it postulated solely on fulfillment in a life hereafter. It is about a world forever undergoing growth and transformation, guided not by the invisible hand of crude economic policy but by an illusive wisdom and a preferred sense of direction that neither scientists nor religionists understand well at this time. Both science and religion are imbued by a desire for mastery, and that inhibits the vision of more wholesome possibilities. It is so much easier to master the past, and for those compulsively addicted to such mastery, the future will always be dismissed as mere fantasy.

Christian Hope

Of all the major religions, Christianity proffers hope as a primary value and disposition for daily living. This is the heart and soul of what the Gospels describe as the Kingdom of God (reviewed in part 2 above). Walter Wink offers the following useful summary:

> Jesus proclaimed the reign of God . . . not only as coming in the future, but as having already dawned in his healings and exorcisms and his preaching of good news to the poor. He created a new family, not on bloodlines, but on doing the will of God. He espoused non-violence as a means for breaking the spiral of violence without creating new forms of violence. He called people to repent of their collusion in the Domination System and sought to heal them from the various ways the system had dehumanized them. (Wink 2002, 14)

Jesus did not promise utopias based on promises that could never be fulfilled, a strategy widely adopted in the politico-economic culture of our time leaving millions disempowered and disillusioned. Christian faith is grounded in the realization of a better future — already in this world — to which all Christians are asked to commit themselves. The following are some of the key areas for co-creative engagement:

- honoring and respecting creation as God's primary revelation, a process with which we work collaboratively, not an object to be manipulated or commodified;
- doing everything in our power to augment relationships based on love and justice, and evolving structures that will support and enhance this relational way of living;
- prophetically denouncing all systems that promote power for the sake of power, condemning people and the earth itself to the estrangement of destructive powerlessness;
- co-creating structures that will liberate people and creation from the bondage of ignorance and oppressive exclusion;
- networking in faith communities that transcend sectarianism, bigotry, and tribalism, challenging people to work collaboratively for the common good of all, including that of the home planet.

In the past, Christian hope was invested in the practice of the faith in one or another denomination, all claiming to represent the true church on earth. Such factionalism is not likely to survive, and where it does it is unlikely to honor the liberating and empowering vision of the New Reign of God. Ecclesial structures will need to be much more fluid and flexible while more explicitly focused on what unites rather than what separates the various creeds and denominations. The philosophy of divide and conquer, which has perforated even the religious domain, can never engender the enduring hope that people hunger for. This is the hope we know deep in our hearts, begotten of the creative God who forever promises us a new and better future.

The fulfillment of that promise is certainly a divine prerogative, but its realization on earth is also a human responsibility, and it can be fulfilled only when we choose to transcend the crippling dualisms inherited from the past and embrace a mode of engagement that includes the social, economic, and political realities of our world. Realistic and enduring hope is postulated not on religious escapism, but on spiritual engagement embracing every aspect of our lifework as planetary-cosmic creatures.

Chapter 30

The Spirit Will Lead You Forth

I maintain that the most adequate response to the current crisis lies in a recovery of the Holy Spirit as a natural, living being who indwells and sustains all life forms. — MARC I. WALLACE

WE CONCLUDED THE LAST CHAPTER echoing the enduring prospect of living hope. Hope, more than any other virtue, is what is needed in these troubled times. While faith is popularly understood as allegiance to religious creeds, hope is born out of the conviction that the living Spirit of God imbues and endows everything in creation. That which animates and sustains all being and continually begets new possibilities for birthing and flourishing is that dimension of the great mystery we invoke as Holy Spirit God. A more dynamic understanding of this living and abiding Spirit is crucial for a more hope-filled future.

Although the Judeo-Christian Bible claims that the Spirit hovered over the void at the dawn of creation, the Christian churches assert that the fullness of the Holy Spirit was not conferred until the first Pentecost about two thousand years ago. The churches also claim that humans receive the Holy Spirit for the first time at baptism. These confused and conflicting claims are further evidence of the reductionism I have named so often in this book. In this case, the Holy Spirit of God is the victim of such reductionism.

American Scripture scholar James Hamilton (2004) argues for a qualitative difference between the presence of the Holy Spirit in the Old and New Testaments. In the Hebrew Scriptures, the Holy Spirit indwells primarily through the temple, whereas in the New Testament the Holy Spirit regenerates in and through the people. Such a separation of people from creation (considered by many to be the core element of the Old Testament covenant) would have been in-comprehensible to our ancient ancestors. Such a reductionism of the availability of God's grace would have been repulsive.

The Inspiring Life Force

Fortunately theology is beginning to reclaim a more foundational role for the Holy Spirit, as that divinely imbued empowering energy oper-ative in creation from time immemorial. Our ancient ancestors readily identified such empowerment in the elements of nature as in wind, fire, and sunlight. Not surprisingly therefore the Scriptures of all the great religions abound with nature-based images and metaphors. The living Spirit of God is depicted as vivifying breath, healing wind, liv-ing water, and purgative fire. Long before pneumatology was ever developed, our graced ancestors discerned the living spirit animating and sustaining everything in creation.

Even modern science reinforces and supports these understandings. Foundational to all life is the force we call *energy*. From the tiniest bacteria to the vast cosmos, energy drives and sustains everything that exists. Rational science is reluctant to investigate the essence of energy; it opts for the safer, less controversial sphere of how energy works, how it is transmitted or contained. Asking what energy is, or how it came to be, leads to a metaphysical exploration in which the rational scientist can no longer fully control the evidence. How can any of us hope to control the Spirit that blows where it wills?

Ultimately, it seems that we require an interdisciplinary mode of analysis as we seek to establish the meaning of energy at a deeper level. What energizes the energy of creation? The ultimate answer surely has to be the Holy Spirit of God. To the scientist this will seem bombastic and to the religionist it feels too impersonal to be taken seriously. Both scientist and religionist are caught in the same illusion, the felt need for power and control. Anything too far be-yond our anthropocentric reach is difficult to entertain in a seriously reflective way.

Again, our attribution of a perfect, ruling God becomes a serious barrier. We know that wind, water, and fire can be both powerfully liberating and incredibly destructive. That apparent contradiction does not seem to have been a problem for our graced ancestors, but for the rational and sophisticated people of our time it is a contradiction that must not be tolerated. It makes God feel weak and unpredictable. Worse still it makes those who rule defective in terms of the absolute control to which patriarchal cultures are so addicted.

So the living animating Spirit becomes the primary force underpinning the will to life at every level. Jürgen Moltmann stated it very explicitly some years ago: God's ruach (breath) is the life force immanent in all the living, in body, sexuality, ecology, and politics. The Spirit in this context is not so much a person as a power, a life force better understood transpersonally rather than impersonally (see p. 100 above).

Our Spirit-Filled Age

For much of Christian history, the Holy Spirit was the dimension of our understanding of God that received least attention. It was that nebulous, bird-like entity that lacked the anthropocentric characteristics that would have made it more credible. God the Father epitomized the power and governance so important for patriarchal cultures; Jesus, son of the ruling Father, had an embodied existence on this earth that could be historically verified (often with more detail than was historically credible); but the Holy Spirit was too big for these otherwise narrow and quantifiable horizons.

When those horizons began to stretch in the latter half of the twentieth century, the Holy Spirit was gradually rehabilitated, with a much more significant role. Among the more daring reconstructions was the proposition of Teilhard de Chardin that we are now living very much in an era of the Holy Spirit. As humanity outgrows its biological conditioning (in which our physicality confers our identity) and grows into higher levels of spiritual maturation (what Teilhard called "psychic evolution"), then the relationship to God as Spirit becomes more central in human experience and more empowering for human growth and development.

This may also be the more informed way to understand much of the language attributed to Jesus in John's Gospel, particularly the allusion to Jesus' immanent departure so that the Spirit could come and lead people in the direction of a fuller truth. Jesus marks the evolutionary moment of bringing to fulfillment all that humans had achieved throughout the 7 million years of biologically driven evolution. Jesus fulfills the past but also points the way ahead to the next evolutionary wave in which mind and spirit will be more central than the physical body. One can see the integration of these new levels in the reality of the risen Jesus.

God as Holy Spirit has a particular appeal for our time because that dimension and articulation of the divine-in-our-midst embodies more readily and tangibly what we are being lured into as evolving creatures today. This is not about God changing. Rather it is about humans undergoing a new moment of transformation and recasting our relationship with the divine in a more empowering way for this new moment of emergence. It is a new way of recognizing and naming the role of the Holy Spirit of God, congruent with the graced experience of this time. Formerly we recognized and named the Spirit differently — as wind, water, fire — images more congruent with our tangible experience of creation itself.

The Spirit That Lures Us Forth

In John's Gospel the Holy Spirit is described as a force that blows where it wills. Unrestricted movement, passionate creativity, and unceasing novelty characterize this divine life force. Thus far my reflections allude mainly to the past activation of spirit power throughout our evolutionary story. Grace triumphs in the power of this animating and enlivening Spirit, but it is always an awakening toward a new and better future.

The Spirit calls us forth, lures us, not from the past but from the future. In terms of life's time structure of past-present-future, when it comes to the dynamic creativity of the living Spirit of God, the future is the dimension that calls for our fullest attention and our deepest discernment. For the German theologian Jürgen Moltmann, the future has become the modern paradigm for transcendence. As a theological concept, grace has been over-identified with the past, more precisely with the repair of what is deemed to have been damaged through sin and wrong action. Grace has come to be regarded almost as the complement of sin. To paraphrase St. Paul, where sin abounded, grace accrued all the more. Grace denotes something of that transcendent power that rescues and redeems us from our sinfulness.

In fact, grace means a great deal more. While denoting healing in terms of our past, it also alerts us to the sacredness of each new moment and invites us to journey forward in purpose, hope, and meaning. Grace is rooted in that empowering wisdom whereby we can see and honor the unfolding pattern of past-present-future. We need all three dimensions to truly experience our graced existence within the blessed abundance of creation.

In the tripartite movement of past-present-future, one dimension has been excessively used, namely, the past. Not surprising, therefore, that the one most neglected is the *future*. And the bridge serving both, namely, the present, may in fact be the most precarious of the three. Why? Because the past that we continually invoke is based on various reductionisms frequently noted in the pages of this book; it is a backward glance that poorly nourishes and sustains us for each present moment. And the future is often vague and nebulous; various forces of knowledge and learning discourage us from exploring it in depth. The present gets congested and congealed between two stultified poles of reference.

Fulfilling the Promise

Most popular approaches to evolution adopt the Darwinian insight, namely, that progress happens through the survival and repetition of those traits and behaviors that serve us best over time. In other words, it seems that evolution is driven from behind (from the past), and, therefore, the past is what we rely on for verification and reliability of the presenting evidence.

The American theologian John F. Haught (1993; 2000; 2003) consistently challenges this stance. Haught suggests that the future also plays a key role, one that is at least as significant as the past, possibly even more so. Just as the past provides the basic patterns upon which nature builds, it is the lure of the future that gives direction and "purpose" to every development. For Haught, this allurement is primarily a religious phenomenon, more accurately, a theological insight: God forever promises, and God never fails to fulfill what has been promised:

> Moreover, theology has conceived of God too much in terms of the notion of a Prime Mover impelling things from the past. Evolution demands that we think of God as drawing the world from up ahead, attracting it forward into the future.... The future, not the dead past, is the foundation upon which the world leans.... Theologically speaking, a promising God who opens up the world to the future is the *ultimate* explanation of evolution. (Haught 2003, 164, 128)

One can detect a similar orientation in human life especially in child development. The child and young person grow toward that which it desires to become, that which life wishes it to become. The future is the primary driving force, and where prospects for the future are weak due to poverty, illness, etc. then frequently arrested growth, lethargy, and even despair are known to ensue.

Teilhard de Chardin (1969), more than any other evolutionary thinker in the twentieth century, posited the future as that dimension which provides direction and goal for cosmic, planetary, and human evolution. More tentatively, others (e.g., Laszlo 1998, 83; Morowitz 2002) use the language of "a preferred sense of direction," endorsing Teilhard's insight that advances in evolution are characterized by an increase in complexity. The future is coming within the scientific gaze, and its key role in the evolutionary process is likely to receive much more attention in scholarship of the future. As early as 1988, the German theologian Jürgen Moltmann wrote:

Generally speaking, the theologies of the Middle Ages were all theologies of love. The theologies of the Reformers, Luther, Zwingli and Calvin were decidedly theologies of faith. But the basic question of modern times is the question of the future. Therefore, Christian theology of modernity must necessarily be a theology of the future. (Moltmann 1988, 23)

As research becomes more interdisciplinary and multi-disciplinary, the future stands a better chance of being honored for what it facilitates. The future signals greater openness, characterized by new options and unforeseen but promising possibilities.

Dreaming an Alternative Future

The Spirit that allures us from the perspective of the ever new future also awakens in our hearts dreams for a future that will often feel threatening to the guardians of conventional reality. The living Spirit lures us into a culture of alternative thinking, conjuring up possibilities that may look both strange and dangerous.

In the culture of orthodoxy, mention of alternatives is considered deviant and subversive. Indeed, all talk about a different and better future tends to be suspect to the orthodox world of politics and religion. When people begin to think differently, they pose a threat to those who feel that they alone have a monopoly on how to manage the prevailing reality. But, as St. Paul reminds us, the luring Spirit is the one who dispenses gifts with prolific generosity, not among some, but among all God's people.

The ability to dream alternatives and the freedom to explore them is the surest guarantee against idolatry. False idols arise and disempower the masses when alternative thinking is suppressed. Particularly, when that thinking evolves into networks and movements, then it will meet with strong resistance.[30] Yet networking continues to flourish, forging new links, connections, and breakthroughs that offer enormous hope. The pioneering work of Paul Hawken of Bioneers (Hawken 2007; *www.bioneers.org*) vividly illustrates the proliferation of networks and their creative potential in the modern world.

This is where the Spirit blows where it wills, where resurrection and new life stand the best hope of thriving today. In such a world, even death takes on fresh meaning — the subject we'll review in the next chapter.

Chapter 31

Preoccupied with Death
and the Afterlife

In nature, death is not an enemy but a friend of the life process.
The death side of the life cycle is an essential component of that
renewal of life by which dead organisms are broken down and
become the nutrients of new organic growth.

— ROSEMARY RADFORD RUETHER

A NOTHER ISSUE requiring fresh attention in the light of a different
eschatologically informed future is our perception of death and
afterlife. Many of the leading ideas are based on a narrow anthropocentrism that regards death as primarily a human issue when in fact
it relates to every life form. Moreover, in religious terms, death has
come to be associated with judgment and afterlife, and these are gross
delusions, militating against a more responsible engagement with life
at every level.

When it comes to death and dying, the human species is divided
between the majority for whom death is a daily occurrence, but who
tend to handle it well psychologically and spiritually, and the Western minority for whom it is a cold clinical fact best forgotten about.
In truth the distortion for both groups is based on a number of
unexamined cultural and religious assumptions.

The Demonization of Death

St. Paul states quite definitively that death is a consequence of sin,
arising from a fundamental human flaw, an evil that only God can
get rid of (Rom. 5:12–17). Few other religious systems are as cate-
gorical as that, yet death carries similar morbid connotations in most

cultures and religions. Death is a kind of curse that someday humans might overcome and then we can live forever. Once again, compulsive anthropocentric drives rear their ugly heads.

Rosemary Radford Ruether (1983, 235–45; 250–58) illuminates the background to this dangerous anthropocentric rhetoric. She highlights what she calls an ontological assumption that deems humans to be superior to nonhuman creatures, with a divine right to live forever. Immortality translates into a patriarchal projection in which humans (particularly males) seek to become gods and thus can rule and dominate forever.

The notion of afterlife finds little support in ancient Hebrew culture, where the ultimate goal of human life is the creation of a more just world order. Crossan (2007, 183ff.) traces the notion of survival in an afterlife to a displacement of the call to co-create with God an earthly dispensation of loving justice — not in some future heavenly domain, but on the earth itself as the location where God's transforming power is forever at work. The Hellenistic split between the real and ideal became the basis for an immortal heavenly realm in which we could transcend the transitory nature of the imperfect earthly order. A flawed cosmology gave birth to what is essentially a flawed eschatology.

This Greek influence strongly impacts on early Christian thought, prioritizing the afterlife and its promise of ultimate fulfillment in a world beyond. This may reflect the culture of early Christian times with pre-Christian influences relating to religious persecution (see Primavesi 2003, 87ff.). Thus the ultimate reward came to be associated with life in another realm beyond the fickle and violent reality of the present times. Meaning was not to be found in the here-and-now; instead it was projected to a future life where all would be well. Hope came to rest not in the reckless present domain, but rather in future life where the male, ruling God would certainly be in charge, and all suffering and death would be eradicated. Thus, even the death of Jesus came to be understood within this questionable line of argument.

The history of Christendom is immersed in a great deal of reckless violence and meaningless death. And today we have good reason to be pessimistic, even hopeless, about death. Most forms of death in the modern world are cruel, barbaric, and capricious, making life seem futile, frequently teetering on the verge of despair. Yet, strangely, it is in the face of the most outrageous suffering, accompanied by so much premature death, that people show the greatest resilience and hope continues to survive and flourish.

Poverty, disease, and violence are the major causes of death in the Southern Hemisphere. Yet the wealthy and powerful North is not without its share of meaningless death. Coronary ailments and various forms of cancer are quite widespread. Much more bewildering however, are the thousands who die from road accidents and violent crime.

For many in the Northern Hemisphere death is a taboo often consigned to numbed silence. It is a grief often borne in isolation and loneliness. We don't know how to talk about death; most people don't want to talk about it. Faced, therefore, with a dramatic event like the untimely death of Diana, Princess of Wales, in September 1987, we see a country in a state of collective grieving, not just for Diana but for the thousands of people we had never properly grieved. Diana's death was the cultural mechanism that let loose the floodgates of repressed grief.

Befriending Death

Ironically, we cannot hope to live better for the future until we also learn to die better. Life and death are complementary values on the same spectrum. As we live so shall we die, but conversely when we integrate death more fully we also learn to live with greater care and compassion.

For a start, we need to outgrow our anthropocentric focus on death. Death is not just about people and personal destiny. Death belongs to the dynamic process that underpins evolution at every level of existence. Death is an integral dimension of the unfolding dynamic of *birth-death-rebirth*. Without death we lack both maturation and new life. The old cannot realize its meaningful end and therefore is in danger of becoming excess baggage that forever weighs us down, sapping up our zeal for life. And the new is not free to take over, because we keep clinging to that which has served its time.

Everything in creation flourishes within the cyclic paradox of birth, death, and new life. Everything, except us humans! We have concocted a whole range of anthropocentric theories, justifying a belief in eternal life not just in a next world but in this one also. We are ensnared within an imperialism that alienates us not just from creation but from our own deepest nature. Our desire to live forever is not of God, but of our deluded desire to be gods. Power has subverted the wisdom of our souls.

Death is our friend, not our enemy. What alienates us in the face of death is the widespread meaninglessness accompanying most forms of human dying, whether in the rich or poor countries. Much of that alienation arises from our inability to befriend death responsibly and creatively. Most meaningless death is not caused by factors beyond human control, e.g., disease, natural disasters, accidents; it arises from our false consciousness leading to destructive human interference. We act wrongly because we think and see in unenlightened ways.

Death in the Cosmic Matrix

In her attempts to re-vision the meaning of death, Rosemary Radford Ruether relocates the issue of survival after death within the larger web of life. Preoccupation with personal survival may be the primary obstacle to a more profound way of understanding death — even on a personal level:

> In effect, our existence ceases as individuated ego/organism, and dissolves back into the cosmic matrix of matter/energy from which new centers of the individuation arise. It is this matrix rather than our individuated centers of being that is "everlasting," that subsists underneath the coming to be and passing away of individuated beings and even planetary worlds.... That great matrix that supports the energy-matter of our individuated beings is itself the ground of all personhood as well. The great

collective personhood is the Holy being in which our achievements and failures are gathered up, assimilated into the fabric of being, and carried forward into new possibilities. (Ruether 1983, 257–58)

In the subatomic world, a particle is never destroyed. Its energy is always transformed into another energy-form. Creation forever recycles its resources — at every level.[31] Even black holes, considered by scientists to be icons of total and ultimate destruction, are now understood to serve other purposes fomenting the orderliness and life potential of galaxies and planetary orbits (see Kunzig 2002). In the creative universe, the potential for re-creation and innovation is enormous; consigning this potential to an afterlife comes dangerously close to blasphemy.

Human life as we know it will come to an end, individually and collectively. So have life forms throughout the entire story of cosmic and planetary evolution. The life force (soul) within us will cease one day and flow into other energy channels in the wider surrounding creation. And from that creative matrix, as Ruether intimates, what was one time my unique energy-constellation (personal identity) will now serve other enlivening possibilities. Rebirthing takes place and life continues to flourish.

The interactive nature of life and death is difficult to discern in a world of so much wanton evil and untimely death. Occasionally we are graced with insights that compel credibility and enhance our understandings. A few years ago, I was privileged to accompany Dorothy as she eased into her death and prepared to depart from this life. She had devoted much of her life to the care of people with handicaps, donating land and money for a special center for care and respite. In her will she asked that her ashes be placed in the land where the center was located.

Later, her family erected a simple headstone bearing her name and the dates of her birth and death. Also inscribed was this brief tribute: "Her ashes lie here; her vision is all around you." In other words, her living spirit is radically alive and transparent in the sheer goodness she made possible by all that happens in and around the care center she had helped to set up. The emptiness of death (the ashes) and the fullness of life (the center) sit side by side. In fact, they always do in this wonderfully fertile planet that we inhabit.

As highlighted in chapter 19 above, even calamitous events like tsunamis, earthquakes, and hurricanes contribute to this indomitable will-to-life. Our ancient ancestors were probably better equipped than we are to engage the paradox of creation, precisely by not seeking excessive control over everything, including afterlife. It is our compulsion for control and domination that comes back to haunt us. If we were more receptive to nature's processes and respectful of their dynamics, we would discern more readily the destruction that is endemic to the paradox of creation; we would learn the skills to live with it in a more convivial way. And, as a result, we would be able to befriend death in a more grace-filled and informed way.

Death and Our Graced Future

Death will continue to adorn the landscape of our existence as it has always done. And redemptive theories, Christian or otherwise, will not get rid of death. If we got rid of death, then life would also rapidly evaporate. The curse of death, the evil therein, is a human projection that we need to withdraw. It is not evil in itself; it is we who make it into a demonic monstrosity.

As graced creatures, we know in the depth of our being how to befriend death. We did it for most of our time on earth. We can do it again. It will involve a radical conversion away from our anthropocentric compulsiveness to play God, to conflate the ego with the Self, to control and dominate everything to our own selfish advantage.

Our theories regarding heaven, hell, and purgatory will also need to be revamped, as the late Karl Rahner and Ladislos Boros attempted to do in the 1970s. Heaven and hell are not places outside the world, but may be reenvisaged as states of being within the one world. Our dead are all around us, living at different vibrational levels.[32] With this insight we might try to dispel the scary stories relating to ghosts and poltergeist and come to reconsider them in a more favorable light. Perhaps they signify unfinished business or unresolved issues, needing further attention across the life spectrum that holds life and death in the one sacred space.

We need to reclaim our deep ancient wisdom whereby we comprehend and appropriate afresh the interdependence of all life forces, including death. We belong to the web of life; we don't own it, less so control it. It is not a commodity for our usufruct and domination; it is a dynamic process upon which we depend for existence, meaning, flourishing, achievement, and dying. And it is absolutely imperative that we do die when we have made our contribution to the evolving process of creation.

Religion projects the meaning of death onto another world; science tends to avoid the subject and, on occasion, sees it as further evidence for a hostile, meaningless universe. There are not many resources in the public forum to empower us to deal with death in a more coherent and responsible way. What is lacking in the public domain, however, is abundantly provided in the inner sphere. Intuitively, we know how to befriend death because we have been doing that for thousands of years throughout our evolutionary emergence. With such a rich ancient resource, we stand a good chance of ridding our world of the meaningless death experienced by far too many people on a daily basis.

Chapter 32

Will We Actually Make It?

We are set irrevocably, I believe, on a path that will take us to
the stars — unless in some monstrous capitulation to stupidity
and greed we destroy ourselves first. — CARL SAGAN

THE PROGNOSIS DOES NOT LOOK GOOD! We may be facing the
verdict of too little too late. The problem is not so much about
humanity in and of itself. The problem is that the life-support mechanisms are so perturbed and damaged that they may not be able
to sustain us much longer. The nourishing womb has been badly
ruptured, even raped, leaving humans in a very vulnerable position.

The problem is aggravated by the fact that so many are so ignorant of what is really going on. In fact, millions simply do not want
to know. For the poverty-stricken masses, it is one more God-damn
problem; they have enough to deal with already. The rich and powerful are very adept at dismissing and ridiculing whatever disturbs their
fabricated comfort. As a species living at this precarious time, our
ignorance is our greatest liability.

Possible Scenarios

Serious global and environmental issues face humanity today, global
warming being the tip of the iceberg at the present time. Ecological
sustainability raises urgent concern in several crucial areas: depletion
and exploitation of natural resources, species extinction at a rate far
in excess of what we have previously known; global warming and
accompanying impact on climate; pollution and the accumulation of
toxic wastes, deforestation and the erosion of topsoil. And these are
just a few of the better-known destructive forces.

231

Together they alert us to the predicament of the living earth itself. Will the earth body survive? At what point does the threat to the earth itself make human life impossible to sustain? These questions are built around a largely unexamined assumption, namely, that humans will somehow survive beyond earth's capacity for self-sustainability. This is a dangerously deceptive delusion, one that undermines the more serious discernment required in our time.

Humans are in fact the most interdependent of all creatures, although clearly we do not behave in a way that honors that fact. We are heavily dependent on all other aspects of the great chain of life. Imbalance or disruption to the planetary ecosystem inevitably destabilizes humanity's ability to live meaningfully on the earth; beyond a certain level of destructability we will not survive. At a critical juncture in the depletion of earth's resources, humanity itself becomes an endangered species. As indicated previously, some theorists believe we have already crossed this lethal threshold.

The earth will survive; we may not. It is not the earth but we ourselves who will first succumb to eco-systemic disruption. The home planet is endowed with a resilience for life far in excess of us humans. In the earth's long story there are indications that the earth will get rid of organisms that do not promote its overall well-being. This may well be what actually happened to the dinosaurs. In their magnificence and overpowering presence, they became too destructive and eventually the wise, intelligent earth decided to get rid of them.

Some commentators suggest that we humans are the dinosaurs of this time. We are the great predators of the present age. Most of the meaningless suffering we experience is not caused by freak elements of nature, but by our own species. We are the multiplying, deranged gene causing various forms of deadly cancer not just for our own species but for other life forms as well. We may well be setting ourselves up for the fiercely protective Earth Mother to dispense with us as she did with other parasitical creatures!

These are grim scenarios but frighteningly real. Unless we radically reverse our crudely destructive behavior, and there is not significant evidence to indicate that we intend to do so, then inevitably we are setting ourselves up to be eliminated by the protective wisdom of the earth itself. Our chances of making it through look rather slim.

Beyond Our Denial

I outline this pessimistic possibility not just as a scare tactic; such tactics tend not to be very persuasive. Instead, I appeal to the more rational and imaginative aspects of our human condition. By facing this cataclysmic outcome, we are likely to become more humble and caring, more aware of what is actually going on, more discerning in the face of such widespread denial, and therefore more transparent to the eventual demise we may have to embrace.

Grief counselors, dealing with people either anticipating or grieving the experience of death (or severe loss) know that denial exerts a terrible toll on our sanity and resilience. Strangely, it is far more healthy and liberating to be able to embrace death in an informed way. If our species is to die out there is a way to prepare for that departure so that we go through it, not as victims embittered and disempowered through denial, but as pilgrims undergoing the dark night that will lead to a new dawn for creation. Yes, this is unashamedly a mystical scenario, one of the few options through which we can handle the impending crisis in a dignified and liberating way.

In fact, if there is to be a reprieve for humanity and we are saved from the destructive outcomes of either self-immolation or elimination by a higher planetary wisdom, then it is likely to be those mystically resigned to going through a great death who will probably bring humanity to a new evolutionary threshold — and hopefully beyond it. In all probability, humanity will gain a reprieve because the earth-body itself will engineer it. The earth (and the cosmos) has frequently come to the rescue in times of impending global crisis, one of the more vivid examples being that of the oxygen crisis some two billion years ago.

We humans, in our presently evolved state *may* make it through, but it will require a kind of rescue that creation in its planetary or cosmic dimensions can, and on occasion, does make possible. And for that rescue to be possible we must make radical adjustments in our lifestyles. Grace itself invites and empowers us to make the quantum leap, as Elizabeth Dreyer vividly reminds us: "Grace demands that one live the very life one is living, but in a new key that is more free, responsible, and open to the transforming love of God. Working to change unjust social and political structures is at the heart of such a life" (Dreyer 1990, 239). Those that cannot rise to that challenge will almost definitely die out, and probably with much of the meaningless pain and suffering that arise from deep denial.

And if the entire species is to die out, then undoubtedly the wise Earth Mother will use the opportunity to move evolutionary becoming on to another level of complexity and a new layer of life will appear on earth. It may be a totally new species, or it may be creatures like ourselves with additional gifts and capacities to engage with life. It will not have been the first time in the great evolutionary story in which death led to new life, the recurring cycle of birth-death-rebirth.

The future is guaranteed! Evolution makes that abundantly clear. Whether or not we humans in our presently constituted state will make it through is not at all clear. We have choices and at this moment in history we need to act urgently and intelligently. Although the odds are stacked against us (we have stacked them against ourselves), creation may come to our rescue. Not, however, without a price to be paid, the need to let go of our addiction to power, dominance, and exploitation. That is the big conversion on which our future depends.

A number of scenarios are possible for the future of humanity. Ancestral grace has a great deal to teach us about the choices we need to make and how we best can make them. We need to relearn once more how to live convivially with our evolving changing earth and cosmos. We have had to make that adjustment many times before; all indications are that we did it in a wise and empowering way. Let's pray for the grace to do now, in an informed and enlightened way, what evolution beckons of us at this time. Let's pray especially for the grace to make the right choices, choices that will enhance rather than undermine a meaningful future.

Hanging On to Hope!

So is hope still possible as we face a precarious future with the odds stacked against us? And how do we sustain a meaningful and realistic hope against such great odds? In oft quoted words of the one-time president of the Czech Republic Václav Havel, we glimpse something of that hope that can be so crucial for our time: "Hope is not the conviction that something will turn out well, but the certainty that something makes sense, regardless of how it turns out."

In a sense that is what this book is all about: depicting a human story that makes sense. Being real about who we are and embracing in a more creative and proactive way our mission as planetary beings. Hope is written into every crevice and hidden recess of our existence. We have had our triumphs — and our failures — and on the grand scale, we have coped remarkably with both.

It seems crucially important that we acknowledge our positive achievements. Not to do so capitulates us not merely into pessimism and possible despair; much more seriously, *it is a blatant act of blasphemy,* an outrageous denial of the God who has seen us through so much and has been with us every step of the way. Hence — my unrelenting fidelity to the notion of ancestral grace throughout the pages of this book.

This outrageous optimism is in no way a denial of the dark side that religion, along with most other formal disciplines, consistently highlights. Yes, we did get it drastically wrong at times, and we are living through an epoch with collective extinction staring us in the face. We are much more likely to face our current shadow against a background of our evolutionary skill and wisdom rather than from within the depravity and sin propagated by religion and cultural nihilism.

Equipped with this ancient wisdom and the miracle of ancestral grace that defies all rationality, we stand a better chance of engaging the urgency our times require of us. We need to become much more real, live in the present, and abandon the patriarchal power games that no longer serve us well. The time is over for playing imperial games with either ourselves or our earth, and victimization is pointless as well. We won't resolve our identity crisis by recriminations, but by graceful acceptance. In facing the truth, the truth will set us free. Above all else we must not condescend to collusive utopias. More than anything else, false utopias undermine hope. False promises underpin many of our utopian dreams; even the postponement of our hopes until the fulfillment of an afterlife can create a false utopia. As suggested in the words of Václav Havel quoted above, the most credible form of hope is that which illuminates meaning in the ordinary, in the daily routine, in the graced nature of each moment.

Perhaps the crucial question is not whether we will make it through, but whether we can muster afresh the outrageous hope we have known so often throughout our long evolutionary journey and allow it to transform us once more in the amazing power of ancestral grace.

Notes

1. Quite a diffuse literature exists on this subject, much of which carries Calvinistic undertones with a strong emphasis on human sinfulness (depravity) requiring God's special rescue (election) through the power of divine grace; see Boise and Ryken 2002; Didonato 2005. Other sources dwell on the historical and theological development, with the emphasis on grace as gift (e.g., Duffy 1993; Haight 1979; Horton 2006; O'Meara 1995; Rahner 1966). Works of a more spiritual nature focus on living gracefully in daily life (e.g., Dreyer 1990; Huebsch 1988). Throughout the 1980s and 1990s liberation theologians in Central and South America contextualized grace in people's desire to rise above oppression; echoes of this wider application can also be gleaned from Fox and Sheldrake 1997 and from Tanner 2005. For Catholic writers, the link between sacraments and grace is strongly emphasized, suggesting that it is primarily through participation in the church's sacramental life that grace is conferred (e.g., Duffy 1993; Cooke 1994).

2. After September 11, 2001, and the attack on the twin towers in New York, many disciplines began to revisit the notion of human depravity. The barbaric, violent scenes of Iraq, Darfur, Lebanon, Sri Lanka, haunt the human spirit in the opening years of the twenty-first century. Not surprising, therefore, to see Christian theologians looking afresh at the related notions of Original Sin and the fundamental flaw. Many follow the seminal lead of the French theorist René Girard and his claims that humans are programmed to behave violently (Alison 1998; Schwager 2006; Ormerod 2007). For a more extensive theological treatment of the subject, see James Arraj (2004), *Can Christians Still Believe?* (chapter 3: "Original Sin"), online book: *www.innerexplorations.com/chtheomortext/chmys.htm.* Also Paul Copan (2003), "Original Sin and Christian Philosophy," online article: *www.paulcopan.com/articles/pdf/Original-sin-christian-philosophy.pdf.*

It seems to me that all these scholars operate out of a conceptual confusion between the fundamental *paradox* and the fundamental *flaw.* They tend to interpret creation's foundational paradox (of creation-and-destruction) as basically flawed, tragic, not meant to be this way. They seem to be working with a narrow anthropology, disconnected from the larger planetary and cosmic context, a more foundational frame of reference to which I allude frequently in this book. For more on the fundamental paradox, see Swimme and Berry (1992); O'Murchu (2002; 2007).

3. Henry Corbin's seminal essay "The Imaginary and the Imaginal" was initially published in 1964; the full text is available at *www.hermetic.com/ bey/mundus_imaginalis.htm*. For further elaboration, particularly by scholars like Carl G. Jung, James Hillman, and Thomas Moore, see Marc Fonda (2005), "Imagination and Aesthetics: The Language of the Soul" at *www.religiousworlds.com/fondarosa/ch2.html*. Further reflections on the nature of imagination are available online at *www.bodysoulandspirit.net/ hypnagogia/what/define.shtml*.

4. The first scholarly paper on this topic was that of R. L. Cann, M. Stoneking, and A. C. Wilson, "Mitochondrial DNA and Human Evolution," *Nature* 325 (1987): 31–36. Since then the subject has received extensive scholarly attention, as can be seen from the web page *www.en.wikipedia.org/ wiki/MitochondrialEve*. For a contemporary treatment, highly scientific yet very readable, see Lane (2005).

5. How scholars differentiate between *Australopithecus* and *Homo*, between the proto-human and the human, is reviewed by Henry M. McHenry and Katherine Coffing, "Australopithecus to Homo: Transformation in Body and Mind," *Annual Review of Anthropology* 29 (2000): 125–46. Also "Before *Homo*" at *www.en.wikipedia.org/wiki/Human_Evolution*.

6. Today, human fossils tend to be dated using a combination of methods including DNA-based techniques and a method known as carbon-14, which has been extensively used since the 1950s; also known as K-ar dating it is based on radioactive decay of potassium-argon elements (see *www.en.wikipedia.org/wiki/Potassium-argon_dating*). Carbon dating is reliable only up to seventy thousand years; in fact, many researchers will use it only on fossils up to forty thousand years old. DNA can be useful for artifacts up to a hundred thousand years old, although rarely used beyond fifty thousand years.

Human fossils are often dated on the basis of corroborative evidence from the local environment, particularly the volcanic ash of rock formations. Some of the mineral deposits pursued include: uranium-235 for materials up 700 million years old, potassium-40, up to 1.3 billion years, uranium-238, up to 4.5 billion years, and thorium-232 up to 14 billion years (see Gibbons

2007, 43–44). More recently, researchers have noted close parallels between trends in climate change and human evolution, especially in reference to *Homo habilis, A. Afarensis* and *Homo erectus* (see *Journal of Human Evolution* 53 [2007]: 443–634).

For Toumai, the oldest human fossil thus far discovered, radiometric dating (potassium-argon) has been used in conjunction with local fauna and the geological conditions of Lake Chad (see Brunet et al. 2002; 2005; Wood 2002; Gibbons 2005; 2007). The environment does not possess any of the layers of ash that typically belong to many of the better known sites in Ethiopia, Kenya, and Tanzania, which is one of the main reasons why the dating of Toumai continues to be hotly debated.

In a previous work (O'Murchu 2005), I dated Toumai at 6 million years old; at the time, it felt like an intelligent guess on the new date scholars would offer for the evolution of the first humans. Since then, the scientific literature tends to cite an original date of 7 million years ago (see John Noble Wilford, "The Human Family Tree Has Become a Bush with Many Branches," *New York Times,* June 26, 2007, D3). That is the figure I adopt in the present work. Even before this book is published that date may be modified, such is the intensity of research and the frequency of new discoveries and breakthroughs at the present time.

7. According to current fossil and genetic analyses the last common ancestor of humans and our closest living relative, the chimpanzee, originated in Africa. A growing body of evidence now indicates that although Africa spawned the first apes, Eurasia was the birthplace of the great ape and human clade. Some 17 million years ago, a land bridge joined Africa to Eurasia, facilitating the movement of apes from Africa into Asia and possibly back again before spawning the primate line that leads to early humans (see David R. Begun, "Planet of the Apes," *Scientific American* 16 [2006]: 5–13).

8. Initially the naming was conferred on Java man, discovered by Eugene Dubois in Indonesia in 1893. Peking man is considered to belong to the same grouping as is *Homo floresiensis,* discovered in the Indonesian Island of Flores in 2003; the latter is generally considered to be a dwarf form of *Homo erectus.*

9. Amid a growing impact of fundamentalist movements infiltrating many parts of Africa, the notion of *spirituality* in Africa is frequently misrepresented. In the past, its richness was underestimated and undervalued by Western missionaries. Authentic African spirituality is distinctly holistic,

relational, earth-centered, celebratory, and empowering. I recommend the following sources: Ephirim-Donkor (1997); Somé (1997; 1999). See also *www.honor-ur-ancestors.com* as well as *www.en.wikipedia.org/wiki/African _religions*. The World Council of Churches (WCC) has sponsored a number of informative studies on the interrelationship of African spirituality with the land (see *www.wcc-coe.org/wcc/what/jpc/echoes-16-05.html*).

10. The Gaia concept of an alive earth was first mooted in the 1970s in the collaborative work of James Lovelock and Lynn Margulis (Lovelock 1979). Initially ridiculed by the scientific community, it is now strongly endorsed by biologists, although still considered far-fetched and superficial by chemists and physicists. In relation to Africa, I invoke the notion of the alive body-organism to highlight that the pain and suffering affecting one dimension of the collective body, in this case the primordial African womb, inevitably leaves all humans feeling ravaged and undermined in terms of planetary health and well-being.

11. Chimps can also use stones for such purposes, and one laboratory-based experiment sought to draw comparisons between humans and chimps on this matter; see Mithen 2005, 127.

12. Scholars distinguish two types of Ice Age art: *parietal,* referring to cave wall paintings, engravings, and relief sculpture, and *mobiliary* art, such as figurines and portable objects (see Fagan 1998).

13. In 1966 about fifty anthropologists gathered for a conference in Chicago to examine the status of the world's hunter-gatherers. An important conclusion coming out of the conference noted that the role of meat in the diets of foraging peoples had been quite exaggerated. The ancient hunt was a much more complex issue than had been assumed heretofore.

Ironically, the conference rapidly became associated with the slogan of "man the hunter," that hunting is innate to the aggressive nature of the human, particularly the male. Sherwood Washburn (1911–2000), at the time working as an anthropologist at the University of Chicago, became the key name linked to the man-the-hunter hypothesis. The papers of the 1966 conference were gathered and published by two students of Washburn, namely, Richard Lee and Irven de Vore (Lee and de Vore 1968). The collection includes a paper read by S. L. Washburn and C. Lancaster, "The Evolution of Hunting," 293–303. For further information on the ongoing debate, see *http://en.wikipedia.org/wiki/Hunter-gatherer.* For one of the most up-to-date studies on this controversial topic, see Hart and Sussman (2005). The social and systemic factors that often evoke human violence have been comprehensively examined by former Stanford psychologist Philip Zimbardo (2007).

14. What Laszlo previously named the "Psi field" (Laszlo 1998) he has now renamed the "Akashic field" (Laszlo 2004), borrowing ancient mystical wisdom of the Far East to describe the etheric, subtle energy that holds everything in creation within an interconnected web of life. This subtle substance is thought to be close to, if not identical with, the notion in quantum physics known as "zero-point energy field" (ZPE), a suggested universal information field still under scientific investigation. Lynne McTaggart (2007) provides an excellent backdrop to many of these provocative but promising scientific insights of the present time.

15. For a useful resume on the current debate about the Great Earth Mother Goddess see *Feminist Theology* (January 2005). The historical context of Paleolithic times is reviewed in detail by Ruether (2005), while the prevailing fascination of contemporary times is comprehensively surveyed by Reid-Bowen (2007).

16. Ironically, Dan Brown's *Da Vinci Code* (Brown 2003) has given a strangely vigorous boost to the notion of the Great Mother Goddess. Despite various critiques highlighting the flaws and deficiencies of this novel, it continues to fascinate and intrigue readers all over the planet. What some reviewers have missed is the *subconscious lure* of this book, which is the reclaiming and rehabilitation of the notion of the Great Earth Goddess. As a cultural archetype of our time, the Goddess may be much more powerful and alluring than we suspect. The implications for theology and spirituality are formidable.

17. The notion of a male priesthood, investing the divine prerogative in humans, and particularly in males, is seen consistently throughout patriarchal times and can also be seen to one degree or another in all the major religions.

18. The influence of Aristotle on our understanding of human nature is clearly at work at the beginning of the eighteenth century when the pioneer of microscopy, Anthony van Leewenhoek, detected tiny organisms curled up in the heads of human sperm. He recognized them as *homunculi,* adaptations of Aristotle's *homunculus.* Aristotle believed that all babies should be like their fathers, unless something interfered with the generative process taking place in the mother's womb. A damp west wind could affect the quality

of the sperm or of the reproductive process, resulting in a less than perfect human being, namely, a *female.*

Down to the present time, Aristotle continues to haunt the human imagination, particularly in the realms of philosophy and religion. Academic textbooks of various disciplines often begin with the Greeks of Aristotle's time, suggesting that this is a foundational landmark of serious significance. One would have thought that many more people in our "educated" world be alert to the cultural short-sightedness of this starting point.

This is the source from which a great deal of female oppression originates. For Aristotle, women are not full human beings, but biological organisms primed to produce and nurture offspring for the male. In terms of sexuality, the prerogative is entirely with the male, propagation through the seed that the male alone possesses. We quickly assume that this is how we always understood things, an assumption that is no longer tenable as we strive to honor the interdependent connectedness that has characterized our species for much of its evolutionary history.

19. Nor must we reserve incarnation just to humans. More accurately, incarnation is a celebration of *embodiment,* in which God embraces the bodies as the primary vehicles through which the living Spirit of God is revealed. God's first embodiment is that of the entire cosmos. Planet earth is also a body, and every creature within the corporeal earth is endowed with body. Our human embodiment is an inheritance of a creative universe, whose existence and flourishing is intimately linked to embodiment. In its fuller meaning, incarnation finds expression in all forms of embodiment.

20. Pilch (2000, 66) indicates that women in the domestic sphere were not subject to some of the requirements of ritual impurity — presumably because they were deemed as nobodies, largely irrelevant creatures whose purity or impurity was of no great cultural or religious significance. For an alternative view, see Tamez (2007).

21. Christians often assume that the synagogue in the time of Jesus must have been similar to what it is today, a place of public worship that Jesus frequented as a zealous religious Jew. Archaeologists have found very few remnants of synagogues in Jesus' time and none in the open countryside where he seems to have carried out most of his ministry. Instead, "synagogue" in the Gospels seems to denote a meeting place for prayer, possibly for worship, something akin to a house-church (see Herzog 2005, 72–74; Johnson 2003, 167–68).

22. The more scientific version of the birth-death-rebirth cycle is known as the theory of punctuated equilibrium — developed by scholars like Eldredge and Gould (1972).

23. In less technical jargon, Ervin Laszlo (1998, 203) makes a very similar observation: "Natural selection is now viewed as a negative rather than a creative factor: It weeds out the non-fit mutant, but does not ensure that mutants that are truly fit are created. The positive factor, biologists realize, is the close coupling of organism and environment within an embracing system that consistently self-evolves. This factor reduces the play of chance in evolution, linking the fluid genome with the systemic mutations that herald major evolutionary leaps."

24. The term "cyborg," which denotes a mixture of the organic and cybernetic, a hybrid of the human and a machine, is first cited in a paper published in 1960 by two aeronautics experts, Manfred Clynes and Nathan Kline (see Graham 2004). Clynes and Kline had earlier explored how technological adaptations might assist human performance in hostile environments like outer space. Technology explorer Kevin Warwick (2002) describes how he implanted a small radio transmitter in his arm which was capable of sending and receiving signals between his nervous system and a computer program. The feminist scholar Donna Haraway (1991) envisages the adaptation of cyborg technology as a means of setting free the human from the narrow dictates of patriarchal mastery and exclusiveness. Philosophical and ethical implications are reviewed on the web page of the Institute for Ethics and Emerging Technologies (IEET): *www.Ieet.org.*

25. Tarlow (2002), drawing on some intriguing insights from the Australian Aborigine culture, offers an inspiring and futuristic overview of protean values at work in business. Also see the extensive analysis of John A. Powell at *www1.umn.edu/irp/publications/multiple.htm.*

26. This socio-economic theory was first developed by a Scottish engineer, Major C. H. Douglas, after World War I. It is often described as the "Basic Citizen's Income," the "Social Dividend," or "Social Credit." It has been extensively studied by economists and is known to be economically viable. A range of political, cultural, and classicist resistances make it unworkable. For more information, see *http://douglassocialcredit.com.*

27. The key research on life stages is that of James Fowler (1981; 1984). A useful feminist critique and overview is available in Nicola Slee (2004). Of particular interest for the present study and the rehabilitation of the adult as adult is the controversial work of Robert Epstein (2007). Epstein

views adolescence as an artificial and unnecessary life stage, suggesting that we replace it with a strategy for integrating the child into adult life from puberty onward. He cites extensive evidence gleaned from various cultures; in all such cases many of the adolescent problems so common in the West are largely unknown. In a sense this endorses the need for much closer attention to the integration of child and adult and may be a more foundational way to address the adult dysfunctionality highlighted by Moore and Gillette (1990).

28. For a more enlightened analysis of the emerging spirituality, I recommend Clarke (2005), Forman (2004), Tacey (2004), Phillips (2006), and Soelle (2001). I wish to alert the reader to the approach adopted by Dreyer and Burrows (2005); in conjunction with other contemporary Christian writers they explore the subject of spirituality (the spiritual life) almost exclusively as a Christian phenomenon, failing to make even minimal connections with the other great religious traditions. I also wish to acknowledge the valuable contribution of Carrette and King (2005), who highlight various contemporary movements that seem to hijack spirituality to foment marketing forces and our commercial drivenness. The notion of spirituality is much in vogue in the secular business world and often deviously used to bolster power or augment commercialism. While the critique offered by Carrette and King is timely and valuable, it fails, however, to discern the cultural nuances of what is transpiring in the secular sphere, and their suggestion that the better way forward is to reappropriate formal religion is a good example of trying to pour new wine into an old wineskin; it simply will not work.

29. Christianity seems to have taken this idea far more literally than other religions. In Christianity the sky-God is portrayed as a male propagator, on the one hand caring and loving, but on the other hand also harsh and judgmental, for much of Christian history a God whose love is postulated on self-loathing and self-inflicted violence.

30. William Cavanaugh (1998) observes that in the attack on so-called communist influences by the Chilean dictator Augusto Pinochet in the 1970s and 1980s, the real target was not rebellious individuals, as the media often intimated, but alternative social and political movements. The individuals were perceived to represent the movements, and the suppression of the movements was the primary target for which thousands of innocent people were used as scapegoats.

31. The recycling of everything in creation should not be equated with a theory of reincarnation. Conversely, a fresh appreciation of the dynamics

through which nature reuses resources gives additional meaning to the notion of reincarnation. In its strictly religious sense, "reincarnation" means that a person continues to be reborn in another embodied form until eventually escaping into the eternal bliss of Nirvana; it is a standard belief in all the great Eastern religions, but also prevailed in early Christian times. My use of the recycling image in the present context is congruent with a creation forever undergoing the process of birth-death-rebirth, rather than a process that some day will end in a finality beyond all reincarnations.

32. American Benedictine monk Brother David Steindl-Rast, in collaboration with Fr. Francis Tiso, an expert in Tibetan culture and language, has been researching what is now known as the "Rainbow Body Phenomenon." See the *Institute of Noetic Sciences (IONS) Review,* no. 59 (March–May 2002); *www.snowlionpub.com/pages/N59_9.php*. It has been noted that some Tibetan lamas, people credited in life for outstanding holiness, went through a rapid bodily transformation shortly after their deaths. First, their bodies shrank in size and eventually disappeared altogether. Steindl-Rast wonders if this discovery might not throw new light on Christian phenomena like the resurrection of Jesus or the alleged assumption of Mary into heaven.

Bibliography

Abram, David. 1996. *The Spell of the Sensuous: Perception and Language in a More-Than-Normal World.* New York: Random House.

Agnew, Neville, and Martha Demas. 1998. "Preserving Laetoli Footprints." *Scientific American* 279, 26–37

Alison, James. 1998. *The Joy of Being Wrong: Original Sin through Easter Eyes.* New York: Crossroad.

Badmington, N., ed. 2000. *Posthumanism.* London: Routledge.

Becker, Ernest. 1971. *Birth and Death of Meaning: An Interdisciplinary Perspective on the Problem of Man.* New York: Free Press.

Bennett, J., et al. 2003. *Life in the Universe.* San Francisco: Addison Wesley.

Berry, Thomas. 2000. *The Great Work: Our Way into the Future.* New York: Harmony Books.

———, and Mary Evelyn Tucker. 2006. *Evening Thoughts: Reflecting on Earth as Sacred Community.* San Francisco: Sierra Book Club.

Bickerton, Derek. 1990. *Language and the Species.* Chicago: University of Chicago Press.

Boise, James, and Philip Ryken. 2002. *The Doctrines of Grace: Rediscovering the Evangelical Gospel.* Wheaton, Ill.: Crossway Books.

Bolen, Jean Shinoda. 2005. *Urgent Message from Mother: Gather the Women, Save the World.* Boston: Conari Press.

Borg, Marcus J. 1994. *Meeting Jesus Again for the First Time: The Historical Jesus and the Heart of Contemporary Faith.* San Francisco: HarperCollins.

———. 2003. *The Heart of Christianity: Rediscovering a Life of Faith.* San Francisco: HarperSanFrancisco.

Borg, Marcus, ed. 1998. *Jesus at 2000.* Boulder, Colo.: Westview Press.

Brown, Dan. 2003. *The Da Vinci Code: A Novel.* New York: Doubleday.

Brown, Steven. 2000. "The 'Musilanguage' Model of Human Evolution." In *The Origins of Music,* ed. N. L. Wallin et al., 271–300. Cambridge, Mass.: MIT Press.

Brueggemann, Walter. 1978. *The Prophetic Imagination.* Philadelphia: Fortress.

————. 1986. *The Hopeful Imagination: Prophetic Voices in Exile.* Philadelphia: Fortress.

————. 2005. *The Book That Breathes New Life: Scriptural Authority and Biblical Theology.* Minneapolis: Fortress.

Brunet, Michel, et al. 2002, "A New Hominid from the Upper Miocene of Chad." *Nature,* vol. 418, 145–51.

————. 2005. "New Material on the Earliest Hominid from the Upper Miocene of Chad." *Nature,* vol. 434, 752–55.

Burr, Harold S. 1991. *Blueprint for Immortality: The Electric Patterns of Life.* New York: Beekman Books.

Campbell, Joseph. 1959. *The Masks of God: Primitive Mythology.* New York: Viking.

Carr, Geoffrey. 2005. "The Proper Study of Mankind." *The Economist,* December 24, 3–12.

Carrette, Jeremy, and Richard King. 2005. *Selling Spirituality: The Silent Takeover of Religion.* New York: Routledge.

Casey, Edward. 2000. *Remembering: A Phenomenological Study.* Bloomington: Indiana University Press.

Cavanaugh, William T. 1998. *Torture and Eucharist: Theology, Politics and the Body of Christ.* Oxford: Blackwell.

Chittister, Joan. 1998. *Heart of Flesh: A Feminist Spirituality for Women and Men.* Grand Rapids, Mich.: Eerdmans.

Chomsky, Noam. 1969. *Aspects of the Theory of Syntax.* Cambridge, Mass.: MIT Press.

————, Adriana Belletti, and Luigi Rizzi. 2002. *On Nature and Language.* Cambridge: Cambridge University Press.

Clarke, Chris, ed. 2005. *Ways of Knowing: Science and Mysticism Today.* Exeter, UK: Imprint Academic.

Claxton, Guy. 2005. *The Wayward Mind: An Intimate History of the Unconscious.* London: Little Brown.

Clayton, Philip. 2004. *Mind and Emergence: From Quantum to Consciousness.* Oxford and New York: Oxford University Press.

Clayton, Philip, and Paul Davies. 2006. *The Re-emergence of Emergence: The Emergentist Hypothesis from Science and Religion.* New York: Oxford University Press.

Conforti, Michael. 1999. *Field, Form and Fate: Patterns in Mind, Nature, and Psyche.* Woodstock, Conn.: Spring Publications.

Cooke, Bernard. 1994. *Sacraments and Sacramentality.* Mystic, Conn.: Twenty-third Publications.

Corballis, Michael. 2002. *From Hand to Mouth: The Origins of Language.* Princeton, N.J.: Princeton University Press.

Corbin, Henri. 1972. "Mundus Imaginalis, on the Imaginary and the Imaginal." (Spring): 1–19 (Dallas: Spring Publications).

———. 1998. *The Voyage and the Messenger: Iran and Philosophy.* Berkeley: North Atlantic Books.

Crossan, John Dominic. 1991. *The Historical Jesus: The Life of a Mediterranean Jewish Peasant.* San Francisco: Harper.

———. 2007. *God and Empire: Jesus against Rome, Then and Now.* San Francisco: HarperSanFrancisco.

Davies, Steven L. 1995. *Jesus the Healer.* London: SCM Press.

Deacon, Terence. 1997. *The Symbolic Species: The Co-evolution of Language and the Brain.* London and New York: Allen Lane/Penguin.

Dear, John. 2004. *Living Peace: A Spirituality of Contemplation and Action.* New York: Image Books.

Delio, Ilia. 2003, "Artificial Intelligence and Christian Salvation: Compatibility or Competition?" *New Theology Review,* no. 16: 39–51.

———. 2008. *Christ in Evolution.* Maryknoll, N.Y.: Orbis Books.

De Waal, Frans. 1996. *Bonobo: The Forgotten Ape.* Berkeley: University of California Press.

———. 2005. *Our Inner Ape: The Best and the Worst in Human Nature.* New York: Penguin.

———, ed. 2001. *Tree of Origin: What Primate Behavior Can Tell Us about Human Social Evolution.* Cambridge, Mass: Harvard University Press.

Didonato, Nicholas. 2005. *The Stronghold of Grace: Rethinking Spiritual Warfare in the Light of Grace.* Bloomington, Ind.: Authorhouse.

Donald, Merlin. 1991. *Origins of the Modern Mind: Three Stages in the Evolution of Culture and Cognition.* Cambridge, Mass.: Harvard University Press.

Donovan, S. K., ed. 1989. *Mass Extinctions: Processes and Evidence.* London: Belhaven.

Dowd, Michael. 2007. *Thank God for Evolution!: How the Marriage of Science and Religion Will Transform Your Life and Our World.* San Francisco/Tulsa: Council Oak Books.

Dreyer, Elizabeth. 1990. *Manifestations of Grace.* Collegeville, Minn.: Liturgical Press.

Dreyer, Elizabeth, and Mark Burrows, eds. 2005. *Minding the Spirit: The Study of Christian Spirituality.* Baltimore: Johns Hopkins University Press.

Du Toit, Cornel W., and Cedric P. Mayson. 2006. *Secular Spirituality as a Contextual Critique of Religion: A Compilation of Papers Presented at the Forum for Religious Dialogue Symposium of the Research Institute for Theology and Religion Held at the University of South Africa, Pretoria 11 & 12 May 2006*. Pretoria: Research Institute for Theology and Religion.

Duffy, Stephen J. 1993. *The Dynamics of Grace: Perspectives in Theological Anthropology*. Collegeville, Minn.: Liturgical Press.

Dunbar, Robin. 1997. *Gossip, Grooming and the Evolution of Language*. London: Faber & Faber.

Edwards, Denis. 1995. *Jesus the Wisdom of God: An Ecological Theology*. Maryknoll, N.Y.: Orbis Books.

———. 2004. *Breath of Life: A Theology of the Creator Spirit*. Maryknoll, N.Y.: Orbis Books.

———. 2006. *Ecology at the Heart of Faith*. Maryknoll, N.Y.: Orbis Books.

Eldredge, N. 1999. *The Pattern of Evolution*. New York: W. H. Freeman.

Eldredge, N., and Stephen J. Gould. 1972. "Punctuated Equilibria: An Alternative to Phyletic Gradualism." In *Models of Paleobiology*, ed. T. J. M. Schopf, 82–115. San Francisco: Freeman.

Ephirim-Donkor, Anthony. 1997. *African Spirituality: On Becoming Ancestors*. Asmara, Eritrea, Trenton, N.J., and London, UK: Africa World Press.

Epstein, Robert. 2007. *The Case against Adolescence: Rediscovering the Adult in Every Teen*. Sanger, Calif.: Quill Driver Books.

Fagan, Brian. 1998. *People of the Earth: An Introduction to World Prehistory*. 9th ed. New York: Longman.

Forman, Robert. 2004. *Grassroots Spirituality: What It Is, Why It Is Here, Where It Is Going*. Charlottesville, Va.: Imprint Academic.

Fowler, James. 1981. *Stages of Faith: The Psychology of Human Development and the Quest for Meaning*. San Francisco: Harper & Row.

———. 1984. *Becoming Adult, Becoming Christian: Adult Development and Christian Faith*. San Francisco: Harper & Row.

Fox, Matthew, and Rupert Sheldrake. 1997. *Natural Grace: Dialogues*. New York: Image Books.

Frenier, Carol. 2005, "Engaging the Imaginal Realm: Doorway to Collective Wisdom." *www.collectivewisdominitiative.org*.

Funk, Robert W. 1996. *Honest to Jesus: Jesus for a New Millennium*. San Francisco: HarperSanFrancisco.

Gardner, James. 2007. *The Intelligent Universe*. Franklin Lakes, N.J.: New Page Books.

Ghiglieri, Michael P. 1999. *The Dark Side of Man: Tracing the Origins of Male Violence*. Cambridge, Mass.: Perseus Books.

Gibbons, Ann. 2005. "Facelift Supports Skull's Status as the Oldest Member of the Human Family." *Science* 308: 179–81.

———. 2007. *The First Human: The Race to Discover Our Earliest Ancestors*. New York: Anchor Books.

Girard, René. 1977. *Violence and the Sacred*. Baltimore: Johns Hopkins University Press.

———. 1986. *The Scapegoat*. Baltimore: Johns Hopkins University Press.

Goodall, Jane. 2001. *My Life with Chimpanzees*. New York: Time Warner Audio Books.

Gould, Stephen J. 2000. *Wonderful Life: The Burgess Shale and the Nature of History*. New York: Vintage.

Graham, Elaine. 2002. *Representations of the Post/Human: Monsters, Aliens, and Others in Popular Culture*. Manchester: Manchester University Press.

———. 2004. "Post/Human Conditions." *Theology and Sexuality* 10: 10–32.

Haight, Roger. 1979. *Experience and Language of Grace*. New York: Paulist Press.

———. 1999. *Jesus, Symbol of God*. Maryknoll, N.Y.: Orbis Books.

Hamilton, James. 2004. "Were Old Covenant Believers Indwelt by the Holy Spirit?" *Themelios* 30: 12–22.

Haraway, Donna. 1991. *Simians, Cyborgs and Women: The Reinvention of Nature*. London: Free Association Books.

Harris, Sam. 2005. *The End of Faith: Religion, Terror and the Future of Reason*. London: Free Press.

Hart, Donna, and Robert Sussman. 2005. *Man the Hunted: Primates, Predators and Human Evolution*. Boulder, Colo.: Westview Press.

Haught, John F. 1993. *Mystery and Promise: A Theology of Revelation*. Collegeville, Minn.: Liturgical Press.

———. 2000. *God after Darwin: A Theology of Evolution*. Boulder, Colo.: Westview Press.

———. 2003. *Deeper Than Darwin: The Prospect for Religion in the Age of Evolution*. Boulder, Colo.: Westview Press.

———. 2006. *Is Nature Enough? Meaning and Truth in the Age of Science*. New York: Cambridge University Press.

Hawken, Paul. 2007. *Blessed Unrest: How the Largest Movement in the World Came Into Being, and Why No One Saw It Coming*. New York: Viking.

Hayles, N. 1999. *How We Became Posthuman: Virtual Bodies in Cybernetics, Literature, and Informatics.* Cambridge: Cambridge University Press.

Hefner, Philip. 2003. *Technology and Human Becoming.* Minneapolis: Fortress Press.

Herzog, William R., II. 1994. *Parables as Subversive Speech: Jesus as Pedagogue of the Oppressed.* Louisville: Westminster John Knox Press.

———. 2005. *Prophet and Teacher: An Introduction to the Historical Jesus.* Louisville: Westminster John Knox Press.

Heyward, Carter. 1999. *Saving Jesus from Those Who Are Right.* Minneapolis: Fortress.

Hill, Jason. 2000. *On Being a Cosmopolitan: What It Means to Be Human.* Lanham, Md.: Rowman & Littlefield.

Horsley, Richard A. 2003. *Jesus and Empire: The Kingdom of God and the New World Disorder.* Minneapolis: Fortress.

Horton, Michael. 2006. *God of Promise: Introducing Covenant Theology.* Grand Rapids, Mich.: Baker Books.

Huebsch, Bill. 1988. *A New Look at Grace: A Spirituality for Wholeness.* Mystic, Conn.: Twenty-third Publications.

Humphreys, Lee, and Paul Messaris. 2006. *Digital Media: Transformations in Human Communication.* New York: Peter Lang Publishing.

Hyde, Lewis. 1983. *The Gift: Imagination and the Erotic Life of Property.* New York: Random House.

Isherwood, Lisa. 1999. *Liberating Christ.* Cleveland: Pilgrim Press.

Jackelen, Antje. 2002. "The Image of God as *Techno Sapiens.*" *Zygon* 37: 289–301.

Jantzen, Grace M. 1998. *Becoming Divine: A Feminist Philosophy of Religion.* Manchester: Manchester University Press.

Johanson, Donald. 2006. *From Lucy to Language.* Rev. ed. New York: Simon & Schuster.

Johnson, Elizabeth A. 1992. *She Who Is: The Mystery of God in Feminist Theological Discourse.* New York: Crossroad.

———. 2003. *Truly Our Sister: A Theology of Mary in the Communion of Saints.* New York: Continuum.

Kaku, M. 1998. *Visions: How Science Will Revolutionize the 21st Century and Beyond.* Oxford: Oxford University Press.

Keen, Sam. 1989. *Fire in the Belly: On Being a Man.* New York: Bantam Books.

Kennedy, Alan. 1974. *The Protean Self: Dramatic Action in Contemporary Fiction.* New York: Columbia University Press.

Knitter, Paul F. 1995. *One Earth, Many Religions: Multifaith Dialogue and Global Responsibility*. Maryknoll, N.Y.: Orbis Books.

Korten, David C. 2006. *The Great Turning: From Empire to Earth Community*. San Francisco: Berrett-Koehler.

Küng, Hans. 1998. *A Global Ethic for Global Politics and Economics*. Oxford: Oxford University Press.

Kunzig, Robert. 2002. "Black Holes Spin." *Discover* 23: 32–39.

Kurzweil, Ray. 2005. *The Singularity Is Near: When Humans Transcend Biology*. New York: Viking.

Lane, Nick. 2005. *Power, Sex, Suicide: Mitochondria and the Meaning of Life*. New York: Oxford University Press.

Lanier, Jaron. 2005. *Truth, Technology and the Visual/Virtual World*. Self-published. Web Page: *www.jaronlanier.com*.

Laszlo, Ervin. 1993. *The Creative Cosmos: A Unified Science of Matter, Life and Mind*. Edinburgh: Floris Books.

———. 1998. *The Whispering Pond: A Personal Guide to the Emerging Vision of Science*. Rockport, Mass.: Element Books.

———. 2004. *Science and the Akashic Field: An Integral Theory of Everything*. Rochester, Vt.: Inner Traditions/Bear & Co.

Leakey, Richard, and Roger Lewin. 1996. *The Sixth Extinction: Biodiversity and Its Survival*. London: Weidenfeld & Nicolson.

Lee, Richard, and Irven DeVore. 1968. *Man the Hunter*. Chicago: Aldine Books.

Lerner, Gerda. 1986. *The Creation of Patriarchy*. New York: Oxford University Press.

Lieberman, Philip. 2006. *Toward an Evolutionary Biology of Language*. Cambridge, Mass.: Harvard University Press.

Lietaer, Bernard. 2001. *The Future of Money*. London: Random House.

Lifton, Robert J. 1999. *The Protean Self: Dramatic Action in Contemporary Fiction*. Chicago: University of Chicago Press.

Lipton, Bruce. 2005. *The Biology of Belief: Unleashing the Power of Consciousness, Matter and Miracles*. Santa Rosa, Calif.: Elite Books (see also: *www.brucelipton.com*).

Lovelock, James. 1979. *Gaia: A New Look at Life on Earth*. New York and Oxford: Oxford University Press.

Maier, Charles S. 2006. *Among Empires: American Ascendency and Its Predecessors*. Cambridge, Mass.: Harvard University Press.

Malina, Bruce. 1996. *The Social World of Jesus and the Gospels*. New York: Routledge.

Mann, Michael. 1986. *The Sources of Social Power.* Cambridge: Cambridge University Press.

Margulis, Lynn. 1998. *The Symbiotic Planet.* New York: Basic Books.

Mauss, Marcel. 1990. *The Gift: The Form and Reason for Exchange in Archaic Societies.* New York: W. W. Norton.

McHenry, Henry M. 2004. "Origin of Human Bipedality." *Evolutionary Anthropology* 13:116–19.

McKenna, Terence. 1999. *Food of the Gods: The Search for the Original Tree of Knowledge: A Radical History of Plants, Drugs and Human Evolution.* Springville, Tenn.: Rider.

McTaggart, Lynne. 2007. *The Intention Experiment: Using Your Thoughts to Change Your Life and the World.* New York: Free Press.

Meyer, M. W., and L. G. Zucker. 1989. *Permanently Failing Organizations.* London: Sage Publications.

Mithen, Steven. 2005. *The Singing Neanderthals: The Origins of Music, Language, Mind and Body.* London: Weidenfeld & Nicolson.

Moltmann, Jürgen. 1988. *Theology Today: Two Contributions Towards Making Theology Present.* London: SCM Press.

———. 1992. *The Spirit of Life: A Universal Affirmation.* Minneapolis: Fortress.

Moore, Robert, and Douglas Gillette. 1990. *King, Warrior, Magician, Lover: Rediscovering the Archetype of the Mature Masculine.* San Francisco: Harper.

Morell, Virginia. 1996. *Ancestral Passions: The Leakey Family and the Quest for Humankind's Beginnings.* New York: Pocket Books.

Morowitz, Harold J. 2002. *The Emergence of Everything: How the World Became Complex.* Oxford and New York: Oxford University Press.

Morris, Simon Conway. 2004. *Life's Solution: Inevitable Humans in a Lonely Universe.* Cambridge: Cambridge University Press.

Myers, Ched. 1988. *Binding the Strong Man: A Political Reading of Mark's Story of Jesus.* Maryknoll, N.Y.: Orbis Books.

O'Meara, Thomas F. 1995. "A History of Grace." In *A World of Grace: An Introduction to the Themes and Foundations of Karl Rahner's Theology,* ed. Leo J. O'Donovan, 76–91. Washington, D.C.: Georgetown University Press.

O'Murchu, Diarmuid. 2000. *Religion in Exile: A Spiritual Homecoming.* New York: Crossroad.

———. 2002. *Evolutionary Faith: Rediscovering God in Our Great Story.* Maryknoll, N.Y.: Orbis Books.

———. 2005. *Catching Up with Jesus: A Gospel Story for Our Times.* New York: Crossroad.

———. 2007. *The Transformation of Desire: How Desire Became Corrupted and How We Can Reclaim It.* London: Darton, Longman & Todd; Maryknoll, N.Y.: Orbis Books.

Ormerod, Neil. 2007. *Creation, Grace and Redemption.* Maryknoll, N.Y.: Orbis Books.

O'Sullivan, Edmund V., et al. 2002. *Expanding the Boundaries of Transformative Learning: Essays on Theory and Praxis.* New York: Palgrave.

Panikkar, Raimon. 1993. *The Cosmotheandric Experience: Emerging Religious Consciousness.* Maryknoll, N.Y.: Orbis Books.

Peterson, Dale, and Richard Wrangham. 1997. *Demonic Males: Apes and the Origins of Human Violence.* Wilmington, Mass.: Mariner Books.

Phillips, Jan. 2006. *The Art of Original Thinking: The Making of a Thought Leader.* San Diego, Calif.: 9th Element Press.

Pilch, John J. 2000. *Healing in the New Testament: Insights from Medical and Mediterranean Anthropology.* Minneapolis: Augsburg Fortress.

Pinker, Steven. 1994. *The Language Instinct.* New York: William Morrow.

Pirani, Alex. 1991. *The Absent Mother: Restoring the Goddess to Judaism and Christianity.* London: HarperCollins.

Plumwood, Val. 2002. *Environmental Culture: The Ecological Crisis of Reason.* New York: Routledge.

Primack, Joel R., and Nancy Ellen Abrams. 2006. *The View from the Center of the Universe: Discovering Our Extraordinary Place in the Cosmos.* New York: Riverhead Books.

Primavesi, Anne. 2003. *Gaia's Gift: Earth, Ourselves, and God after Copernicus.* New York: Routledge.

Raffaele, Paul. 2006. "The Smart and Swinging Bonobo." *Smithsonian* 37: 66–75.

Rahner, Karl. 1966. "The Concept of Mystery in Catholic Theology." *Theological Investigations.* Vol. 4. London: Darton, Longman & Todd.

Rappaport, Roy A. 1999. *Ritual and Religion in the Making of Humanity.* New York: Cambridge University Press.

Rees, Martin. 2004. *Our Final Century: Will the Human Race Survive the Twenty-first Century?* London: Arrow Books (imprint of Random House).

Regan, Hilary D., and Terence J. Kelly. 2002. *God, Life, Intelligence in the Universe.* Canberra, Australia: ATF Press.

Reid-Bowen, Paul. 2007. *Goddess as Nature: Towards a Philosophical Thealogy.* Burlington, Vt.: Ashgate.

Richmond, Brian, and William Jungers. 2008. "*Orrorin Tugenensis: Femoral Morphology and the Evolution of Hominin Bipedalism.*" *Science* 319: 1662–65.

Rohr, Richard. 2004. *Soul Brothers: Men in the Bible Speak to Men Today.* Maryknoll, N.Y.: Orbis Books.

Rohrbaugh, Richard, ed. 1996. *The Social Sciences and New Testament Interpretation.* Peabody, Mass.: Hendrickson.

Rose, Steven. 1997. *Lifelines: Biology, Freedom, Determinism.* New York: Penguin Books.

Rose, Steven, and Hilary Rose, eds. 2000. *Alas, Poor Darwin: Arguments against Evolutionary Psychology.* London: Jonathan Cape.

Ruether, Rosemary Radford. 1983. *Sexism and God-talk: Toward a Feminist Theology.* Boston: Beacon Press.

———. 2005. *Goddesses and the Divine Feminine: A Western Religious History.* Berkeley: University of California Press.

Sahtouris, Elizabet. 1998. *EarthDance: Living Systems in Evolution.* Alameda, Calif.: Metalog Books.

Sale, Kirkpatrick. 1991. *Dwellers in the Land: The Bioregional Vision.* San Francisco: Sierra Club.

Schüssler Fiorenza, Elisabeth. 1994. *Jesus: Miriam's Child, Sophia's Prophet.* New York: Continuum.

———. 2001. *Wisdom Ways: Introducing Feminist Biblical Interpretation.* Maryknoll, N.Y.: Orbis Books.

Schwager, Raymund. 2006. *Banished from Eden: Original Sin and Evolutionary Theory in the Drama of Salvation.* Leominster, UK: Gracewing.

Sheehan, Thomas. 1986. *The First Coming: How the Kingdom of God Became Christianity.* New York: Random House.

Sheldrake, Rupert. 1988. *The Presence of the Past: Popular Uses of History in American Life.* London: Collins.

———. 1999. *A New Science of Life: The Hypothesis of Formative Causation.* Rochester, Vt.: Inner Traditions/Bear & Co.

Shlain, Leonard. 1998. *The Alphabet versus the Goddess: The Conflict between Word and Image.* New York: Allen Lane.

Slee, Nicola. 2004. *Women's Faith Development: Patterns and Processes.* Aldershot, Hants (UK), and Burlington, Vt.: Ashgate Press.

Smart, Ninian, and Steven Konstantine. 1991. *Christian Systematic Theology in a World Context.* London: HarperCollins.

Soelle, Dorothee. 2001. *The Silent Cry: Mysticism and Resistance.* Minneapolis: Fortress.

Somé, Malidoma Patrice. 1997. *Ritual, Power, Healing and Community.* New York: Penguin Books.

———. 1999. *Healing Wisdom of Africa: Finding Life Purpose through Nature, Ritual, and Community.* New York: J. P. Tarcher.

Stewart, John. 2000. *Evolution's Arrow: The Direction of Evolution and the Future of Humanity.* Canberra, Australia: Chapman Press.

Stringer, Chris, and Robin McKie. 1998. *African Exodus: The Origins of Modern Humanity.* London: Routledge.

Sullivan, Clayton. 2002. *Rescuing Jesus from the Christians.* Harrisburg, Pa.: Trinity Press International.

Swimme, Brian. 1996. *The Hidden Heart of the Cosmos: Humanity and the New Story.* Maryknoll, N.Y.: Orbis Books.

Swimme, Brian, and Thomas Berry. 1992. *The Universe Story: From the Primordial Flaring Forth to the Ecozoic Era — A Celebration of the Unfolding of the Cosmos.* San Francisco: Harper.

Sykes, Brian. 2004. *The Seven Daughters of Eve.* London: Gorgi Paperback.

Tacey, David J. 2004. *The Spirituality Revolution: The Emergence of Contemporary Spirituality.* New York: Brunner Routledge.

Tamez, Elsa. 2007. *Struggles for Power in Early Christianity: A Study of the First Letter to Timothy.* Maryknoll, N.Y.: Orbis Books.

Tanner, Kathryn. 2005. *Economy of Grace.* Minneapolis: Augsburg Fortress.

Tarlow, Mikela. 2002. *Digital Aboriginal: The Direction of Business Now.* New York: Warner Books; London: Piatkus.

Tarnas, Richard. 2006. *Cosmos and Psyche: Intimations of a New World View.* New York: Viking.

Tattersall, Ian. 2006. "How We Became Human." *Scientific American* 30: 66–73.

Teilhard de Chardin, Pierre. 1969. *Christianity and Evolution.* London: Collins.

Tiger, Lionel, and Robin Fox. 1971. *The Imperial Animal.* Delta Books (Dell).

Volf, Miroslav. 1998. *Exclusion and Embrace: A Theological Exploration of Identity, Otherness and Reconciliation.* Nashville: Abingdon.

Wallace, B. Alan. 2007. *Hidden Dimensions: The Unification of Physics and Consciousness.* New York: Columbia University Press.

Wallace, Mark I. 2002. *Fragments of the Spirit: Nature, Violence, and the Renewal of Creation.* Harrisburg, Pa.: Trinity Press International.

———. 2005. *Finding God in the Singing River: Christianity, Spirit, Nature.* Minneapolis: Fortress.

Ward, Peter. 1995. *The End of Evolution: On Mass Extinctions and the Preservation of Biodiversity.* London: Weidenfeld & Nicolson.

Warwick, Kevin. 2002. *I, Cyborg.* London: Century Books.

Wheatley, Margaret J. 1992. *Leadership and the New Science: Learning about Organization from an Orderly Universe.* San Francisco: Berrett-Koehler.

White, Lynn. 1967. "The Historical Roots of the Ecological Crisis." *Science* 155: 1203–7.

Wink, Walter. 1998. *The Powers That Be: Theology for a New Millennium.* New York: Doubleday.

———. 2002. *The Human Being: Jesus and the Enigma of the Son of Man.* Minneapolis: Augsburg Fortress.

Wong, Kate. 2006a, "Lucy's Baby." *Scientific American* 295: 56–63.

———. 2006b. "The Morning of the Modern Mind." *Scientific American* special edition, 16, no. 2: 74–83.

Wood, B. 2002. "Homonid Revelations from Chad." *Nature,* vol. 418: 133–35.

Wray, Alison. 2002. *The Transition to Language.* Oxford: Oxford University Press.

Wright, Roland. 2004. *A Short History of Progress.* New York: Carroll & Graf.

Yancey, Philip. 1997. *What Is So Amazing about Grace?* Grand Rapids, Mich.: Zondervan.

Zihlman, Adrienne L., Mary Ellen Morbeck, and Alison Galloway. 1996. *The Evolving Female: A Life-History Perspective.* Princeton, N.J.: Princeton University Press.

Zimbardo, Philip. 2007. *The Lucifer Effect: Understanding How Good People Turn Evil.* New York: Random House.

Zimmer, Carl. 2002. *Evolution: The Triumph of an Idea.* London: Heine-mann.

Zinn, Howard. 2002. *The Power of Nonviolence: Writings by Advocates of Peace.* Boston: Beacon Press.

Index

Abell, Paul, 38
Abram, David, 64, 76
Acheulean age, 27, 45, 53
addictions of Empire, 165
addictive behavior, source of, 195
adolescence, 244n27
adult
  in creation, 194
  dealing creatively with, 193–94
  education of, 196–99
  inner child and, 195–96
Africa
  birthplace of human species, 36, 37–38
  diviner in religions of, 146
  as humans' collective home, 40–42
  resolving present plight of, 41–42
  spirituality of, 41, 239–40n9
afterlife, 225
agricultural revolution
  results of, 88–90, 201
  shadow side of, 9
agriculture, 85–86
  ancestral grace and, 89–90
  dark side of, 86, 87
Aiello, Leslie, 73
Akashic field, 60, 241n14
Alemsgeded, Zeresenay, 37
alienation, 11, 122–23, 134, 202
al-Saud, Salman, 61
Altamira, 47
altruism, present in all cultures, 34
ambiguity, coping with, 56–58
ancestral grace
  agriculture and, 89–90
  all food sacred in, 151–52
  allowing respect for paradox, 99
  embodying affirmation of will-to-life, 52

granting wisdom underlying creation, 62
honoring earth's complexity and interdependence, 86
Jesus embracing, 159, 162
preceding Jesus, 114
reclaiming power of divine at work in transforming humanity, 147
reclaiming the Jesus of, 95–97
requiring wider perception, 115
restlessness as aspect of, 39
undermined by rationalism, 84
wisdom of, crucial for future evolution, 52
woman as icon of, 48
working in deep time, 28
Anderson, John M., 89
animal drawings, 49
anthropocentrism, 7, 12
  evidenced by human figureheads, 63
  leading to exploitation, 61
  overcoming, 31
  related to language theory, 75
  rise of, 87–88
  urge to control as element of, 57
apocalyptic mind-set, 210–11
apostles, failing to grasp message of the Kingdom of God, 124
archetypal living, distinguished from Christian perfection, 108
archetypes, 107, 110–11
Ardipithecus, 21
Ardipithecus ramidus, 29
Aristotle, 16
  envisioning the nation state, 185
  influence of, on understanding human nature, 241–42n18

259

Aristotle (*continued*)
  on sex as biological function, 25
  understanding of the human person,
     134
art
  early discoveries of, 46–47
  spirituality and, 48–50
artifacts, progression in, 48–49
artificial intelligence, 176, 177
Asfaw, Berhane, 59
Asia, originally considered as origin of
     humans, 37–38
astronauts, observations of, 61
Auden, W. H., 8
Augustine, 4
Australo Garhi, 44
Australopithecus, 17, 39
Australopithecus afarensis, 36–37
Australopithecus africanus, 37
Australopithecus boisei, 38
Australopithecus robustus, 38
autonomous personhood, 134
autopoiesis, 213
avatars, 145

Bacon, Francis, 88
Bahn, Peter, 49
Bateson, Gregory, 80
Baum, Gregory, 109
Beauvilain, Alain, 21
Beckett, Samuel, 156
Berry, Thomas, 167, 169, 196
Bickerton, Derek, 75, 76–77
biomes, 187
bioregionalism, 187–88
bipedalism, 30, 38–40, 42
birth-death-rebirth cycle, 56–57, 90,
     94, 226
  at all stages of evolution, 139–40
  creative process of, 102
  guaranteeing freedom and creativity,
     115
birthing, as most generic activity of the
     divine, 102–4
black holes, 228
Black Madonna, 103

Bodhisattvas, 145–46
Bolen, Jean Shinoda, 82
bonobos, 23–25, 33
Borg, Marcus, 145, 159
Boros, Ladislos, 229
Bower, Bruce, 39
BP, 45n
Breuil, Abbé Henri, 49
Broom, Robert, 37, 38
Brown, Dan, 82
Brown, Frank, 59
Brown, Steven, 74
Brueggemann, Walter, 50, 160
Brunet, Michel, 21
Buddha, the, 62–63, 145
Buddhism, 145–46
Burr, Harold S., 24

Campbell, Joseph, 55, 69
Carr, Geoffrey, 34, 86
Carrette, Jeremy, 121
Carson, Rachel, 171
Casey, Edward, 14
Cavanaugh, William, 161, 244n30
cave art, 47, 48
Chauvet Cave, 47
child, moving beyond preoccupation
     with, 196–97
chimpanzees, 22, 24–25, 33
Chittister, Joan, 83
Chomsky, Noam, 75
Christ, Carol, 81
Christian church, providing shaky
     foundation for ideas of grace and
     redemption, 6
Christian Gospels, contradictions in,
     108
Christian heritage, rethinking time
     restriction of, 26
Christian humanism, 110
Christianity
  anti-world spirituality of, 119–20
  arrogance of, 146–47
  clinging to the past, 125
  early, related to classical Greek
     culture, 136

integrating into wider human culture, 134

offering hope for daily living, 213–14

releasing from cultural bondage, 149

surviving deviant enculturations, 117–18

Christians, professional, 94

Christian spirituality, search for, 159–60

christological doctrine, 136

civilization

concept of, fundamentally flawed, 7

cultural model of, postulated on imperial power, 191

Claxton, Guy, 19, 60

Clements, Frederic, 187

clericalism, 118

Clynes, Manfred, 243n24

co-creation, 212, 214

co-evolution, 27, 168, 172, 179

cognitive fluidity, 51

co-learning relationship, 197

collective unconscious, 59–60, 62

commensality, 125, 151–52

communal challenge, 64–65

communion, 169

conscious choice, 168

consciousness

altered states of, 153

defining, 59

self-reflexive, 64–65

Constantine, 128

convergence, characterizing evolution, 8

cooking, 55

cooperation, 31, 170

Corballis, Michael, 73

Corbin, Henry, 14–15

cosmic-planetary story, divine grandeur in, 13

Coulson, Sheila, 46, 80

Cradle of Humanity Museum, 72

creation

changing human approach to, 7

Christian approach to, 104

coming home to, 121–22

flawed because of humans, 5–6

fundamental flaw in, fallacy of concept, 93

God at work at, in every stage, 8

innate intelligence within, 61–62

misconstruing meaning of, 122

stories of, 101–2

sustained by grace-filled energy, 8

thriving on diversity, 149

creative outbursts, contained by rationalism, 13

creative vacuum, 60

creativity, religious endorsement of, 50–51

creoles, as stage in language development, 76

Crossan, John Dominic, 124, 151, 154, 211, 225

cultural isolation, 68

cyborg, 176, 243n24

Dark Side of Man, The (Ghiglieri), 54

Dart, Raymond, 37

Darwin, Charles, 168–69

Davies, Steven, 154

Da Vinci Code, The (Brown), 82, 241n16

Deacon, Terence, 75

death

associated with judgment and afterlife, 224–25

befriending, 226–27, 229

in the cosmic matrix, 227–29

demonization of, 224–26

embracing, 233

graced future and, 229–30

meaning of, projected onto another world, 230

treatment of, 57

de Bruyn, M., 37

Deby, Idriss, 21

de Castro, José Bermúdez, 66

deep time, 26–28

Delio, Ilia, 180

democracy, limits of, 184–85

Demonic Males (Peterson and Wrangham), 54

denial, as self-survival strategy, 207
de Perthes, Boucher, 53
de Sautuola, Don Marcelino, 47
despair, embracing, 110
deviant behaviors, projecting into past, 116
de Waal, Frans, 23–24, 33, 55
Diana, Princess of Wales, 226
differentiation, 169
discos, as sites of repressed ritual, 156
divide and conquer, 89–90, 95, 201
divine
    addiction to male personifications of, 104
    as creator, 101–2
    as spirit power, 99–101
divine-human integration, all humans capable of, 147–48
divine meaning, accessing, through being human, 109–10
diviner, 146
Djimdoumalbaye, Ahounta, 21
Donald, Merlin, 74
Douglas, C. H., 243n26
Douglas, Mary, 32
Dowd, Michael, 31, 52, 170
Dreimulen, 38
Dreyer, Elizabeth, 10, 234
dualism, 100, 119, 205
    between perfect God and flawed human, 120
    conventional worldview of, 139
    largely unknown in pagan spirituality, 81
Dubois, Eugene, 239n8
Duffy, Stephen, 123
Dunbar, Robin, 73, 76, 77
du Toit, Cornel, 179–80

earth
    convivial relationship with, as survival resource, 208
    objectification of, 87–88
    perceived as holy and sacred, 79
    survival of, 232
earth spirituality, 83

ecclesial structures, increased need for flexibility in, 214
Eckhart, Meister, 102
eco-systemic destruction, 232
Edwards, Denis, 106, 154
Eisler, Riane, 81
Eldredge, Neils, 22, 171–72
Eller, Cynthia, 81
embodiment, 242n19
energy, 217–18
energy fields, 24
environmental issues, 231–32
epics of entropy, 192
Epstein, Robert, 243–44n27
eschatological outlook, 211–13
Essai sur le don (Mauss), 31–32
Eucharist, 151–52
Eurasia, as source of great ape and human clade, 239n7
Europe, impression of, 68–70
Europeans
    indigenous, 66, 67–68
    suffering from deflated warrior archetype, 70
evolution
    continuance of, 168–69
    Darwin's inadequate approach to, 169
    divine creativity at every stage of, 17
    driven from the past, 220–21
    God's role in, 113–14
    growing perspective of, 167–68
    quantum leaps in, 22
    story of, carved by mystery and potential, 14
    thriving on creativity, 17–18
    women at heart of, 16
evolutionary story, rightness of, 8–10
exile, biblical, as metaphor for human estrangement from God, 120
extinction, 171

the Fall, 5–6, 120–21
Falwell, Jerry, 208
Fiorenza, Elisabeth Schüssler, 106, 154
fire, 56

food, despiritualized in contemporary culture, 152
fossils, dating of, 238–39n6
FOXP2, 75
Frazer, James, 49
Frenier, Carol, 15
Freud, Sigmund, 53
Funk, Robert, 137
future
co-creating, 170, 172
dreaming of alternatives, 222–23
guaranteed by evolution, 234
options for, 171–73
role of, 221

Gaia, 240n10
Gandhi, Mohandas, 35
gender complementarity, 32–34
genetic mutation, 168
Gerasene demoniac, story of, 152–53
gesturing, 73
gifting, 31–32
Gillette, Douglas, 195
Gimbutas, Marija, 81
Girard, René, 6, 50
global governance, 188–91
globalization, 188
God
alienation from, 120
in double bind, 93
feminine face of, 102–4
human face of, reclaiming, 109–10
love of, overlooked, 6
molded in human image, 136, 139
New Reign of, 105
presence of, as empowering Spirit, 101
worshiped as a great woman, 81–83
Goddess, archetype of, 79
Golden Bough, The (Frazer), 49
Gould, Stephen J., 8, 171–72
grace. *See also* ancestral grace
available from the church, 3
biblically understood as divine graciousness, 4
characteristics of, 4–5

as divine gift, 138
dualistic overtones regarding, 3–5
in Eastern vs. Western Christianity, 4
linked with sacraments, 237n1
losing meaning in contemporary world, 6–7
perceived as coming from the cross, 138
reclaiming, 7
related to the Fall, 5–6
requiring openness and transparency in human spirit, 58
as survival skill, 10
Graham, Elaine, 180
Great Earth Mother Goddess, 101–2
cult of, 48
inhabiting cosmic and planetary creation, 87
personified in Lady Wisdom, 106
reemergence of archetype, 103–4
worship of, 81–83
great extinctions, 140
Great Sky God, 87. *See also* sky-God
Greece, classical, 9, 167
Guru Nanak, 146

Habilis, 44–45
Haile-Salassie, Y, 44
Hamilton, James, 216
Haraway, Donna, 243n24
Haught, John F., 212, 221
Havel, Václav, 235
Hawken, Paul, 222–23
Hawkins, Yisrael, 209
healing, 81, 97, 124, 125, 151, 152
Herzog, William R., 159
Heyward, Carter, 94
Hill, Jason, 173, 200
Hillman, James, 15
Hinduism, 145
hmmmmm, 67, 74
holiness, gauge of, 88–89
Holy Spirit, 101, 216–20
homecoming, 121–23
hominin, 21
Homo antecessor, 66

Homo erectus, 38–40

Homo ergaster, 39, 51, 53–57, 74

Homo habilis, 39, 51, 74

Homo heidelbergensis, communication of, 74

Homo sapiens, 40–41, 51
  dating, 59
  as icon of holy wisdom, 62
  representing cumulative wisdom, 64–65
  speaking skills of, 67

hope, 216, 235–36

Horney, Karen, 6

House of Yahweh, 209

human-animal relationship, depictions of, 49

humanism, Christian, 110

humanity, viewed as depraved and corrupt, 11

humans
  altering behavior of, 178
  as archetypal statement of divine empowerment, 110
  behavior of, presumed to improve over time, 140–41
  as beneficiaries of original blessing, 51
  blood-thirstiness of, 54
  called to inner renewal, 31
  co-birthing of, Christian perspective on, 104–5
  creativity of, 168
  depravity of, 237n2
  as dinosaurs of our time, 232
  disenfranchisement of, 185–86
  earliest evidence of creativity and innovation, 45–46
  embracing paradox, 142–43
  emerging, relating interdependently with creation, 30–31
  energy field of, 24
  fundamental flaw of, as human invention, 115
  graced for wholeness, 110
  great figureheads of, 62–63
  hardwired to detect injustice, 34
  history of, related to last 2,000 and 5,000 years, 26, 50, 78, 113–14, 139, 166–67
  identity of, caught between strain of two cultures, 134–35
  interdependence of, 232
  Jesus as archetype of, 97–98
  making sense of human story, 235
  mechanizing, 176–77
  mind potential of, 60–61
  need of, to escape or transcend earthiness, 202
  needs for love and work, 53
  not descended from apes, 22
  preoccupation with violence and patriarchy, 24–25
  presumptions about ancestors, 193
  primarily oriented toward cooperation, 30–31
  primate ancestors of, 16–17
  as relational creatures, 203
  reprieve for, 233–34
  as social manipulators, 55
  spirit of playfulness in, 155
  tracing origins of, 15–17

hundredth monkey syndrome, 28

hunting, 54–56

Hutchinson, Clyde, 16

Huxley, Aldous, 80

Huxley, Julian, 181

Ice Age art, 44, 47, 102, 240n12
  fascination with women and female fertility, 81
  motivation for, 49–50
  religious significance of, 50

identity, inherited from relationality, 64

imagination, 13–15

immortality, as patriarchal projection, 225

Imperial Animal, The (Tiger and Fox), 54

imperialism, civilized, 191–92

incarnation, 113, 115, 144–47

incarnational religion, prone to bizarre predilections, 209

incarnational spirituality, 160
individual, threat to, 64
individualism, 65, 202, 204
inner child, 195–96
instinct, as dimension of archetypal
  meaning, 73
intelligence, human, potential of, 60–61
intelligent behavior, tracing, 56
intelligent unconscious, 19, 60
interconnectedness, losing sense of, 88
interiority (*autopoiesis*), 169
intimacy, alternative, 204
intuition, return of, 13–14
Iraq, post–Saddam Hussein, 184
Islam, 146, 204

James, William, 80
Jansen, Cornelius Otto, 119
Jansenism, 119
Jantzen, Grace, 144
Jaspers, Karl, 145
Java Man, 239n8
Jesus, 62–63
  archetypal dream of, over-
    spiritualized, 111–12
  as archetypal human, 97–98, 107–12
  assumed to be ardently religious, 157
  attempting to demolish patriarchal
    hegemony, 128
  celebrating high point in Christian
    evolutionary development, 117
  challenging purity laws, 131
  coming to bring fulfillment rather
    than salvation, 116
  declared Pantocrator, 128
  declaring and embodying a New
    Reign of God, 111
  disassociating himself from his Jewish
    roots, 131
  divinity of, preoccupation with, 98,
    107, 109, 137, 141, 147
  dream of new heaven and new earth,
    126
  eliminating dangerous memory of,
    131–32

embodying life lived by ancestral
  grace, 94
embracing ancestral grace, 159
embracing paradox, 141–42
as empowering liberator, 132
faith in, 161–62
five central features in life and ministry
  of, 160–61
fulfilling human achievement, 140
grounded in ancestral grace, 162
as healer, 153–54, 160
humanity of, 107, 141
integrated into the fundamental flaw,
  95
liberation proclaimed by, 125
literalizing life and ministry of, as
  example of patriarchal minimalism,
  114
living in world of signs and wonders,
  150
marking culmination and fulfillment
  of a process, 114
ministry of, centered on commensality
  and healing, 151–54
as model of inspired birthing, 104–5
as movement initiator, 161
as mystic, 160
new vision of, 125
as non-Caucasian, 161
patriarchy's distortion of, 94
placing in Wisdom tradition, 106,
  154
portrayed as anti-religion, 157–59
as prophetic subversive portraying
  ancestral grace, 154
rebirthing dream of God for all
  creation, 140
reclaiming deeper meaning for,
  117–18
as rescue for all humans, 5–6
rescuing from patriarchy, 95–97
Resurrected, as exemplar of human
  destiny, 117
re-visioning, in larger context of
  creation, 99
as ritual-maker, 150–54

Jesus (*continued*)
  self-understanding of, 136–37
  as social prophet, 160–61
  as storyteller, 105–6
  strained relationship with his family,
    159
  transcending worldview of his time,
    126
  viewing life in terms of paradox,
    139–40
  as wisdom teacher, 160
Johanson, Donald, 37
Johnson, Elizabeth, 106, 154
Jung, Carl, 14, 59–60, 73, 107
Jungers, William, 39
Jungian psychology, 107
justice-making, commitment to, 143

Kaku, Michio, 176–77
Kali, 103
Kalkin, 145
Keen, Sam, 82
Kimeu, Kimoya, 53
King, Martin Luther, Jr., 35
King, Richard, 121
King, William, 66
Kingdom of God, 105. *See also* New
    Reign of God
  as companionship of empowerment,
    124
  Jesus' miracle ministry situated
    within, 154
Kingship, Jesus undermining, 159
Kline, Nathan, 243n24
Knitter, Paul, 107–8
Konstantine, Steven, 146
Korten, David, 12, 165
Krishna, 62–63, 145
Kromdraai, 38
Küng, Hans, 148
Kurzweil, Ray, 177, 178, 182–83

Lady Toumai, 20, 21, 24, 26
Lady Wisdom, 106
Lane, Nick, 16
language, 75–77

Lanier, Jaron, 176–77
Lascaux, 47
Laszlo, Ervin, 27–28, 60
Leakey, Louis, 44–45
Leakey, Mary, 38
Leakey, Meave, 45
Leakey, Richard, 45, 53, 59, 90, 171
Leakey family, 38
learning, teacher and student jointly
    responsible for, 197
leprosy, 153
Levi-Strauss, Claude, 140
Lewin, Roger, 90, 171
Lieberman, Philip, 75
Lietaer, Bernard, 32, 189
life, as complex, open-ended system,
    169–70
life force, 217–18
lifelines, 169
Lifton, Robert J., 179
Lipton, Bruce, 31, 162
literalism, misleading nature of, 129–30
Lovelock, James, 240n10
Lucy, 34, 37
Lucy's Baby, 37
lure of the future, 212
Luthuli, Albert, 161

man, as hunter, 54–56
Mann, Michael, 191
Man the Hunter (Lee and DeVore), 54
Margulis, Lynn, 31, 170, 240n10
martyrdom, cult of, 204
Mary, role and depictions of, in
    Christian faith, 103
mass extinctions, 52
matriarchy, adopting model of, 33
Mauss, Marcel, 31–32
McKenna, Terrence, 176–77
McLuhan, Marshall, 188
McTaggart, Lynne, 162, 241n14
meat-eating, 55
mechanization, 176–77
Mereschkowsky, Konstantin, 170
Merleau-Ponty, Maurice, 63, 64
metamorphosis, 171–72

millennial fantasies, 209
Miller, Alice, 6
Mills, James, 208
mime, 74
minimalism, 10, 114
mistakes, confirming Jesus' authenticity, 142
Mitchell, Edgar, 61
Mithen, Steven, 45, 51, 67, 73–74
mitochondria, 16
Mitochondrial Eve, 16
mobiliary art, 240n12
modern arts, as repressed ritual, 156
Mohammed, 62–63
Moltmann, Jürgen, 218, 219–20, 221–22
money, symbolic spiritual significance of, 32
Moore, Robert, 195
Morgan fisherfolk, 18
morphic resonance, 28
Morris, Simon Conway, 8
mothering, desire for, 82–83
Movement for the Restoration of the Ten Commandments, 209
Mrs. Ples, 37
multifaith dialogue, 148–49
multi-regionalists, 40
mundus imaginalis, 14
music, 67, 73–74
musilanguage, 74
Myers, Ched, 152

nanobots, 178
Napier, John, 45
Nariokotome Boy, 53
natality, process of, 144
nation state, dwindling status of, 185–86
natural selection, 168–69, 243n23
nature, humans' convivial relationship with, 18
Neanderthals, 40, 51, 66
  characteristics of, 69
  culture of, 67
  end of, 68
  link with *Homo sapiens,* 67–68

music among, 73–74
  providing inspiration, 70–71
  ritual burials among, 79–80
  tasks performed by, 66–67
networking, 192
New Reign of God, 105
  based on radical inclusiveness and egalitarianism, 126
  as call to humility and service, 142
  goal of, 148
  holy translated into wholesomeness, 162
  as Jesus' relational matrix, 137
  reenvisioned, 123–25
new world order, 209–10
Ngandong, 40
nonduality, endorsing, 173–74
nongovernmental organization, 189
nonverbal patterns, 73–74
nonverbal strategies, leading to growth, 74–75
nonviolence, commitment to, 34–35
normalcy, disrupting regimes of, 130–31
nurture, 169

Oldowan technology, 45–46
omnipotence, as anthropocentric projection, 141
omniscience, as anthropocentric projection, 141
open common table, Jesus' sharing of, 151
Original Sin, effects of, 120–21
Ormerod, Neil, 6
Orrorin tugenensis, 29–30
O'Sullivan, Edward, 198
Otto, Rudolf, 80
"Out of Africa" hypothesis, 40–41

Paabo, Svanta, 75
Pacha Mama, 103
pagan, 78
paganism, reinstated, 78–79
painting, carrying spiritual significance, 46
paleoanthropologists, work of, 20

Paleolithic era, 33
parables, 126, 128–31
paradox
  confused with flaw, 237–38n
  dealing poorly with, 58
  humans embracing, 142–43
  inability to control, 94
  Jesus embracing, 141–42
  as part of life cycle, 57
  source of transformation, 52
parietal art, 240n12
past, anthropologists' and psychologists'
    negative view of, 18
patriarchy
  addiction to, 90
  assumptions of, 12–13
  of chimpanzees, 22
  as dark age, 116
  distorting Jesus, 94
  embracing the past, 167
  emerging from rise in agriculture,
    86–88
  flawed perception of, 93–94
  great delusion of, 194
  influence of, on religions, 88
  Jesus trying to distance himself from,
    109
  rescuing Jesus from, 95–97
  as source of alienation, 18
  subverting birthing power of the
    divine, 103
  unquestioned assumptions about, 9
Pelagius, 4
permanently failing organizations, 192
personal survival, preoccupation with,
    227–28
phallic symbolism, 69–70
Pickford, Martin, 29
pidgins, 76
Pilch, John J., 53
Pinker, Steven, 75, 76
Pinochet, Augusto, 244n30
Pirani, Alex, 82
Plato, understanding of the human
    person, 134–35
posthuman, 176, 178

prehistoric faiths, shaman in, 146
primary representation system, 76
primate grooming, 73
primates, research into, 21–22
Primavesi, Anne, 31
primitive, term misapplied, 140–41
primitive animism, 100
prophets, Islamic, 146
protean, 181
protean self, 179
proto-language, 73–75
Psi field, 241n14
psychosexual bonding, 204, 205
punctuated equilibrium, 171–72
pure space, 60

Rahner, Karl, 4, 229
Rainbow Body Phenomenon, 245n32
Rama, 145
Rappaport, Roy A., 46
rationality, cult of, 11–13
Reagan, Ronald, 208
redemption, theology of, 6
Rees, Martin, 171
Reid-Bowen, Paul, 81, 87
reincarnation, 244–45n31
relationality, role of, in human nature,
    135–37
relationships, lateral, 205–6
religion
  alliance with Darwinian science,
    203–4
  approach of, toward death, 230
  co-opted into dominant patriarchal
    culture, 88
  formal, 78
  fundamentally flawed, 7
  partnering with technology, 179–80
  prehistoric, 78
  suppressing human creativity, 50
religious fervor, regressive possibilities
    from, 208–9
religious reductionism, 6
restlessness, 39
revelation, narrow and constricted sense
    of, 212

Richmond, Brian, 39
ritual, 77
   healing, 153
   involving threshold times and
     boundary places, 80
   in Jesus' time, 150–51
   oldest evidence of, 80
   in present day, 155–56
ritual-making, 79–81, 155–56
ritual purity, 158
Robinson, John T., 37
rock painting, 46
Rohr, Richard, 136
role-modeling, 67
Rose, Steven, 169
Ruether, Rosemary Radford, 81, 225,
   227–28

Sabbath rest, 158
Sahtouris, Elizabet, 202
Sale, Kirkpatrick, 187
*Saving Jesus from Those Who Are
   Right!* (Heyward), 94
Schwarz, Ernst, 23
science, approach of, toward death, 230
Scriptures, dangers of literalizing, 155
self-organization, 169
senses, used to appropriate knowledge
   and wisdom, 63–64
Senut, Brigitte, 29
Seven Daughters of Eve, The (Sykes), 16
sexes, change in complementarity of,
   accompanying rise in agriculture,
   85–86
sexuality, purpose of, 25–26
shaman, 55–56, 146
shamanism, 49
Sheehan, Thomas, 157
Sheldrake, Rupert, 28
Shelford, Victor, 187
sign language, dating of, 72
Sikhism, 146
sin
   forgiveness of, 158
   losing meaning in contemporary
    world, 6–7

Singularity Is Near, The (Kurzweil), 178
Sixth Great Extinction, 90, 171
sky-God, 9, 87, 128, 202, 244n29
Smart, Ninian, 146
social bonding, language and, 76–77
Soelle, Dorothee, 108, 122, 160
song, 67
soul, 14, 62
soulful consciousness, 111
soulfulness, 62
Spirit, experience of, 100–101
spirit-power, 41, 50
spiritual, ritualizing of, 79–81
spirituality, 78
   affected by cultural reductionism, 79
   art and, 48–50
   awakening of, 198–99
   paradigm shift in, 83
spiritual vacuum, attempts to fill, 121
spoken language, limitations of, in
   accessing inner wisdom, 74
spoken word
   evolution of, 75
   related to nature sounds, 76
statuettes, 48
Steindl-Rast, David, 245n32
Sterkfontein, 37–38
Stewart, John, 31, 170
Stone, Merlin, 81
Strier, Karen B., 55
suffering, as part of great life cycle, 57
suicide bomber, 204, 210
Swartkrand, 38
Swimme, Brian, 169
Sykes, Bryan, 16
symbiogenesis, 170
symbolic, liberating power of, 84
synaesthesia, 63–64

Tara, 103
Tarlow, Mikela, 179, 197, 200, 205
Taung Child, 37
technology, shadow side of, 181–82
Teilhard de Chardin, Pierre, 117, 171,
   182, 218, 221
temple, Jesus' cleansing of, 159

Tobias, Philip, 45
tools, 39, 44, 45, 53
Toumai, 20–21, 39
transformation, embracing, 172
transformative learning, 198–99
transhuman, 181
transnational corporations, 185
transpersonal archetype, 84
transpersonal wisdom, 181
tribalism, 200, 205
trust, necessity of, 165–66
tsunami (December 2004), Morgan
    fisherfolk's reaction to, 18
Turing, Alan, 177
Turkana Boy, 53
tyranny of the academy, 50

uniqueness, inherited from relationality,
    64
United Nations, 188–89
universal victimhood, 6
Upper Paleolithic era, artistic
    achievement in, 47
upright stride, 42–43

van Leewenhoek, Anthony, 241n18
Venus figurines, 48
verbal speech, dating of, 72
Vogelherd caves, 48
Volf, Miroslav, 7
Volynov, Boris, 61

Wallace, B. Alan, 60
Wallace, Marc I., 78–79, 101

Ward, Peter, 171
warfare, birth of, 86
warrior archetype, 69, 70
Warwick, Kevin, 243n24
Washburn, Sherwood, 240n13
White, Lynn, 120
White, Tim, 21, 29, 53, 59
Whitehead, Alfred N., 191
Wink, Walter, 97, 109, 124–25, 213
wisdom, innate nature of, 84
Wisdom literature, 106
Wisdom tradition, placing Jesus in, 154
woman, archetypal significance of, 48
women
    at heart of evolutionary story, 16
    Ice Age art's fascination with, 81
    Jesus' interaction with, 158–59
    role of, in food gathering, 54–55
work
    joy of, 53–54
    separating from the living wage,
        190–91
work ethic, alternative, 190
World Trade Organization, 185
Wrangham, Richard, 55
Wright, Roland, 191

Yancey, Philip, 10

zero-point energy field, 241n14
Zhoukoudians, 40
Zihlman, Adrienne, 54–55
Zimbardo, Philip, 50, 241n
Zinj, 38